Engineering Global
E-Commerce Sites

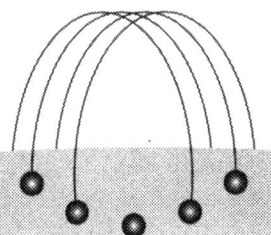

Engineering Global E-Commerce Sites

A Guide to Data Capture, Content, and Transactions

James Bean
Foreword by Jorden Woods

MORGAN KAUFMANN PUBLISHERS

AN IMPRINT OF ELSEVIER SCIENCE

AMSTERDAM   BOSTON   LONDON   NEW YORK
OXFORD   PARIS   SAN DIEGO   SAN FRANCISCO
SINGAPORE   SYDNEY   TOKYO

Senior Editor	Lothlórien Homet
Publishing Services Manager	Edward Wade
Senior Production Editor	Cheri Palmer
Editorial Assistant	Corina Derman
Project Management	Matrix Productions
Cover Design	Frances Baca
Cover Image	Getty/Charles Sleicher
Text Design	Mark Ong (Based on a design by Stuart L. Silberman Graphic Design)
Composition/Illustration	Technologies 'n' Typography
Copyeditor	Sharilyn Hovind
Proofreader	Jennifer McClain
Indexer	Bill Meyers
Cover Printer	Phoenix Color Corporation
Interior Printer	The Maple-Vail Book Manufacturing Group

Designations used by companies to distinguish their products are often claimed as trademarks or registered trademarks. In all instances in which Morgan Kaufmann Publishers is aware of a claim, the product names appear in initial capital or all capital letters. Readers, however, should contact the appropriate companies for more complete information regarding trademarks and registration.

In no event shall the publisher or the author be liable for any direct, indirect, special, consequential, or inconsequential damages. No warranties are expressed or implied, including warranties of merchantability or fitness for a particular purpose.

Morgan Kaufmann Publishers
An imprint of Elsevier Science
340 Pine Street, Sixth Floor
San Francisco, CA 94104-3205
www.mkp.com

© 2003 by Elsevier Science (USA)
All rights reserved.

07 06 05 04 03   5 4 3 2 1

No part of this publication may be reproduced, stored in a retrieval system, or transmitted in any form or by any means—electronic, mechanical, photocopying, or otherwise—without the prior written permission of the publisher.

Library of Congress Control Number: 2002115469
ISBN: 1-55860-892-3

Transferred to Digital Printing 2007

*To my wife and partner, Sue, and to my children,
Lisa, Kimberly, and David*

Contents

Foreword xi
Preface xiii
Acknowledgments. xv

Chapter 1   Global E-Commerce and the Web. 1

The Web Is Global 2
Seven Frequent Global Web Site Design Mistakes 4
  Mistake #1: Assuming a Market Is North American Only 5
  Mistake #2: Assuming an Audience Is Exclusively English Speaking 5
  Mistake #3: Assuming "Globalization" Simply Means Support for
    Multiple Languages 7
  Mistake #4: Ignoring Geography and Time Zones 8
  Mistake #5: Neglecting the Importance of Information and Transaction Data 9
  Mistake #6: Transacting Business Exclusively in U.S. Dollars 10
  Mistake #7: Lack of Awareness of Regulatory Acts 11
A Web of Diverse Data 11

Chapter 2   Defining the Terms *Global, Regional, International,* and *Local* 15

Global 15
Regional 17
International 18
Local 18

Contents

Languages and Dialects... 19
Internationalization and Localization in Brief.................. 21
    Character Sets... 23
    Internationalization and Localization Skills................... 25

Chapter 3   Global Standards 27

Types of Information and Data Standards........................ 30
Common Consumer-Oriented Data Concepts......................... 35
    Name of an Individual (Person)................................ 37
    Identifier for an Individual (Person)......................... 39
    Residence, Postal, or Delivery Address........................ 40
    Telephone Number.. 44
    Country... 47
    Currency.. 49
    Language.. 52
    Unit of Measure... 52
    Date.. 54
    Gender.. 56

Common Business-Oriented Data Concepts......................... 57
    Identifier for a Business..................................... 58
    Industry Code... 59
    Bank Account Number... 60

Customer Preferences, Locale, and Market Affinities............ 61
SLKD Auto Rental Example—Locale................................ 63

Chapter 4   Globalized Data and Transactions 65

Presentation and Capture of Global Data........................ 65
Global Customer Relationship Management (G-CRM)................ 66
Typical Global B2C, Web-Based Customer Relationship............ 68
Typical Global B2C Technology Cycle............................ 70
SLKD Auto Rental Example—Global Data........................... 74
    Locale Identification... 75

Product Selection. 77
Customer and Order Data Capture 78
Confirmation. 91

Chapter 5 Globalization Process and Techniques 93
Defining Global Business Requirements 94
Identifying Potential Markets. 97
Developing Market Profiles 99
Market Validation 101
Formalizing the Design Approach 108
Functional Requirements. 110
Global Data Requirements. 119
Reintegration of Requirements 136
Global Transaction Design 137

Chapter 6 Transaction Engineering. 143
XML-Based Transaction Solutions 144
Change Is Inevitable 169
Global Transaction Engineering Principles to Avoid. 171
Beware! 175

Chapter 7 Enterprise Application Integration 177
Global Data Integration 179
Extensive Use of Standards and Classifications 186
Operational vs. Analytical. 191

Chapter 8 The Complexities of Mobile E-Commerce 193
The Wireless Globe 194
Wireless Design Complexities. 195

Contents

WML 196

Appendix A   Global Standards References 199

Appendix B   Resources and Recommended Reading 205

Glossary 211

Index 217

Foreword

Revolutions, though seemingly abrupt from a historical perspective, can span many years or decades within the lifetime of an individual. Paradoxical as this may seem, the full acceptance of a phenomenon is most often significantly predated by the same forces and ideas in a more nascent form.

Global e-commerce is one of these concepts that is set to become a revolution, yet today still lacks the necessary broad-based understanding and support from the world business community. In short, global e-commerce is in the process of accumulating the necessary adherents and critical momentum leading up to its explosion on the world scene.

Beginning in 1997, I began implementing global Web sites and then developed technology and methodologies for global e-commerce. During this time I often wished that I had a book to which I could refer customers, partners, and colleagues so that they could better understand the key concepts for success.

Even when I began lecturing on global e-commerce in 2000, there was still no definitive book on the subject. The moment I have been waiting for has finally arrived. This book by James Bean presents the critical concepts and implementation criteria that you will need to understand prior to embarking on any global e-commerce initiative. Global e-commerce is not only very powerful, it is complex, multithreaded, and full of compromises.

This book is a critical step toward a broader and more complete understanding of a force that has the potential to reshape the world both economically and politically. The tools for developing a competitive advantage with global e-commerce already exist; what has been missing up until now has been easily accessible information and best practices for generating successful global e-commerce projects.

In writing this book, Bean has developed a road map that will take you from basic concepts and key parameters to a strategic overview of methodologies, and then to implementation technologies and techniques. The first five chapters should be sufficient to bring most business-oriented readers up to speed, while the final three chapters of the book should be of particular interest to technical implementers. It is in these final chapters that James shows how to apply the latest standards and XML-based approaches to creating successful global e-commerce initiatives.

With this valuable resource you are now armed to the teeth with twenty-first-century globalization insight. The time is ripe for being at the leading edge of the next revolution. I wish you the best of luck on your journey and much success in the days ahead.

Jorden Woods
Cofounder
GlobalSight

Preface

It is becoming evident that the next evolution in business is a global Web economy. With the development of the Web, the ability to transact business with customers anywhere in the world has become not only a reality, but also an imperative. However, there are still numerous challenges, preconceptions, and biases that need to be resolved.

Developing and publishing open or unrestricted content to the Web makes that information globally available. However, this does not mean that the information can be readily understood or used by all people around the world. Nor does it mean that the information driven by any random Web site can be captured, exchanged, or integrated with other enterprise business processes.

An obvious challenge to a global Web economy is language. Language is a requisite medium for consumer-to-consumer and business-to-consumer communication. Language is also fundamental to developing global customer relationships. However, the most common misconception regarding globalization is that the ability to provide Web page content in a variety of languages is the sole solution to globalization success. This book acknowledges the importance of language and similar presentation capabilities, but goes beyond the typical language-focused approach to include the globalized information and transactional data integration that are required to facilitate and conduct global e-commerce. Both are necessary in developing a successful global Web site.

Web site globalization is first and foremost a process. As a process, it incorporates planning, research, design, and development. The process also includes and references internationalization and localization, as well as variations and extensions of the more traditional concepts of data standards and data integration.

This book defines the tasks, activities, techniques, and deliverables that must be resolved in order to succeed. It is important to note that variations of this process abound.

The electronic age, particularly the Web, provides the ability to capture and process tremendous volumes of information, from anywhere in the world and at incredible speed. As a result, traditional enterprise business systems are often inundated with massive amounts of information that is highly diverse in structure, format, and context. In order to identify and describe the sources and targets of this information and to effectively transact business, the associated information (data) must also be globalized.

This book was developed from the point of view of a traditional United States–based company that has decided to extend its business to include Web-based e-commerce. These "traditional" enterprises are often unaware of the opportunities and challenges of a global economy, and when confronted with the challenges, they are suddenly in dire need of solutions. It is important to note that this perspective could be shifted to apply equally to business enterprises in countries other than the United States.

The focus of this book is on 1) the evolution of the Web as a medium for transacting global business, 2) acknowledging the importance of language as a component of the Web's globalization process, and 3) the critical importance of globally diverse data. Without a well-defined globalization strategy, the ability to effectively identify, attract, acquire, and integrate new customers from a global marketplace is difficult at best and more than likely not possible. The audience includes (but is not limited to)

- Web or e-commerce planners/strategists
- Web or e-commerce architects
- Web or e-commerce developers
- Data architects and database designers
- Enterprise application architects

Keeping this primary audience in mind, some subjects are covered more deeply than others, based on what is useful for people in these roles. IT and business managers working with the above may also find much that is of interest.

This book has a companion Web site at www.mkp.com/globalcommerce. Here you will find useful links and errata.

Acknowledgments

I would like to acknowledge the publishing staff at Morgan Kaufmann, in particular Lothlórien Homet for her enthusiasm, guidance, and patience and Corina Derman (thank you!). I would also like to acknowledge family members, business partners, and friends who have been supportive of my work over the years, including Sue Bean, Jack Bauer, David Bean, Lisa Bean ("SA"), Kimberly Bean ("Bug"), Beth Bauer, Norm Johnson, Sandy Johnson, Barb Wakefield, Dick Schreiber, Nick Torrez, Lara Tang, Gloria Michalak, Wally Sellman, Caren Shiozaki, Jerry Halterman, Mike Ruttledge, Deb Barra, Dennis Barra, Patrick Vincent, Mike Nicewarner, Lori Gubernat, John Gubernat, Jerry Blidy, Dave Blidy, and many others (you know who you are).

In addition, I would like to acknowledge the following industry and technology standards organizations: W3C, IETF, ISO, ANSI, NIST, ITU, UPU, UCC, BIPM, OASIS, and the many others. Without the contributions of these organizations, we would not have achieved the current advances in collaborative Web-based business and technology.

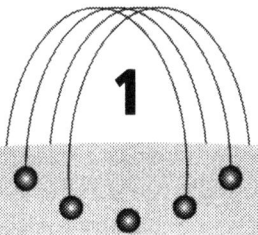

Global E-Commerce and the Web

The advent of e-commerce at the turn of this century brought about a revolution in business processes and redefined our notion of a customer. The most important technology and business innovations that enabled this revolution are the extension of the Internet to the Web and the electronic transaction of business known as e-commerce. With this combination of technology and business, viewing of information, communication, advertising, marketing, and business transactions can be initiated at any time of the day and from anywhere in the world by a consumer with access to the Web. Not only can business be transacted rapidly and without the constraint of physical borders, but also Web-based e-commerce is considered to be significantly more economical and efficient than traditional business processes.

In order to better understand the implications of global e-commerce, it is important to gain a solid foundation in the basic concepts. As companies introduced more applications to the Web, it became apparent that describing and presenting their products and services was the most rudimentary form of Web application. The next logical progression was the ability to accept and process business transactions (what quickly became known as e-commerce). In the simplest terms, *e-commerce* is the ability to use the Web as a marketing channel and as a sales interface to initiate and transact business between providers and consumers. The most common e-commerce models are *business-to-consumer (B2C)*, *business-to-business (B2B)*, and *consumer-to-business-to-business (C2B2B)*, or what is often described as a *portal*. B2C applications are still the most common consumer-oriented e-commerce models, although B2B and C2B2B applications are quickly gaining ground.

As a simple B2C scenario, a business presents information describing their products and services, accepts and validates transactions, ships products and services, and receives payment. From the other point of view, a prospect or customer visits a business Web page, identifies products or services of interest, makes appropriate selections, agrees to terms, initiates a transaction for purchase, provides payment, and accepts delivery. As evidenced by this simple scenario, the initial B2C e-commerce model is similar to traditional consumer-oriented business processes. The obvious differences lie in the ability to conduct business without having to physically visit a "brick-and-mortar" institution, along with the efficiencies resulting from advertising over the Web, rapid execution of transactions, and the decreased number of required support personnel. Eliminating the visit to a brick-and-mortar institution is even more significant when considering that physical distance between the business and the consumer is typically of little consequence. In fact, the business and the consumer could be geographically located in the same physical community or on opposite sides of the world.

A simple variation of the B2C model can also be used to describe a B2B application. With the B2B model, the "consumer" would be another business rather than an individual or person. One business markets and provides goods and services to another. In addition, both participants of a B2B e-commerce model may also be collaborators or trading partners. That is, they may operate under a formal or informal contract, and with agreed-upon terms such as scheduling, pricing, delivery, and support. Other frequently observed characteristics of a B2B e-commerce model are volumetrics. The size and exchange frequency of B2B transactions between one business and another tend to be far greater than typical individual consumer transactions.

The Web Is Global

For many traditional brick-and-mortar businesses, the basic Web-based e-commerce models presented a seeming panacea for transacting global business. This was especially true of the traditional consumer-oriented business, where the cost of doing business internationally was significantly complex and potentially prohibitive. However, this new consumer business model also introduced a number of what at first appeared to be "subtle" opportunities and challenges. It is important to note that the Internet originated primarily from U.S. sponsorship (it evolved as a separation from a Department of Defense DARPA network). As a result, the original perspective taken in the development of many Web sites was narrowly focused on a North American market rather than the diversity of the globe. This North

American influence resulted in most original B2C Web pages being expressed using English as the primary language for product marketing and sales. This parochial English-language emphasis and North American view of the Web are still frequently observed today.

Today, many North American companies view the Web as a cost-effective medium for engaging in business with the same types of consumers that they have in the past. Unfortunately, this view does not recognize the opportunities afforded by a far broader global marketplace. Focusing on an English-speaking, North American market will rarely target prospective consumers from other countries and cultures and capture them as customers. Additionally, with the recent emphasis on growth and prosperity through a global economy and free trade, the ability to recognize and address globally diverse markets can make or break the traditional brick-and-mortar business. However, the long-standing barriers to global business of geography, language, and culture still present daunting challenges.

The first challenge to understanding the global nature of the Web is recognizing its lack of physical constraints. Surf the Web for any length of time and you will discover Web sites expressed using complex character sets, and URLs with domains such as .uk (i.e., United Kingdom), .au (i.e., Australia), .fr (i.e., France), and .de (i.e., Germany). (Domains are the terminating part of a URL or Web address.) It soon becomes obvious that the Web is not physically constrained or bound by geography, language, or culture. As the term *World Wide Web* implies, the Web is by default unbounded and global. However, either some business leaders and technologists are unaware that the Web is global, or they are ambivalent to a globally diverse market. To help describe the concept of a global Web, I often use the simple statement in Figure 1.1.

As described in Figure 1.1, if a Web site URL is either indexed by a search engine or available as a link from another Web page, and the Web site has unrestricted access, then it is available for viewing by any Web user with browser access, and from any location in the world where there is an available Internet connection. The online user browsing the Web site might be located in another country, may be of any culture or nationality, and may or may not speak English as a primary language. As you might imagine, this presents a tremendous opportunity to use the Web as a marketing channel, as a medium for communication, and as a method for presentation that is not limited to the geographic or physical location of either potential customers or the originating business.

Assuming a business enterprise is interested in attracting global prospects as customers, the next challenge is providing an environment that is aligned with the preferences of a globally diverse audience. Addressing this challenge requires the identification of characteristics and preferences that will help to attract globally

> **If your Web page or site**
> - Is published as a link on other sites
> - Is indexed to a search engine
> - Does not have restricted access or security
>
> **And**
> - Your potential consumer has Web access
>
> *Then, by default, your Web page or site is global.*

Figure 1.1 The global Web

diverse viewers as prospects and then capture them as customers. The most common consumer characteristics include country of residence, preferred language, dialect, and preferred currency. Additionally, depending upon the offered product or service, there may be a number of other important demographic characteristics. Once the necessary global consumer characteristics and preferences have been identified, the content of the Web site can be presented in a manner that targets that audience. Design and development techniques applied to address the language-related needs of a globally diverse audience are referred to as *internationalization* and *localization*, which are described in Chapter 2.

Once a global audience has been identified and the Web page content has been translated to the audience's preferred language, the next challenge is the ability to acquire, process, and integrate globally diverse data. The solution to this challenge is a set of design principles and techniques, which are the main focus of this book. However, before jumping into the complex world of data concepts and standards, it is important to understand the most common Web globalization challenges and mistakes.

Seven Frequent Global Web Site Design Mistakes

Even though a business enterprise may have recognized the global nature of the Web, it may deploy Web applications without consideration for the many opportunities and challenges presented by the global marketplace. The result is a Web site that presents product and service information in a manner that is limited to the originating country, language, and culture of that business. Such Web sites are marginally effective at attracting a broader global audience, and the development effort is often considered to be a globalization failure. The potential global customer will either be unable to interpret the Web site content, be unable to navigate the site, or abandon the Web browser session if there is significant difficulty in understanding or completing a transaction.

The real problem in this case is not failure to recognize that the Web is global, but rather the lack of a rigorous globalization process and design principles. The potential customer is mistakenly assumed to interpret Web page information in the same manner as a traditional North American customer. Web sites of this type can generally be identified by seven common design mistakes, as follows.

Mistake #1: Assuming a Market Is North American Only

The first globalization mistake for a North American organization is assuming that those who view its Web site and Web page content are exclusively from North America. If the business enterprise is physically located in North America and has traditionally focused on English-speaking North American prospects and customers, most likely the presentation, content, and navigation of its Web pages will be aligned or biased to a North American audience.

As an example, consider the hospitality industry in Las Vegas, Nevada, USA. When in Las Vegas, it is quite obvious that there is a very large contingent of international visitors. One could presume that international visitors and vacationers present an enormous potential market for the hospitality industry, and more specifically for this U.S. resort location. These observations are supported by many noticeable international cultural influences (e.g., frequent currency exchange, multiple spoken and written languages, a broad selection of available cuisines, etc.).

However, Web sites for several of these resorts, hotels, and restaurants are expressed only in English and present pricing exclusively in U.S. currency. With such Web sites, the assumption is that the customer understands the English language to a degree that warrants interest and allows for functional navigation of the site. Even if the potential customer is reasonably comfortable with the English language (as limited examples, an English-speaking resident of the United Kingdom, Australia, or New Zealand), they must perform cumbersome manual currency conversions in order to estimate and plan for the cost of their visit. When considering a potential visitor from another country, this type of Web site is largely ineffective.

Mistake #2: Assuming an Audience Is Exclusively English Speaking

A second mistake is assuming that the Web site audience is exclusively English speaking. Even though the target market might include predominantly English-

Table 1.1 Global Internet statistics on language

Language	People with Internet access (approximate)	Percentage (approximate) of world online population
English	228 million	40.20%
Total non-English languages	339 million	59.80%
European languages	192 million	33.90%
Asian languages	146 million	26.10%
Total*	560 million	

Source: Global Reach, March 2002, *www.global-reach.biz/globstats/index.php3*
* Totals may include other numbers not shown here.

speaking countries such as England, Australia, and New Zealand, there are many residents of these and other countries who read and speak other languages. Some traditional North American companies will design and implement Web sites and Web page content using English as the primary language. An English-only site will present difficulty for many potential customers and may inadvertently offend others (the business may be viewed as "arrogant" because the Web page content is presented or expressed only in English).

Of important note are metrics that describe online users according to primary or preferred language. According to Global Reach, a leading company in the global market research arena, as of May 2002, the number of English-speaking online Web users was approximately 228 million, or 40.2% of the total online population, as compared with 339 million, or 59.8%, of non-English-speaking users (see Table 1.1).

At approximately 40% of all online Web users, the English-speaking online population is obviously significant. However, it is important to note that there has been an observable decline over time in the ratio of English-speaking users to all online Web users. In some respects these metrics can be misinterpreted. The total number or population of English-speaking online Web users is actually trending upward (as opposed to the percentage). However, when compared as a percentage or ratio to the total number of non-English-speaking populations that have recently gained access to the Web, the trend appears to be declining. When evaluating these metrics, consideration should be given to examples such as Asia and Africa, where there are significant local populations that are gaining access to the Web.

Mistake #3: Assuming "Globalization" Simply Means Support for Multiple Languages

After acknowledging that multilingual support is an important and fundamental globalization activity, and even when Web site content has been translated into the primary languages of the target market, another mistake is assuming that multilingual support alone makes a Web site a success in terms of globalization. This assumption could not be further from the truth. It is undisputed that presenting Web content in the preferred language of the target customer is an important requirement. Multilingual support represents the principal medium for communication and contact with the global customer as a preliminary method for developing a relationship.

However, multilingual support is not the entire solution. In addition to language and translation activities, there are a number of globalization-related characteristics identified by customer preference or locale that need to be incorporated in order to succeed. The presentation of currency amounts (with the appropriate currency symbol, decimal positions, and decimal separator), telephone numbers (using accepted format for display of international telephone numbers), and dates are common examples of important global presentation characteristics. Extending the example of welcoming an international visitor to a Web page for a resort in Las Vegas, design questions such as those in Figure 1.2 must be addressed.

- Are quotes, pricing, and similar currency amounts presented in both U.S. dollars and the preferred currency of the customer?

- Are currency symbols and appropriate decimalization presented?

- Are the company contact and customer service telephone numbers presented in acceptable international format?

- Do all telephone numbers assist users in determining whether they need to dial a local international access number and the target country code?

- Are scheduling, reservation, and confirmation dates presented in the preferred or local format of the customer (e.g., yyyy-mm-dd, mm-dd-yyyy, dd-mm-yyyy)?

Figure 1.2 Sample subset of globalized Web site questions

Mistake #4: Ignoring Geography and Time Zones

Another common globalization oversight is not recognizing the importance of geography and its relationship to time zones. Often the Web sites of large U.S.-based companies will be unavailable at certain times, such as Sunday night from 2:00 A.M. until 4:00 A.M. eastern standard time (EST), in order to perform backups and maintenance. Taking a site down for maintenance during the sample time frame appears to be an ideal opportunity to perform site updates and backups given the work schedules of technology support personnel located in the United States. However, if the Web site becomes unavailable during this time and the target market includes consumers located in central Europe, they will be unable to access the site during their primary hours for Web use.

Some technologists will argue that they have dynamic rollover or multiple Web servers to carry off-hour site traffic. Given the state of Web technology today, this is an excellent solution. These organizations have recognized the potential problem and can afford the necessary technology redundancy. However, the scenario is more troublesome for those organizations that cannot afford these costly solutions yet still consider themselves (or want to be) "global."

Another important consideration regarding time zones is the identifying time stamps applied to business transactions. As manufacturing and distribution companies continue to adopt "just-in-time" (JIT) principles and given the rapid transaction capabilities of the Web, there may be instances of time stamps from a Web server or application server at the physical Web site being applied to transactions at varying locales. For a more business-oriented site (such as a B2B site), this opens the potential for inaccuracy in reporting inventory movement such as "dock-to-stock" and "dock-to-dock." In rare situations, depending upon the method for determining and applying the time stamp, the transfer of inventory from one physical storage location to another, or from a vendor to a customer warehouse, could be time-stamped as "received" before it was actually shipped, resulting in numerous reporting and planning anomalies.

Including time zones as a design consideration for the time stamping of transactions at first appears to be common sense, yet the error in the previous example is possible. As an additional observation, this scenario is even possible within the United States, which falls under several time zones. Although the most recognized continental U.S. time zones are eastern standard (EST), central standard (CST), mountain standard (MST), and pacific standard (PST), there are many exceptions, which vary by state, county, region, and locality.[1] Such exceptions are often found during seasonal time zone changes such as daylight saving time.

Further complicating the concept of time zones is an incorrect assumption that geographic alignment is always in one-hour offsets. There are some geographic areas with time zone offsets other than one hour, such as Calcutta, India, where the offset from UTC (coordinated universal time) is +05:30, and Katmandu, Nepal, where the offset to UTC is +05:45. As a result, time-stamp information should include not only the local time, but also the full offset to UTC. This can help to avoid the pitfall of computing all time zone offsets and associated time stamps with one-hour offsets.

Mistake #5: Neglecting the Importance of Information and Transaction Data

The mistake with the most significant impact on enterprise application and data integration is neglecting the importance of standardized information and transaction data. Beyond the obvious necessity for multilingual support is the ability to acquire, process, and integrate globally diverse information and data. The most common examples of consumer-oriented information are an individual's name, address, and telephone number. While it is important to attract a global customer with Web site content that is translated into their preferred language, the ability to capture information from and about the global customer is critical to developing a relationship and transacting business.

Names, addresses, and telephone numbers vary widely as to context, format, structure, and allowable content. Using the example of an individual's name, combinations of geographic locale, culture, religion, social status, military status, and ethnicity can introduce significant variations and complexity. In the United States, a commonly recognized name format includes three basic name particles (first name, middle name or middle initial, and last name). Even this example is inefficient when considering the cultural population mix of North America. Some cultures may require multiple middle and last names (especially those influenced by religion or with a Central or South American background). Among many other variations are hyphenation and concatenation of multiple last names, name connectives, family line (where last names become the first name of successive generations), a single name, use of only a last name, and the concept of a maiden name, which is the last name of a spouse prior to marriage.

---

[1] U.S. Code Collection, Title 15, Chapter 6, Subchapter IX, Section 260a, Advancement of time or changeover dates, Legal Information Institute, Cornell Law School; *www4.law.cornell.edu/uscode/15/260a.html*.

Residence, delivery, and postal addresses are of even greater complexity. One all too common address format in the United States is composed of only three lines of information (addressee, street address, and the combination of city, state, and zip code as the third line). Even in the United States, what should be obvious to most technologists is that this three-line address format (frequently found on Web page and preprinted paper forms) is significantly flawed when considering such simple variations as apartments or business addresses (including corporate complexes, buildings, suites, and floor numbers).

Perhaps the most significant flaw of the common three-line U.S. address format is the descriptive label or text for the zip code. The Zoning Improvement Plan (zip) originated with the U.S. Postal Service and was first implemented in 1963 as process to simplify and expedite the sorting and delivery of mail. In many countries outside the United States, zip codes are not only unrecognized, but are often confused with a well-known file-compression format. An internationally recognized and more accurate text description or label for the same address information is "postal code."

These information and transaction data concepts, as well as several other common consumer-oriented data concepts, are described in further detail in Chapter 3.

Mistake #6: Transacting Business Exclusively in U.S. Dollars

Another frequent Web design oversight is monetary expression that is limited to the U.S. dollar currency type. In order to effectively conduct e-commerce over the Web, a site's content must include monetary amounts for quotation, pricing, and the like. Monetary currency is a complex topic for a number of reasons. One is the rate at which the value of one currency can fluctuate against another. If a U.S. business quotes a price to a customer that is based on the U.S. dollar, it may choose to fix that price in that currency by term or contract. Payment for a corresponding transaction would then be settled exclusively with U.S. dollars (potentially after a direct currency conversion and exchange from another currency type to the dollar). This technique is quite common and avoids some of the transaction and regulatory complexities involved with currency fluctuation and exchange.

Alternatively, other businesses may find it is advantageous to quote prices for products and services in both a base currency such as the U.S. dollar and the customer's preferred currency or the currency of the customer's locale (e.g., English pound, Australian dollar, etc.). When considering this or a similar scenario, it becomes important to notify the customer of the base currency type and rate at which the quoted amounts are determined, with the annotation that alternative currencies are provided as a courtesy and are subject to market fluctuation until the transaction is completed.

Using the earlier example of an international customer planning a vacation (frequently referred to outside the United States as holiday) to a Las Vegas resort, viewing quoted prices presented exclusively in U.S. dollars is far from convenient. In order to plan and estimate the cost of the impending visit, the potential customer must perform a separate, manual conversion to their local or preferred currency. Additionally, depending upon the base currency, currency and market fluctuations may result in significant variance by the time travel has been initiated.

Mistake #7: Lack of Awareness of Regulatory Acts

Although it is suggested that beyond multilingual support, global information and transaction data are the most significant design and development issues, it is also suggested that regulatory acts may present the greatest level of complexity. Compounding this challenge are the number, variations, and limited availability of published materials for international regulatory acts (e.g., by nation, region, or municipality). Seeking information on some legal and regulatory topics as they apply in an international setting is difficult but not impossible. However, there are many topics that may be of issue, including the following:

- Privacy
- Taxation and tariffs
- Import/export regulations
- Import/export duties and tariffs
- Employment, wage, and benefit issues
- Nondisclosure and competitive secrecy agreements
- Liability (personal, professional, business, and other)
- Warranties and guarantees
- Fraud and fraud protection
- Copyrights, trademarks, and patents
- Consumer protection
- Information retention
- Financial reporting and disclosure
- Incorporation, business ownership, partnership, equity, and DBAs
- Discrimination and bias

It is therefore recommended to seek guidance from an authoritative source such as an attorney who specializes in international law.

A Web of Diverse Data

It is important to note that a global market can be represented by multiple geographic locations, languages, and cultures. As a result, multilingual support is a fundamental and important focus of internationalization and localization efforts. However, multilingual support is not the only important design consideration. There are many other critical success factors. The capture, processing, and integration of globally diverse data into the enterprise are also necessary in order to succeed with global e-commerce. Although the content of a Web site may have been translated to the primary languages of the target markets, an inability to correctly capture a customer's name, address, and telephone number (among many other data concepts) will frequently result in the prospective consumer abandoning their browser session or in incomplete or highly inaccurate transactions.

Many European and Asian business enterprises are all too familiar with the challenges of global diversity. Businesses from these regions have a long history in transacting global business and rarely limit their market focus to consumers of a single language or culture. While in practice it is often far from perfect, the ability to market, sell, acquire, and trade products and services among geographically, culturally, and linguistically diverse communities has become a virtual requirement for businesses outside of North America. However, this ability can become a significant challenge for many traditional U.S.-based enterprises.

A common observation is that many traditional North American businesses have a parochial view of the international consumer. One of the most fundamental oversights is assuming that English is the primary language for conducting business. It has historically been assumed that advertising materials, product information, and correspondence produced in English is acceptable to any potential consumer, without consideration for their geographic location or language preference. Recent recognition that all online Web consumers do not speak English as their primary language has resulted in an increased focus on multilingual support and translation. While language is often considered a critical component for effectively attracting and capturing international customers, there are many other critical globalization concepts.

From a technology perspective, the Web originated as a sharable, open, and viewable repository of knowledge that leveraged HTML and the Internet as its underlying technology and infrastructure. Initially, most Web applications presented information to someone with a Web browser. They were used primarily to describe companies and to advertise products and services. These initial Web applications focused on the rendering of information for presentation to the individual as an online user or consumer. If you had access to the Internet (Web) and an HTML-capable browser, you could navigate among various nodes and view the resources posted there as information (HTML pages). This capability to find and view massive amounts of information signified a revolution in collaborative communication and knowledge sharing. Information was no longer limited to printed publications, person-to-person communication, radio, or television.

The advent of the Web also presented tremendous opportunity. After having been deemed available for commercial use, many businesses quickly identified the Web as a cost-effective method for advertising to a consumer-oriented market. These businesses could rapidly develop marketing information and have it available for presentation to any Web user who might be interested. Traditional forms of advertising and marketing such as mailing lists, form letters, brochures, printed magazine and newspaper advertisements, and televised commercials could be supplemented with this new advertising medium, at a fraction of the cost. The Web user soon became aware (sometimes painfully) that the Web no longer held purely academic or noncommercial information. In defense of these business organizations, without opening the Internet and Web to commercial endeavors, the support costs for the underlying technology would no doubt have become overwhelming and the commercial progression of the Web may have stalled or become cost prohibitive.

Although the Web has always been to some degree global, recent emphasis on the importance of a global economy has provided motivation for the evolution of Web-based business to global e-commerce. As shown in the coming chapter, language and culture play significant and fundamental roles in global e-commerce. Similarly, global information and transaction data are also of critical importance. The challenges associated with integration of global information and transaction data are highly diverse structures, format, context, and allowable content. Examples of the most common consumer-oriented data include the following:

- Name (of individual)
- Address
- Telephone number
- Currency
- Date
- Units of measure

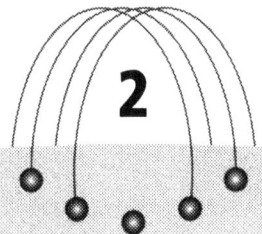

Defining the Terms *Global, Regional, International,* and *Local*

The lexicon associated with globalization can be somewhat puzzling. Terms such as *global, regional, international,* and *local* are used frequently and at times interchangeably. Confusion and frustration by the uninitiated business leader or technologist is often warranted. Many globalization, internationalization, and localization practitioners mistakenly make the assumption that their audience is well versed in their particular discipline and will often use these terms in the abstract to imply that some form of global diversity exists between the topics they present. To help clarify the use of this vocabulary, I include several explanations. However, before focusing on exact definitions for each term, it is important to consider the term's context, application, or use.

Global

The term *global* is often used interchangeably with *international*. Intuitively, it is interpreted as representing all locations, nations, cultures, and peoples of the world (see Figure 2.1). While an admirable goal, this is not a practical application of the term as applied to business and especially to e-commerce. The reality is that the Web is indeed global, but developing a single Web site or application that targets every country, culture, and language of the globe is most likely not achievable (at least not with just a reasonable effort). More appropriately, use of the term *global* as in *global marketplace* is intended to describe broad collections of regions, nations,

Chapter 2 Defining the Terms *Global, Regional, International,* and *Local*

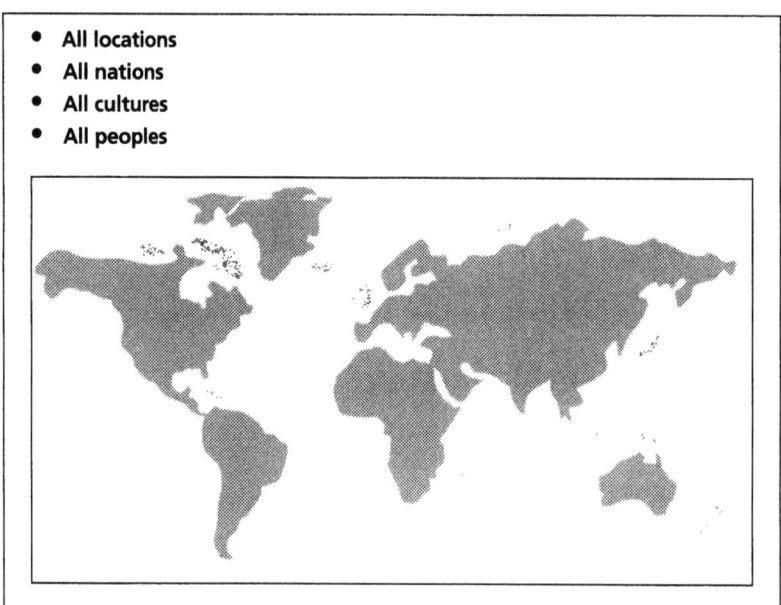

Figure 2.1 A global perspective

cultures, and peoples that are not restricted by geography, language, or culture. The phrase *global marketplace* will often refer to targeted combinations of regions, nations, and locales rather than the entire globe. Consider an application of Pareto's Law (often referred to as the 80/20 rule), where 80% of the world's population could be addressed with Web page content that is engineered to target 20% of the known languages and cultures.

Globalization is often abbreviated as G11N (reflecting the first letter g followed by 11 characters and ending with the letter n). Globalization is actually a process that identifies and targets many nations, regions, cultures, and peoples. A typical Web globalization effort will include identification of target prospects and customers that embody a vast number of cultures and languages, development of representative market profiles, affinity analysis, and formalization of business and technology requirements for Web presentation and data.

A globalization effort will address both presentation and data. Presentation infers the linguistic, cultural, and expressive characteristics required to attract and communicate with a global customer. These characteristics are well founded in language. Additionally, a requisite companion to presentation is data (also referred to as "data content"). Data content implies the underlying global data and transaction information that is fundamental to completing transactions and, when integrated with other traditional enterprise data, enables related business processes. The significance of globalized data is the focus of this book.

Regional

Like the term *global*, the terms *region* or *regional* may refer to combinations of nations, cultures, and peoples. However, the most common uses of these terms apply primarily to geography (geographic proximities, borders, closely located nations, or defined market areas). In some cases, a subset of national borders, countries, or locations may define a region (see Figure 2.2). In other cases, a region is defined by a set of business or marketing characteristics that may cross, subset, or combine countries (e.g., "European region," "Asian region," "North American region," etc.). It is important to note that the countries or borders defined by a region are often of close geographic proximity. However, this is not a specific constraint or restriction.

The process of defining regions (sometimes known as *regionalization*) involves the identification of target markets as sets of nations, geographic areas, and cultures

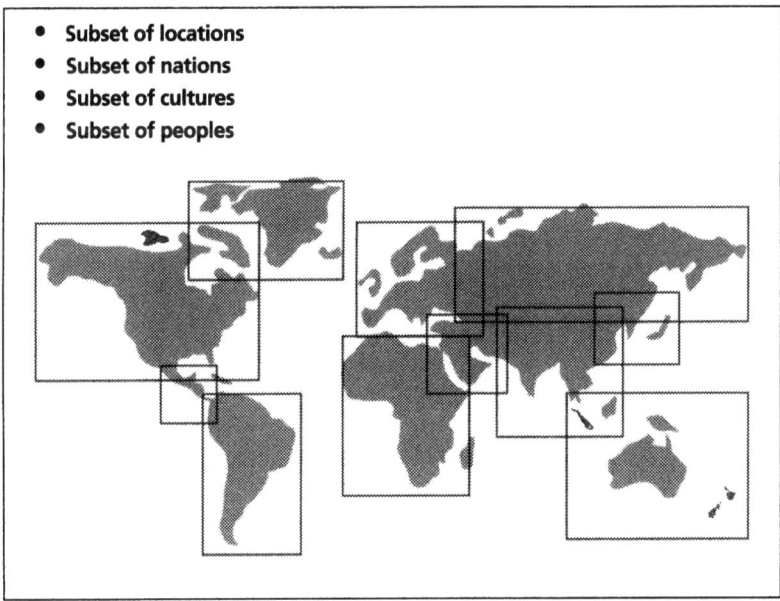

Figure 2.2 A regional perspective

with observable affinities. The most notable regional affinities are geography and economy. A traditional approach to regionalization can be somewhat abstract and generally driven by enterprise market analysis, market segmentation, prevailing sales territories, or the physical location of personnel or product storage facilities. As defined by some companies, regions may also overlap or may be geographic subdivisions of countries (e.g., the U.S. regions "East," "West," "Midwest," "South," and "Southwest").

International

A simple definition for the term *international* is "of or representing multiple nations or countries." As implied, an international market will consist of or focus on more than one country (i.e., nation). In order to attract the citizens of those countries as potential customers, a number of design and development principles come into play. *Internationalization* (often abbreviated and referred to as *I18N*, reflecting the first letter *i* followed by 18 characters and ending with the letter *n*) is a process that describes, aligns, or repositions products and services with the languages and cultures of multiple nations or in some cases regions. Extending internationalization to the Web, the primary focus is to design and engineer Web sites that target customers from various countries, with modular content that may be further tailored to individual languages and cultures.

A simple example of an international market that exhibits affinities with English as a primary language might include the United States, Canada, England, Australia, and New Zealand. With this example, the noted countries are not contiguous as to location, and a number of other languages and cultures may be represented. However, when considering English as a frequently used or spoken language (see Figure 2.3), it is an obvious affinity. As a base language, English is common to the sample market. However, there are other important characteristics to consider. English comprises multiple dialects, with variations in spelling, context, and colloquialism. Also, languages other than English may be of significant use, varying monetary currencies may be used, and the display format of a date can vary. These and other characteristics are identified as possible variations by the internationalization process. However, they are usually resolved later by the localization process.

Local

A *local* market is one that is well defined and specific to a location and corresponding regional preferences such as language and currency. In short, an international market can be further defined by a collection of locales. Internationalization

- A set of nations or countries
- Language and/or cultural affinities

Country	Primary or common language
United States	English
Canada	English
England	English
Australia	English
New Zealand	English

Figure 2.3 An international perspective

identifies geographic locations, cultural characteristics, and affinities as *locales*, which in combination act as the drivers for more granular localization. The localization process incorporates design and development techniques that focus on language translation and cultural presentation characteristics. *Localization* is often abbreviated and referred to as *L10N* (reflecting the first letter *l* followed by 10 characters and ending with the letter *n*.

In its simplest sense, a locale can be thought of as a combination of location (often a national or regional subdivision), language, dialect, and, potentially, additional preferences such as currency (see Figure 2.4). The defining components of a locale can be used to drive language translation and presentation-level characteristics necessary to address a larger globalization effort. Also of importance are the combinations of locale characteristics within the same country or geographic location. Given the previous example, there may be multiple locales within the United States, defined by combinations of language and dialect.

Languages and Dialects

As a medium for communication and collaboration, language is important. Without the ability to exchange and interpret a common context and meaning, communication will fail. When considering consumer-oriented e-commerce, targeting

- Location (country or regional subdivision)
- Language
- Dialect code
- Currency code, date format, or other characteristics

Location	Primary or common language	Dialect code	Currency code
United States	English	US	USD, 840
Canada	English	CA	CAD, 124
England	English	UK	GBP, 826
Australia	English	AU	AUD, 036
New Zealand	English	NZ	NZD, 554

Figure 2.4 A local perspective

prospects and customers who speak and read languages other than that of the business enterprise is critical to success.

Written and spoken language is more than an assembly of words and phrases. Language also incorporates context and meaning. As a language, English is complex in that when applied in different locales and by different cultures, some words and phrases may have different meanings. To take a simple example, *boot* may be interpreted to represent "a form of footwear" in the United States and "the storage area of an automotive vehicle" in England. More subtle language and context variations can be found within different locales. There are also countless colloquialisms, non-traditional uses of terms, and slang that can be observed.

A frequent assumption is that every country has an official national language, but this is not true. Some countries may have several recognized or official languages, while others may not have any (consider Switzerland, where several languages are used but there is no language known as "Swiss").

To assist with the formal or data-related identification of language, a set of standard language codes have been developed by the International Organization for Standardization (ISO) and used in a number of applications.[1] These language codes

---

1 International Organization for Standardization, ISO 639 Language Code; *www.iso.ch/*.

are invaluable as a classification of primary language. However, they do not readily address or recognize language variations by culture or locale. Some linguists will argue that these variations are spoken rather than written. However, this is not always the case. As evidenced by the previous *boot* example, variations can occur in context. Other variations can be found in spelling (e.g., "globalization" vs. "globalisation"). For the technologist responsible for a translated application, this can present a number of additional problems.

Internationalization and Localization in Brief

Internationalization is not limited to language—it also incorporates a process to identify locales and cultures that will result in the need to uniquely describe or align content. The definition of a locale as a set of characteristics is fundamental to the internationalization process. Some of the more common characteristics used to identify a locale include geographic location, language, dialect, and currency. The locales defined to each target market must be identified in order to push an effort from internationalization to a more specific localization process, where tactical language translation will occur. As might be imagined, the ability to identify the consumer's locale as a set of characteristics is fundamental to a globalized Web site. As global prospects or customers enter the Web site, they must be given the opportunity to select preferences that will identify their locale and/or provide simple navigation to a more specifically localized version of the site content.

The most obvious internationalization techniques focus on separation of core constructs and content from those that must be localized. The noncore or locale-specific constructs are then externalized so that language and culture customization can be implemented while mitigating impact to the primary content or application. In summary, internationalization identifies and takes on the perspective of several locations and cultures and prepares for localization, while localization focuses on the unique presentation requirements of each locale (see Table 2.1).

Internationalization includes various concepts that will be addressed or resolved more specifically by localization:

- Display and print "real estate" (display and print area). Translation from one language to another often results in expansion or contraction of character count and word lengths.
- Collation and sort sequences. Some languages introduce character sets and character sequences that may not follow traditional high- to low-order sorting.

Chapter 2 Defining the Terms *Global, Regional, International,* and *Local*

Table 2.1 Internationalization vs. localization

	Market				
Internationalization	United States	Canada	England	Australia	New Zealand
Localization					
Language	English	English	English	English	English
Country code	U.S.	CA	UK	AU	NZ
Currency code	USD-840	CAD-124	GBP-826	AUD-036	NZD-554

- Browser types. The common types and versions of Web browsers may vary widely by locale. This may be due to availability of a particular browser technology, experience and comfort with a browser, or economic conditions. Internationalization processes will often consider coding that is browser independent.
- Bandwidth and download speeds as they apply to the complexity of Web page content, the number of images, and image size.
- Image colors, color separation, and image density as it applies to display resolution. Some colors do not display well on certain monitors, and some image types may not render as intended depending upon the display resolution.
- Identification of locale-specific language translation of externalized or modular text, messages, dialogs, and error management.
- General usability and navigation principles. Avoiding the use of icons that are not globally recognized (e.g., an octagonal red sign representing "end" or "stop"). Add language-specific image text and alternate titles. Consider the implications of data entry and navigation as they may apply to alternate keyboards.

When following a rigorous internationalization process, the subordinate localization processes formalize the tasks and activities required to develop, present, or express globally diverse content. Among other important activities, consideration is also given to product and brand alignment, where simple language translation may not suffice. Beyond the technology complications of language translation, there are many areas where localization personnel will identify and avoid inaccurate translation of text from one language to another, misinterpretation due to context or culture, and misapplication of a word or phrase that is nonsensical or possibly offensive.

Internationalization and Localization in Brief

In order to properly attract a global consumer, product and service information should be presented in the preferred language and priced in the preferred currency of that consumer. In addition to preferred or local language, there are a number of cultural presentation characteristics that must also be considered by the localization process (e.g., character sets, symbols, punctuation, icons, and date format).

Character Sets

In order to accurately present, display, or print textual information, the appropriate character sets, characters, and glyphs must be used. These are often misunderstood or ignored. There have been many Web sites that have attempted to display or render textual information as translated from English into non–Latin character languages such as Greek, using the base ASCII English character set (ASCII lower set). The result is a set of translated terms using English characters (presented as glyphs) that do not reflect the necessary character forms and diacritics specific to the language in question.

A *glyph* is the visual or pictorial form or representation of a character. Glyphs are the characters that we see when reading a word. This may sound confusing to someone who is only familiar with the English language, but consider that with some languages a character such as *e* might be displayed with different representations or visual forms depending upon the word in which it is used, the position of the word within a sentence, phrase, or statement, or possibly the emphasis placed on the word. (In a simple example, in English the character X can be represented by many different glyphs, using font style and size as presentation variants (see Figure 2.5).)

Additionally, characters can be described by groups of collective encodings known as *character sets*. A character encoding is a uniquely defined numeric value (generally described by either an integer or hex value) that corresponds to a character or symbol. Character encodings allow for the automated storage, transfer, interpretation, manipulation (such as parsing or string manipulation), and rendering (display or print) of primarily text information. Put simply, each character is represented by a code. Depending upon the character encoding scheme used, each character code is unique and is part of a set to which the character is defined.

A *font* is a method of applying display and print styles to a character regardless of character set. Consider that the font face of Arial, the font size of 12 points, and the font style of bold the could be applied to ASCII characters. Similarly, the same font characteristics could also be applied to characters of the ISO Latin character sets; ISO-8859–1, -2, -3, and so on. It is important to note that the application of font characteristics implies operating system support and display support.

Chapter 2 Defining the Terms *Global, Regional, International,* and *Local*

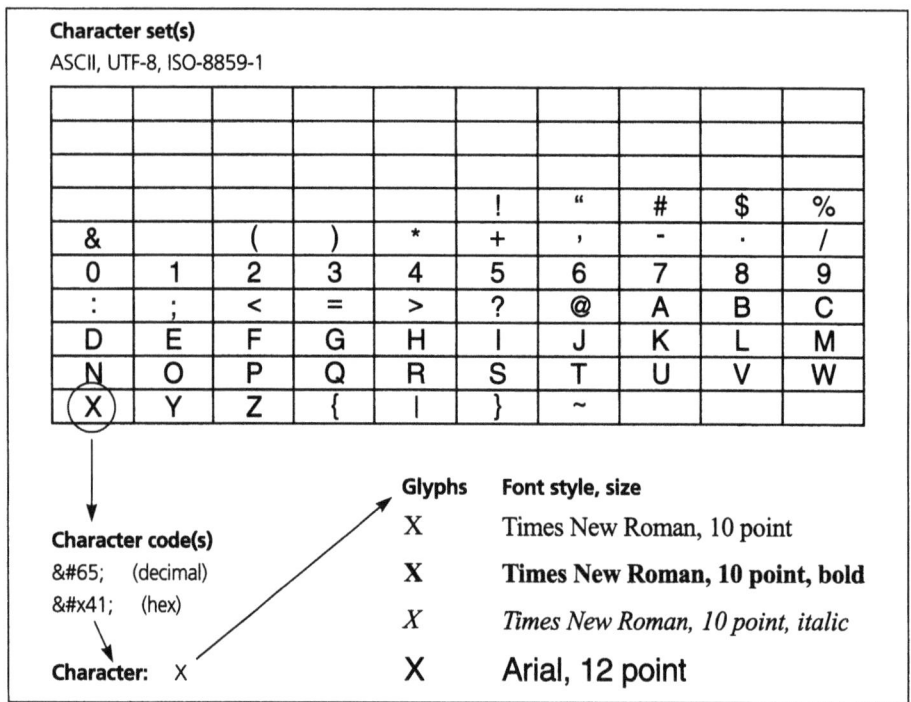

Figure 2.5 Character sets and glyphs

Additionally, font characteristics may not be applicable to the characters or graphic symbols of some languages.

A form of logical intelligence has been used to group characters and codes within character sets. A common scheme used to define a character set is a combination of the set of characters comprising a base alphabet, the basic numeric symbols (ordinal scale), and other common or frequently used symbols (punctuation, currency, etc.). In many cases, these character sets also exhibit some level of language affinity. In some examples, a single character set may include the characters and common symbols of the base alphabet for several similar languages. Some character sets may define characters that can be used by more than one language, and other character sets include symbols of a common theme (e.g., currency symbols and mathematical symbols). However, this scheme is not always so. There are still other character sets that primarily represent a single language (e.g., Devanagari, Thai, Tibetan, etc.).

Internationalization and Localization in Brief

The encoding of characters and the use of character sets present variations based upon underlying technology, combinations of technologies (storage of characters as data vs. rendering of characters for viewing or print). The more common types include the following:

- Unicode (from the Unicode Consortium, generally the most language independent and platform agnostic)
- ISO International Character Set Registry, which is often applied to HTML (ISO-8859–1, . . .-2, . . .-3, etc.)
- Codepages (primarily OEM groupings and ordered sets of character codes that exhibit language affinities)
- Fonts (applied as presentation and print variants, resulting in different glyphs)

In summary, a character is an alphabetic symbol. It is identified by a character code (encoding). A character set is a collection of character encodings that in total are intended to include the base alphabet of one or more languages. A font is a set of styles for rendering (display or print), and a glyph is the graphic representation of a character with styles applied (the representation that you see).

As you might imagine, the development of Web page content translated into multiple languages can be quite complex. When you consider the language, spelling, and presentation characteristics, along with cultural implications of context and colloquialisms, it becomes obvious that language translation for Web-based global e-commerce requires a specialized skill set.

Internationalization and Localization Skills

Internationalization and localization are not trivial processes. The language translation and cultural aspects of these processes require a significant level of expertise. It is suggested that when following a globalization process that includes language- and translation-related activities, it may be of advantage to augment the project team with skilled internationalization and localization experts. While there are a number of reputable industry and service organizations that compete in this area, the level of provable experience versus the cost, the resulting quality, and the speed of delivery may come into question.

When looking to augment existing staff with internationalization and localization resources, validation of skill and expertise are important. Traditional methods of work history validation and reference are highly recommended (including examples of previous work, references from organizations where services have been performed, confirmation of education, etc.). In addition, it may be of value to request and verify in-locale or in-country experience. Forms of verification for in-locale or in-country experience may include the following:

- Passport with entrance and exit stamps
- Copies of work visas
- Military documentation
- Academic identification cards and transcripts from in-country institutions
- International and country-specific automobile operator's license
- Documentation of residence, employment, or alternate citizenship
- Documentation of nationalized medical insurance
- In-country family records (e.g., birth certificates, marriage licenses, or registration for parents and siblings)
- Telephone records

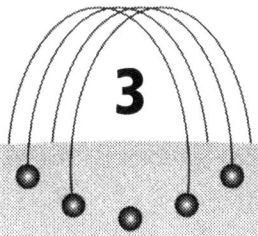

Global Standards

As shown in Figure 3.1, globalization splits into two distinct paths that are rejoined at a later stage of application development. These two paths are representative of 1) presentation/expression and 2) information. Following and then reconverging the paths is critical to a successful Web globalization effort. As emphasized in the previous chapters, multilingual support is fundamental. However, multilingual support is not the only critical component to a globalization solution. Of equal significance and potential complexity is globalized information (data- and transaction-oriented content and metadata). Metadata are the characteristics and rules that describe and constrain data (e.g., the value "840" is data, while the name of the element that holds the value of "840," the data type of that element, and the maximum allowable character length of that element are examples of metadata).

By definition, information can be considered as a fact or collection of facts that when combined in some logical form or manner can be interpreted, used, and applied. It is important to note that some facts are defined as "atomic," in that they cannot be logically decomposed. Similarly, data are the granular components of information that align with a specific definition, follow a defined format, or are valued from a defined set. From a practical perspective, a postal address that includes street address, city, state, region or county, postal code, and country is considered information.

Similarly, a street address line from a complete postal address may be classified as either information or data, depending upon how it is used. If the street address

Chapter 3 Global Standards

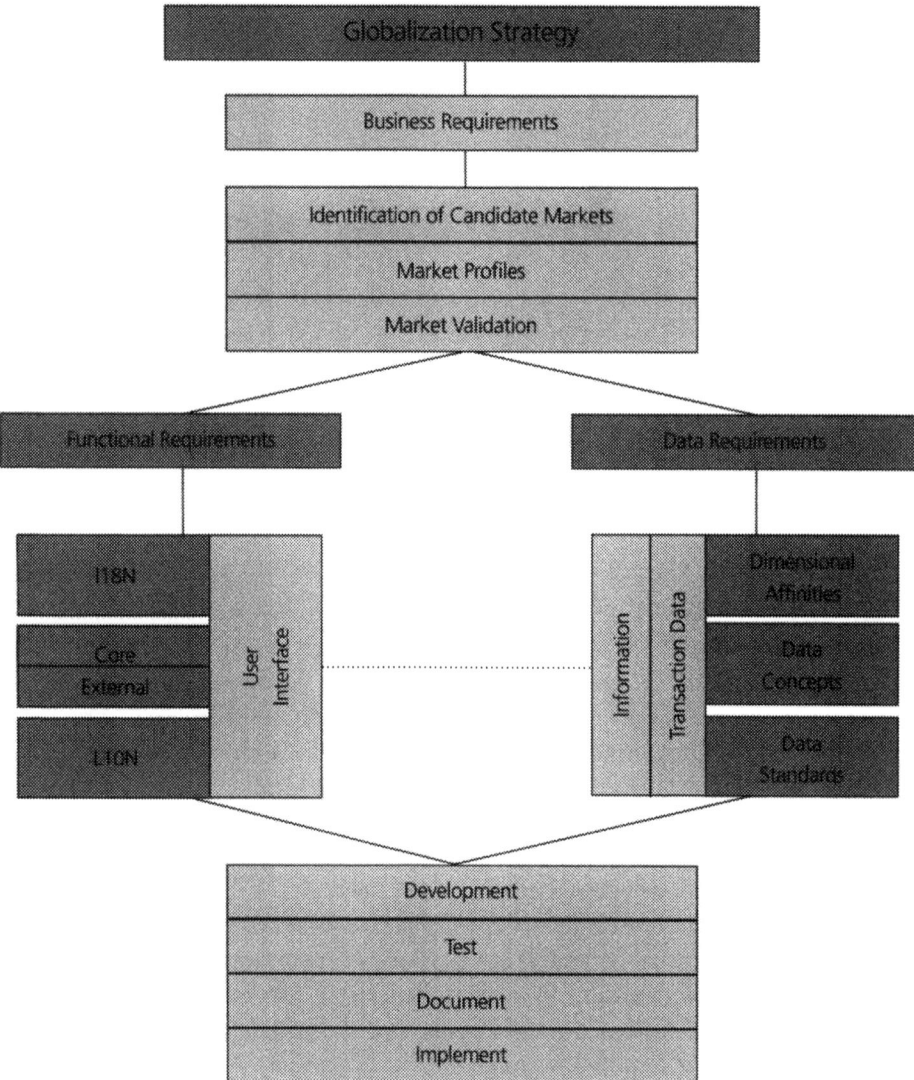

Figure 3.1 Globalization strategy (© 1996–2002 by James Bean)

line is not or cannot be decomposed into more granular particles, then the address line is considered information. However, if it can be decomposed into street number, street name, street type, and street direction, then each of these individual parts are considered data. In this simple example, the individual components of a street address are not logically decomposable, are aligned with a specific definition, follow a defined format, and are valued from a defined set.

The tactical implementation of a globalized Web site requires the identification of a Web user's locale and preferences. These globalization characteristics are used to determine which language as well as which global, international, or industry information and data standards to apply. Although the identification of locale and preferences are critical to the tactical operation of a globalized Web site, as you'll see in Chapter 5, there are a number of important planning and design activities that must occur first.

Once the locale for a Web site visitor has been identified, the visitor can be identified as international or not, and some basic information about the visitor can be determined. Additional cultural and demographic information can be determined by visitor-selected (or -provided) preferences such as preferred currency and unit of measure (both of which are critical for business relationships that involve the sale of products and services). When the identified locale is combined with visitor-selected preferences, a *global customer relationship* (G-CRM) can be developed. The relationship between the business and the customer will then drive site navigation, presentation of language-specific content, and similar methods of personalization.

As the customer relationship proceeds to the actual transaction of business, the ability to accurately capture and integrate globally diverse data is critical. The most common method for capturing consumer data from a Web page is a Web form (HTML, XHTML, or other). Forms should be organized by the general type of information that is required (name, address, telephone number, etc.). However, if the Web form used to capture name, address, and telephone information from the prospect or customer has been engineered with a parochial bias toward the United States, it is highly doubtful that the noted customer information can be captured accurately, if at all. If the entry fields and descriptive text on the form do not align with the associated data of the customer, there is also a significant probability that the customer will abandon entry of the requested information in frustration. Even if the prospect or customer can "force" entry of the requisite information into various elements of the Web form, it is likely that the data will be inaccurate, incomplete, or misaligned with the necessary elements. Further, editing the collected information and integrating it with other enterprise data will no doubt be impossible.

The solution to the global information problem is not language translation. Rather, the solution is both strategic and tactical. The strategic component identifies the international markets to be addressed by the Web site. The tactical component includes the identification of the customer's locale and culture and the presentation, capture, and alignment of supporting global information with the appropriate data standards. This two-part solution is a key component of the Web globalization process. However, before understanding the strategic activities surrounding global data integration, it is necessary to understand data standards.

Types of Information and Data Standards

Information and data standards are defined by metadata. *Metadata* is frequently described as "data about data." However, this description is incomplete. A more appropriate definition is "the defining description, structure, format, rules, and set of allowable values as characteristics of information." Without recognizing these important characteristics, information would be abstract, intangible, unstructured, and potentially unusable collections of characters and digits.

In order for information to be usable, it must conform to a set of metadata rules. Even text strings conform to basic metadata rules (e.g., allowable characters, minimum and maximum length). Information that originates from or is representative of varying locales and cultures of the globe can be highly diverse. Consider the postal addresses for the many different countries of the world. These addresses can vary as to the number of address lines, allowable content for each address line, the mandatory or minimum content of each address line, and the sequence in which address lines should be ordered for proper use. Many international postal address formats can be defined by a common structure, but there are others that are unique. Each of these formats is represented by a standard. Without implementing the Web page form elements in a manner that represents the postal address standard specific to a customer's locale, that customer would not be able to enter (or accurately enter) their postal, residence, or delivery address. This example is one of many. Without the application and adherence to standards, businesses are not able to accurately capture, edit, share, and exchange globally diverse data. Even more important, without these standards, the ability to integrate and process global information along with more traditional enterprise data is either cost prohibitive or not possible.

Most business- and transaction-oriented information is described by one or more standards, which are of different types. It is important to note that many standards can be described by more than one type. The basic standard types are as follows:

- Identification (recognized or unique identifiers)
- Code sets (code values, decode descriptive text)
- Valid values (the domain of allowable data values)
- Structures (rules, sequence, order, composition)

- Vocabularies (eXtensible Markup Language, Electronic Data Interchange)
- Formats (sequences of characters, patterns, presentation characteristics)
- Expression (icons, symbols)
- Cultural (calendars, dialects, privacy issues)

Identification standards are used for the specification and assignment of numeric or alphanumeric values intended to provide identity or uniqueness for individuals, products, financial accounts, and locations. The assignment of an identifier is generally done via a standard scheme or by some form of registration authority. In some cases, identification standards include some form of format or intelligence. In the United States a common form of identification for a person is their Social Security number. This number is assigned to an individual and is used for a variety of purposes, including tax reporting, identification of credit history, and for benefits as defined by the Social Security Administration. It is important to note that the current scheme for assigning Social Security numbers as identifiers does not adequately provide for universal uniqueness. There have been cases of the numbers being mistakenly assigned or used by more than one individual, and other cases where Social Security Numbers of deceased individuals are reassigned after a prescribed period of time. Some European countries have implemented a somewhat similar Health Insurance number.

Some of the more common examples of identification standards include the following:

- EAN/UPC—retail product number
- SIC/NAICS—industry code
- Person identifier
- BBAN/IBAN—basic and international bank account number
- U.N. ports and locations

Code sets are numeric, alpha, or alphanumeric codes that have corresponding text descriptions (decodes). The purpose of a code set is to identify or classify what would be descriptive text by a value that is unique and consistent. These values can then be interpreted and processed by automated programs, eliminating the potential for capturing or attempting to process abstract or intangible information. In some cases, code sets may be extensions of or subordinate to other code sets. While not always the case, a common example is that of a hierarchy, where the parent, or higher-level, code represents broader descriptive information and the subordinate, or lower-level, code represents more granular decomposition of the parent.

Consider the international standard for language codes (ISO 639). The names that describe known base languages of the world are strings of text. While the most common implementation of this standard will decode to English text names for each language, versions of this standard might have language names translated into the language of local implementation (e.g., German, French, Spanish, Japanese, etc.). However, even if the language names have been translated from English to another language for a specific implementation, in order to conform, the translated language names must be of the same definition and context and the language code values must not be modified in any way.

Using the example of English, if the language names of the ISO 639 standard were translated to French for a specific local implementation, the ISO 639 three-character language code for English would be "ENG." The base language name would be "English," but the translated language name would be "Anglais." In either case and in order to conform to ISO 639, the language code would remain "ENG." Common examples of code set standards include the following:

- ISO 639 Language Code
- ISO 3166 Country Code
- ISO 4217 Currency Code
- ISO 5218 Gender Code
- SIC/NAIC—industry code
- time zone

Valid values are the domain or collection of allowable data values for an atomic data component. Although not mandatory, most valid value standards are also code set standards. Even though a valid values type of standard may only list the allowable data values for a component of data, without the corresponding decode descriptive text for each value, practical use of the standard would be limited. Consider the international standard for gender (ISO 5218). In order to conform to this standard, there are currently only four allowable data values (0, 1, 2, 9), which are nondescriptive and lack implied intelligence: a value of "1" denotes "male," "2" denotes "female," "0" denotes "not known," and "9" denotes "not specified." However, without the corresponding decode descriptive text (code sets), the data value "1" would have little meaning to an uninitiated viewer. Many valid value standards are derived from code sets.

Structure standards are the architectural rules that define the logical assembly, the sequence or order, and the allowable content of granular information and data particles into usable information. Revisiting the example of an address, without defining the content of each address line and the order in which each line must appear in the collective address group, an address intended for the purpose of delivery would be unusable.

Other similar standards can be used to specify the sequence and allowable components of a person's name. The name of an individual can vary widely based upon culture, family heritage, religion, marital status, academic position, and military rank. Some of the more common structural standards include the following:

- UPU postal address
- Personal name
- Salutation
- Honorifics, title, suffix
- Honorifics, title, prefix
- Family and group structure

Vocabulary standards define a context, language, or vocabulary for transacting business. A vocabulary will generally conform to a defined set of contained data elements and structure. In this case, *structure* is defined as the position and relationship of elements within a context. Traditional e-commerce utilized Electronic Data Interchange (EDI) standards to define the different types and content of electronic business transactions. EDI vocabulary standards tend to be rigorously defined and adhere to a fixed set of structures. With the advent of eXtensible Markup Language (XML), this scenario has been extended not only to include standard vocabularies, but also to allow custom extension of these vocabularies. Examples of common XML vocabularies (many others have also been defined) include the following:

- Name and Address Markup Language (NAML)
- Customer Identity Markup Language (CIML)
- Customer Profile Exchange (CPEX)
- Electronic Business using eXtensible Markup Language (ebXML)
- Person name (HR-XML)

Format standards are patterns used for the capture and rendering of information. Consider the presentation of the date. The "Y2K problem" highlighted the common error of using a two-digit year without identifying the century. The international standard for dates (ISO 8601) defines several formats and extensions of date information (such as date and time). However, a common format for automated processing and storage of date information is specified as YYYY-MM-DD (two-digit century plus two-digit year, followed by month and day). This format allows for common left-to-right and incremental decimal collation sequences, such as ordering a list of dates. However, the rendering of date information has dependencies to locale. In the United States, the display of date information varies, but common formats include the following:

- Month Literal DD, YYYY (February 01, 2003)
- MM-DD-YYYY (02–01–2003)

In other countries, the presentation format for a date can vary as well. Examples found in the United Kingdom for rendering dates include the following:

- DD Month Literal YYYY (01 February 2003)
- DD-MM-YYYY (01–02–2003)

As can be determined from the combination of these two sets of date formats, if a Web user were presented with a date formatted according to the U.S. pattern of MM-DD-YYYY, it is possible for misinterpretation or error (e.g., does the sample date 02-01-2003 represent January 2 or February 1?). Obviously, if all nations, cultures, and Web users of the world rendered dates using the ISO 8601 format of YYYY-MM-DD, potential for misinterpretation and error would be significantly reduced (or possibly eliminated). Date is only one of several important format standards. The most common include the following:

- ISO 8601 date and time formats
- ITU E.123 international telephone number presentation format
- Currency punctuation and symbols

Expression standards are generally visual and interpretive. The most common methods are icons, symbols, and similar graphics. Some expressions conform to widely recognized international standards (e.g., the recycle symbol ♻ is recognized by many international Web users.) However, the area of expressions introduces significant potential for misinterpretation. One commonly used yet often incorrect technique is to display images of national flags on a Web page and then allow the user to click the image and branch to a language-specific set of Web pages. The problem with this technique is a general misunderstanding of the underlying relationship to standard languages. Not all countries have a standard language and many others may have more than one standard language. Consider Switzerland, where there is no single official language defined as "Swiss," yet French, German, and Italian are very common. An international Web user originating from Switzerland might click the flag image for that country, then be presented with Web content in other than their primary language. Similar examples may apply for many other countries.

Other common examples of U.S. icons and symbols include the use of a mailbox with the flag up to represent "new mail." This image is recognized in many countries but not all. Another common U.S. symbol is an open door to represent "exit" or "log out." However, this image is largely misunderstood in many Asian countries.

Cultural standards are aligned with locale and are more specific to individual preference. Consumer or personal privacy is a significant issue that has gained recent emphasis. The issue is not limited to a specific country, culture, or locale, but it is not readily addressed in the same manner worldwide. Also, in some cultures, the issue of privacy may not be of such significance. Other examples of cultural standards are those that support dialect as an extension of language, and calendars.

Dialect is a controversial topic among those in the globalization industry. Some experts suggest that dialects are spoken variants of language and that the core, or base, language is the only necessity. Others (including myself) suggest that dialect is not only spoken, but also introduces variations from base language in spelling and context. Even when a Web site has been engineered using English, if it follows the U.S. dialect, users from other English-speaking countries such as England, Australia, and New Zealand may not find that the Web content has been personalized to their preference, and simple spelling and context variants may cause marketing blunders.

Common Consumer-Oriented Data Concepts

The origin and scope of information and data standards are of four basic categories: global, national, industrial, and internal enterprise (see Table 3.1). Global standards are those that classify and describe the metadata characteristics of data concepts that may apply to or be generally used by more than one nation or country. National standards originate from and tend to apply to data concepts that are specific to one nation or country. Industry standards are representative of an information or data concept that is specific to an industry, collaborative group, or set of trading partners, or that may be technical. Many industry standards can also apply to more than one nation or country. Internal enterprise standards may also apply to more than one nation or country. However, internal enterprise standards are engineered by a specific business and focus on internal classifications of information, information exchanges between business units, and internal processes. The one common thread for each of the described standards categories is that regardless of origin or scope, most may apply to more than one nation or country.

When a business engineers a B2C Web site that targets international consumers, the ability to present product and service information, capture consumer information, and complete a transaction implies a dependency on information and data

Table 3.1 Standards varieties (abbreviated list of examples)

Global standards

IBAN	International bank account number
ISO 3166	Country code
ISO 4217	Currency code
ISO 5218	Gender code
ISO 639	Language code
ITU E.123	Notation for national and international telephone numbers
Time zone	Time zone abbreviations, names, assignment, offsets

National standards

FIPS PUB 5-2	State abbreviations
Title 15, Ch. 6, Sub. Ch. IX, Sec. 260	U.S. Code, Advancement of Time and Changeover Dates
USPS ZIP, ZIP+4	U.S. Postal Code Zoning Improvement Plan

Industry standards

EAN	European Article Number
GTIN	UCC—Global Trade Item Number
NAICS	North American Industry Code
UM	Unit of Measure
UPC	Uniform (Universal) Product Code

Internal enterprise standards

N/A (fictitious)	Application system type code
N/A (fictitious)	Customer relationship type code
N/A (fictitious)	Payment method code
N/A (fictitious)	Payment terms code

standards. Without the ability to align with and support standards, any captured consumer information is abstract, is subject to inaccuracy, and presents significant difficulty when attempting to integrate and process that information. There are a number of consumer-oriented data concepts and supporting standards that are fundamental to effective global e-commerce. It is important to note that several of the standards supporting these consumer-oriented data concepts can apply equally well in a B2B scenario.

Common Consumer-Oriented Data Concepts

The consumer-oriented data concepts of significance include the following:

- Name of an individual (person)
- Residence or postal address
- Telephone number
- Country
- Currency
- Language
- Unit of measure
- Date

It is important to note that not all standards are freely available as open and public specifications. Many are in the public domain, while others are proprietary or copyright products that may require some form of registration or even a fee for use. The reader is encouraged to carefully consider the legal implications and potential costs for acquiring official copies of standards.

Name of an Individual (Person)

The name of an individual can be a highly complex set of information. Significant variations in names can result from culture, religion, family lineage, marital status, and many other issues. The most common U.S. name format will generally include a first name, middle name (or initial), and last name. It is suggested that this name format is minimally acceptable and in many cases is not valid even within the United States. Given an international context, the structure and format of an individual's name is subject to numerous complexities. Variations can include the number of components or parts of a name, the sequence or order in which the parts are assembled, the allowable character length of each part, connectives between name parts, prefixes and suffixes (to support salutation, titles, and honorifics), and the text labels that describe or inform a person as to the appropriate entry of name parts into Web page elements.

Further complicating the data concept of a name is the lack of information and data standards. Some organizations have identified and described the noted complexities, others have implemented structures that allow for multiple occurrences of name components or particles, and still others have either ignored or were unaware of name complexities. One of the best attempts to describe the complexity of a name and propose a solution is that of Dublin Core elements.[1]

---

1 Dublin Core Metadata Initiative, DCMI People's Names, Andrew Waugh, February 3, 1998, © DCMI, 1995–2001; *dublincore.org/documents/1998/02/03/name-representation/*.

Chapter 3   Global Standards

Free-form entry of name

Name	Dr. John Quincy Adams von Doe Sr.

Predefined entry of individual name segments

Please Enter Your Name

Prefix, Title	Dr.
Given Name	John
Middle Name	Quincy Adams
Family Name	von Doe
Suffix, Title	Sr.

Selectable entry of individual name segments

Please Enter Your Name

Prefix, Title ▼	Dr.
Given Name ▼	John
Middle Name ▼	Quincy
Other Name ▼	Adams
Family Name ▼	von Doe
Suffix, Title ▼	Sr.
Other Name ▼	
Other Name ▼	

Figure 3.2 Sample design for capturing an individual's name

From a practical perspective, the Web site designer may consider several different alternatives for capturing a person's name (see Figure 3.2). Each alternative has obvious advantages and disadvantages. One is to capture the name as a single large text element. This alternative is the simplest from the perspective of the user or consumer but does not allow for effective use and processing of the name. If the name is combined with other data, such as an address, and used for multiple purposes, such as sorting, identification of previous existing customer information, or identification of family groups, this technique is prone to errors. Another alternative is to predefine several name components (similar to the common U.S. name format described previously but allowing for multiple occurrences of each name component). This is a more effective data entry technique and allows for more granular capture of name components, but the type and number of predefined name components may not apply to many cultures. Some cultures do not recognize or use first and last names in the same manner, and do not use the descriptive titles "first name," "middle name," and "last name." A more appropriate global solution is to describe associated name components by more commonly recognized text labels of "given name" and "family name." Additionally, some cultures place a last name (family name) to precede the first name (given name). A third and perhaps the "purest" alternative is to provide a set of Web form entry elements that also include a drop-down list of descriptive name types next to each. Default name type values can be determined by locale to reflect the most common audience. The content type and ordering is determined as the user selects the description from the drop-down box combined with the logical entry sequence of the name elements. This last alternative provides for the most granular and accurate entry of a name. However, it can be considered cumbersome by the user.

Although a single rigorous standard for capturing an individual's name is not in place, each of the noted techniques (as well as others) may be valid alternatives. Also of importance are the more metadata-specific characteristics of an individual's name such as the maximum allowable character length of a complete name or each name component. In some cultures (such as India), the character length of a name can be extensive. Individual name components exceeding 20 characters in length are not uncommon. Rather than identify one technique as the best, additional consideration should be given to factors such as

- Purpose (use of the name information)
- Integration (ability to integrate name information with other more traditional enterprise data)
- Usability (acceptable level of entry complexity for the target audience)
- Performance (application performance required for edit, validation, parsing of name components, and processing)

Identifier for an Individual (Person)

The name of an individual is fundamental to conducting consumer-oriented business over the Web. However, for some business applications, a name is largely ineffective at providing specific identification of an individual. Of frequent use in the United States (especially for financial business), the Social Security number (SSN) is used as a method of individual identification. While this application of the SSN as an identifier is common and can be effective, there are exceptions where such information is inaccurate (e.g., there have been cases where SSNs have been reused or issued more than once, resulting in anomalies). Many other countries have similar methods of identifying an individual, although the format and allowable content can vary tremendously. When forms of personal identification are required, consideration should be given to sources such as

- Social Security number
- Health Insurance number (a.k.a. National Insurance number, National Health Insurance ID, etc.)
- Automobile operator's license
- Aircraft operator's license
- Military ID
- Academic institution ID
- Employee ID
- Professional association membership ID
- Passport and visa number

In addition to the forms of identification listed above, it may be necessary to acquire additional and supporting information such as country of issue, locale of issue, effective date, and expiration date.

It is important to note that requesting, capturing, and using forms of personal identification are highly controversial. Such information is considered to be of issue to personal privacy. Even when it is considered legal and ethical to capture forms of personal identification, considerable effort should be given to security, encryption, and privacy. Regulatory acts regarding the use of personal identification information vary from country to country. When such information is necessary to conduct business, guidance from legal professionals is recommended.

Residence, Postal, or Delivery Address

In order to identify a location or point of delivery for a product or service, or to provide additional information (e.g., posted correspondence), a residence or postal address is required. Address forms are most often dictated as standards by government or other authoritative postal agencies. In the United States, the U.S. Postal Service specifies the format of an address according to several standards publications.[2] U.S.

---

2   United States Postal Service Publications 28, 40, 201, 221; *usps.com/*.

addressing standards describe general structure as to the number of address lines, recommended content of each line, and standard postal codes.

A common U.S. postal address format comprises three or four address lines. The first line contains identification of the addressee (generally a name), lines two and three contain street address information (including street number, street direction, street name, street type, apartment, suite, and similar information), and the fourth line contains a combination of city, state, and zip code. Even within the United States, this address format may be marginally effective. Complex business addresses may require additional addressing information, such as corporate complex, building, and mail stop.

Outside the United States, this format is largely unusable. Depending upon locale, the number of address lines may be as many as six. Additionally, the content and sequence of each address line can vary widely. From the perspective of a postal authority or delivery service, inability to correctly capture and format an address can result in misdeliveries, nondelivery, or rate penalties for additional processing. From the perspective of the business enterprise, these same issues apply. Additionally, if the Web site has not been engineered in a manner that supports address formats aligned with standards for a particular locale, the consumer may be prohibited from entering their address in the necessary form or may abandon entry in frustration.

As with an individual's name, there is no single address standard that applies to every country and locale in the world. One of the best sources of global address information is the Universal Postal Union (UPU), a branch of the United Nations that coordinates between international postal authorities and publishes combinations of address format standards and postal authority contact information on their Web site, *www.upu.int/*.

In order to accurately capture a postal address, a Web site designer must consider alternative techniques. One is to adopt a predefined number of free-form address lines that allow for any text entry or address content the consumer determines is appropriate. This technique may be effective when the only purpose for the address information is to describe a location for a delivery. However, even when limited only to delivery, validation of any entered address information is difficult and the content is subject to inaccuracy. Also, without some form of complex parsing, the address information captured from this technique is largely unusable for any other purpose (see Figure 3.3).

Another more effective technique combines a predefined number of street address lines (allowing for the greatest number of lines required to meet an international address) with separate elements to contain geographic and location-specific information such as city, country, and postal code, along with a limited number of regional elements such as county, state, province, territory, or region. The intended content of the country element and similar predefined regional elements (e.g., U.S.

Chapter 3   Global Standards

Please Enter Your Address

Address to	Dr. John Quincy Adams von Doe Sr.
Address	Jones Medical Complex
Address	123456 S.E. Broadwind Blvd.
Address	Building 6, Suite 9-B
Address	Phoenix, AZ 85000
Address	USA

Figure 3.3 Sample design for capturing an address, allowing free-form text entry

states, Canadian provinces, Australian territories, Mexican states, etc.) would be determined by a drop-down list of selectable values. For specific locales, only those elements required to describe those geographic, location, or regional characteristics would be required (i.e., a localized Canadian Web site would not require address elements and drop-down lists for U.S. states, Mexican states, or other such regions). Free-form regional elements would allow for any text entry but would be described by a drop-down list of selections (see Figure 3.4).

There is no single standard that defines all delivery, residence, and postal addresses, regardless of country or locale. Although a predefined set of free-form address line elements is the closest single solution to describe all international addresses in a locale-agnostic manner, it is the poorest from the perspective of data quality. The alternative technique of combining free-form address lines with predefined regional address elements is a far better solution but is subject to user entry complexity. Deriving locale-specific versions of the address format (using international address information from the UPU) that limits entry to only those address elements of an identified locale is a better solution.

When Web sites must be engineered to consider numerous locales, development costs can be excessive. In those cases, it may be possible to engineer a set of address formats that may be used by several locales. This technique may introduce address elements not required by all locales, resulting in some usability challenges, but careful design and identification of market profile and locale affinities can help to mitigate problems.

In addition to general address design techniques, there are a number of related challenges. Rarely do international address formats include granular detail of

Common Consumer-Oriented Data Concepts

(a)
Please Enter Your Address

Address to	Dr. John Quincy Adams von Doe Sr.
Address	Jones Medical Complex
Address	123456 S.E. Broadwind Blvd.
Address	Jones Square
City	London
Postal Code	EC1 8SY
Country	GBR–United Kingdom

Other Region
Other Region

(b)
Please Enter Your Address

Address to	Dr. John Quincy Adams von Doe Sr.
Address	Jones Medical Complex
Address	123456 S.E. Broadwind Blvd.
Address	Building 6, Suite 9-B
City	Phoenix
Postal Code	85000
U.S. State	AZ–Arizona

Figure 3.4 Sample designs for capturing an address when the locale is unknown or multiple locales must be considered (a) and when the locale is known (b)

important metadata characteristics (even those described by the UPU). Also of importance are characteristics such as the maximum number of characters allowed for each address line, the sequence of data particles within a street address line (e.g., street number preceding the street name, street direction following the street number, etc.), and postal encoding schemes. When considering that there are well over 100 possible international address formats, these characteristics can introduce additional globalization design and engineering complexity. It is suggested that each of these complexities is justification for performing rigorous market research and aligning markets with locale-specific affinities.

Similar to the design issues and complexity of an individual's name, any address design technique should also consider factors such as

- Purpose (use of the information)
- Integration (ability to integrate highly diverse address information with other, more traditional, enterprise data)
- Usability (acceptable level of entry complexity for the target audience)
- Performance (application performance required for edit, validation, parsing of address components, and processing)

Telephone Number

A common misconception in the United States is that all telephone numbers are defined as a collection of three parts (area code, prefix, local number) and that a telephone number presented in the form of "(999) 999-9999" is understood worldwide. However, outside of North America—the countries and regions participating in the North American Numbering Plan (NANP)—the format of a telephone number can vary tremendously. Additionally, depending upon the point of origin and the destination for an international call, international access codes may also vary. Another common marketing technique used in the United States is to acquire and represent telephone numbers that are translated to dial pad alpha characters as a form of name or shorthand telephone number reminder. This is a terrible technique from the perspective of an international user. The abbreviations and colloquialisms used are rarely interpreted in the necessary context, and some dial pads may not display the alpha character encoding for numeric telephone number digits.

Consider that telephone numbers are critical to conducting business in any form. Given that Web sites may be located anywhere in the world and there may not be a corresponding physical location that a consumer can visit, the telephone offers an important method of communication. Business Web sites should include contact information so that consumers, prospects, and other interested parties can make contact. At a minimum, contact information should include a postal address, one or more telephone numbers, and one or more e-mail addresses. To assist international users, all telephone numbers should be presented in official notation for international telephone numbers as described by the International Telecommunications Union (ITU). The ITU coordinates and manages numbering plans, supporting

Common Consumer-Oriented Data Concepts

technical specifications, and related issues for telephone communications of the world. In the case of international telephone numbers (or national telephone numbers that must be presented to and used by international callers), there are defined standards for notation (format and presentation), access codes, country codes, and telephone number digits.[3]

Assume that the business enterprise and telephone contact is located in the United States. In this example, the North American Numbering Plan describes the telephone number as a dialing sequence to include the following:

- International access code (also known as "country code" or "long distance access code," optional depending upon the origin and destination of the call)
- Area code (three digits)
- Prefix (also known as "subscriber exchange," three digits)
- Local number (also known as "subscriber number," four digits)

Depending upon the telephone system used within the business, there may also be an internal "extension" that is used to route a call within the enterprise. When implemented, the internal extension is not dialed until a connection to the telephone system within the business has been established.

Given this definition for a telephone number and the description above, the presentation format most often used is "(999) 999-9999." When an international caller attempts to dial this number (with the call originating from outside North America), there may be additional digits that need to be dialed. Generally, a call originating outside North America and placed to the United States will require an international access code, country code, area code, local prefix, and local number. Depending upon the country or locale where the call originates, these additional digits may vary. The international access code may vary by country, locale, or service provider, and the country code for the United States of "1" is not unique (Canada also uses a country code of "1").

Even when the locale-specific preferences of an international consumer can be identified, the user may be accessing the Web site from a location other than that of the locale. In this scenario, the international access code could be different from the international access code of their locale. Rather than attempt to predefine an international access code for a consumer, a more appropriate technique is to identify in

---

[3] International Telecommunications Union, E.122—Measures to reduce customer difficulties in the international telephone service; E.123—Notation for national and international telephone numbers, e-mail addresses, and Web addresses; and E.164—The international public telecommunication numbering plan; *www.itu.int/*.

which position of the telephone number the international access code, country code of the call destination, and remainder of the telephone number would be dialed. Additionally, punctuation such as parentheses and dashes can be misinterpreted, and the number of digits for each segment of a telephone number can vary. As a result, the general recommendation of the ITU E.123 specification for notation of international telephone numbers is to present telephone numbers with no punctuation or telephone number segment separators that could be misinterpreted as a dialable symbol. Examples of telephone number segment separators found in the ITU E.123 specification are spaces (white space).

Alternatively (and potentially in conflict with E.123), it is suggested that depending upon the font and character width and display resolution, spaces are not easy to identify visually. Another approach is to use a period (".") as the telephone number segment separator. A period is easier to identify and is generally acceptable by most international users. In addition to telephone number separators, a plus symbol ("+") is understood to be a placeholder for the international access code and should be prefixed to the country code. The resulting international presentation format for a U.S. telephone number is "+1.999.999.9999." In this example, the international user would recognize and replace the plus symbol with the international access code specific to the origin of the call. Even though a period is not described by the E.123 specification, most users understand that it is not a dialable character.

When a Web page is designed to acquire an international telephone number, there are two basic alternatives. The first allows for a single free-form telephone number entry element. This element would allow the user to enter a telephone number in the format that they are familiar with for their locale. Conceptually, this technique aligns well with the ITU specifications. However, it is prone to error if the user enters punctuation specific to the format of their "national" telephone number rather than the international format. They may incorrectly include dialable digits or local access codes that are not valid for an international caller. Additionally, if the business enterprise should desire to perform marketing analysis to identify calling area affinities (perhaps to develop outbound call marketing reports), the telephone number data would require complex parsing. A more appropriate technique would be to provide separate elements for the entry of locale-specific telephone number segments. To simplify user entry, country codes could be predefined to a drop-down list allowing for selection rather than entry. In many cases, a common format with clearly described telephone number segments could be used by multiple locales (see Figure 3.5).

Also of importance is the maximum possible length of a telephone number. The current ITU E.164 specification (ITU international public telecommunication numbering plan) limits the maximum possible number of telephone number digits

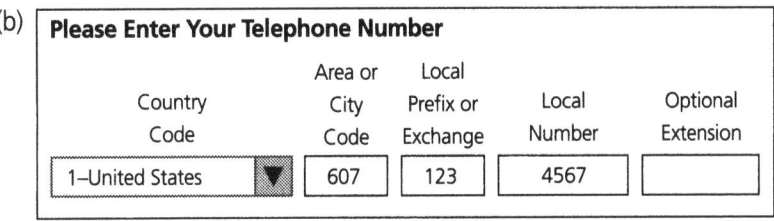

Figure 3.5 Sample designs for capturing a telephone number with free-form text entry (a) and standardized text entry (b).

to 15 (excluding the international prefix). However, earlier versions of the ITU E.163.3 specification stated: "The maximum number length shall be 15 digits. However, some administrations may wish to increase their register capacity to 16 or 17 digits."[4] It is assumed that this allowance for additional telephone number digits was to support the possibility of future renumbering, extension of the telephone number specification, or the possibility of technology shifts requiring additional digits. Regardless of the international telephone number technique selected, it is recommended that the maximum allowable number of digits should be at least 15.

Country

The country is a key component of a locale and is also a key component of an international address (i.e., residence, delivery, or postal address). A *country* is an accepted geopolitical designation that includes the declaration of a nation and national borders. Countries recognized by the United Nations have official names, as well as common abbreviations or acronyms (e.g., the United States of America is also known as "USA"). For international postal addresses, the destination country must be specified. Some postal agencies will allow the use of either the official

---

4 International Telecommunications Union, E.164, Numbering plan for the ISDN era, Section 3.3, Number length; *www.itu.int/*.

country name or its abbreviation. As with any text, entry of country name is subject to misspelling, character transposition, and inaccuracy.

The ability to identify a country in a standard manner and to process information and data specific to that country is necessary for conducting global e-commerce. Entry of country names as part of international address information will not provide the necessary granularity and specificity. Consider, for example, United States, where free-form text entry of country could result in these variations: "United States," "United States of America," "America," "USA," and "U.S." Attempting to sort, aggregate, and store international address data by country would not be possible with all of these variations.

The most common solution to standard identification of a country is a code set standard defined and maintained by the International Organization for Standardization (ISO). The ISO 3166 Country Code standard assigns a three-digit numeric code, a three-character alpha code, and a two-character alpha code to each recognized country of the world.[5]

The content and organization of the ISO 3166 Country Code standard provides support for cross-referenced translation of country names to country codes. Effective design techniques can include drop-down lists that allow a user to select the appropriate country as partial identification of their locale or to identify the country of an international address. Within the Web page (in HTML), the drop-down list includes translation from country name to the appropriate code. The Web user views the descriptive name, while the application can cross-reference and capture the standard country code (see Figure 3.6).

Similar techniques can be used to define and select a country code as it applies to a telephone number. When the locale is fully definitive and there is no possibility that the country for an address will vary from that of the locale, the country code could be predefined within the logic for the Web page. Even with the effective use of the Country Code standard, the Web page designer needs to identify which of the three ISO 3166 country codes are needed (e.g., three-digit numeric code, three-character alpha code, or two-character alpha code). Another important characteristic of countries and country codes is change. As evidenced by recent history, countries are not static. Although change is not frequent nor of significant volume, when

---

[5] International Organization for Standardization (ISO); *www.iso.org/*.
ISO 3166, Country Codes, TC46 Technical Committee; *www.iso.ch/iso/en/stdsdevelopment/tc/tclist/TechnicalCommitteeDetailPage.TechnicalCommitteeDetail?COMMID=1757*.
ISO 3166, Country Codes, MA Maintenance Agency; *www.din.de/gremien/nas/nabd/iso3166ma/a3ptnorm.html*.

Common Consumer-Oriented Data Concepts

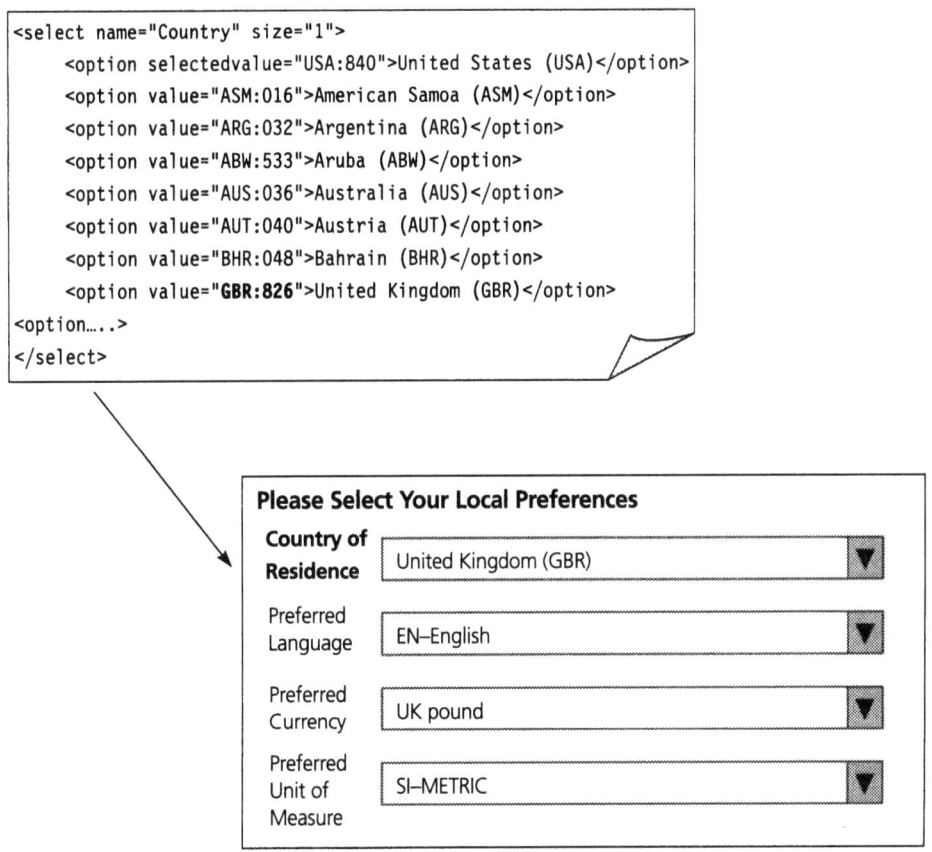

Figure 3.6 Sample design for selecting a country of residence, allowing the user to select preferences as part of locale identification

country code information is embedded within Web page content, ongoing maintenance is inevitable. Where possible, externalized structures used for selection and validation of country information are recommended.

Currency

Like country, currency is also a key component of a locale. A currency is a monetary instrument used to conduct business (e.g., payment for goods and services, investment, earnings, declaration of "value," etc.). Currency can be described by two standards types: code set and format. Currency also has a name, can be identified by a code, and may have format characteristics (e.g., currency symbol, digits of decimal scale, and decimal punctuation). Interestingly, not every country has an official currency, nor are all defined currencies exclusive to one country. As an example, the euro is currently the official currency of twelve European Union member countries. Also, as with country codes, currency codes are subject to change.

The most common solution to standard identification of a currency is a code set standard defined and maintained by the International Organization for Standardization (ISO). The ISO 4217 Currency Code standard assigns a three-digit numeric code and a three-character alpha code to each official country of the world.[6]

The content and organization of the ISO 4217 Currency Code standard provides support for cross-referenced translation of currency names to currency codes. Effective design techniques can include drop-down lists that allow a user to select a preferred currency as partial identification of a locale. Within the Web page (in HTML), the drop-down list includes translation from currency name to the appropriate currency code. The Web user views the descriptive name, while the application can cross-reference and capture the standard currency code (see Figure 3.7).

The ISO 4217 Currency Code standard does not provide information regarding the presentation characteristics of a currency, nor metadata such as decimalization. Both of these characteristics are important for the correct presentation of currency information (e.g., product or service pricing) and for the capture of currency amounts. I am unaware of a specific standard that describes all currency characteristics, however, such information may be derived from many different resources. Also of interest is that presentation characteristics such as currency symbol and fractional decimal punctuation may vary between locales. For those locales that use a comma as the fractional decimal separator, it may be necessary to present fractional U.S. dollar amounts using the comma rather than a period.

The level of decimalization for currency also varies. Often mistaken is that all currencies are decimalized and support two fractional digits (i.e., 1/100ths). Many currencies are decimalized and support two fractional digits. However, other currencies are decimalized and support three fractional digits, while still others are not decimalized and do not support any fractional currency amounts. In order to determine the proper currency symbols, fractional digits separator, and the number of fractional digits, the best technique is to maintain an externalized validation table that

---

6   International Organization for Standardization (ISO); *www.iso.org/*.
    ISO 4217, Country Codes, TC68 Technical Committee; *www.iso.ch/iso/en/stdsdevelopment/tc/tclist/ TechnicalCommitteeDetailPage.TechnicalCommitteeDetail?COMMID=2183*.
    ISO 4217, Currency Codes, UN/ECE United Nations Economic Commission for Europe; *www.unece.org/ cefact/rec/rec09en.htm*.

Common Consumer-Oriented Data Concepts

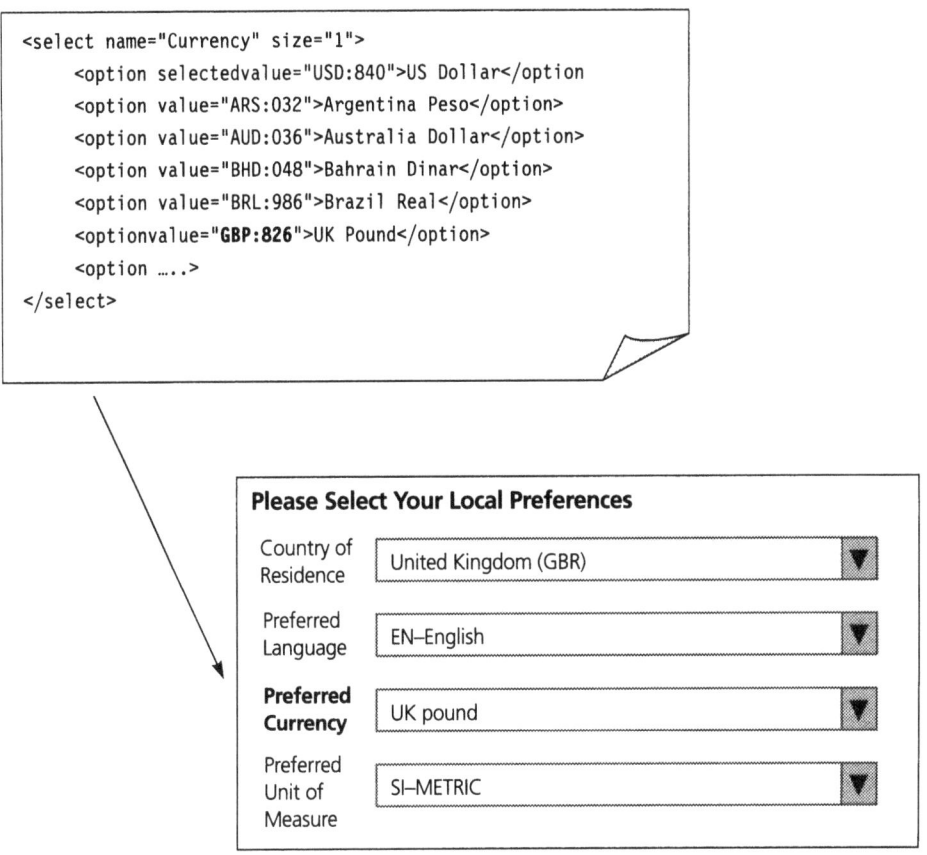

Figure 3.7 Sample design for selecting a preferred currency, allowing the user to select preferences as part of locale identification

associates locale to currency code. This table would then reference both base and locale-specific currency characteristics:

- Currency code
- Locale identifier
- Currency name
- Currency symbol
- Number of fractional decimal digits (fractional decimal scale)
- Fractional digits separator (punctuation)

Another common complication of multiple currency support is currency conversion (exchange). Many globalized Web sites provide multiple-currency support, with conversion of base currency amounts to the user's preferred currency. The logic for currency conversion is not complex (generally multiplication using a factor). Yet, the determination of applicable exchange rates and associated legal issues such as liability, errors and omissions, and contractual obligation all introduce potential risks and challenges. Multiple-currency support with currency conversion is highly recommended. However, the reader is strongly cautioned to investigate and resolve potential legal issues.

Language

Along with country, currency (and unit of measure, yet to be discussed), preferred language is critical to the identification of an international Web user's locale. Beyond the obvious need for multilingual support and translation (tasks and techniques beyond the scope of this book), language is again a key component of a locale. Languages are also supported by an international code set standard (ISO 639 Language Code). There are different versions of the ISO Language Code standard and extensions to the standard, as well as other "competing" language code sets. When limiting the context of language to "base" languages, the ISO 639 Language Code standard is sufficient. It provides a two-character code for all major languages. Alternatively, the ISO 639-2 Language Code standard provides a three-character code.[7]

When an international Web user identifies or selects a preferred language (as part of their locale), the Web application can then redirect that browser session to a set of language-specific Web pages. If more dynamic technologies are used, internationalization servers can assemble and serve language-specific content to the user's browser session. Similar to country and currency, allowing the Web user to identify or select their preferred language from a drop-down list can be an effective design (see Figure 3.8).

Unit of Measure

In combination with country, currency, and preferred language, unit of measure completes the minimum number of identifying characteristics for a locale. The unit of measure is fundamental to support international product description, sales, and service over the Web. When considering global Web applications, the assumption that all physical measurements are English or U.S. ANSI (inches, feet, yards,

---

[7] International Organization for Standardization (ISO); *www.iso.org/*.
ISO 639-2, Language Code, TC37 Technical Committee; *www.iso.ch/isolen/stdsdevelopment/tc/tclist/ TechnicalCmmitteeDetailPage.TechnicalCommitteeDetail?COMMID=1459*.
ISO 639-2, Language Code, RA Registration Authority; *lcweb.loc.gov/standards/iso639-2/langhome.html*.

Common Consumer-Oriented Data Concepts 53

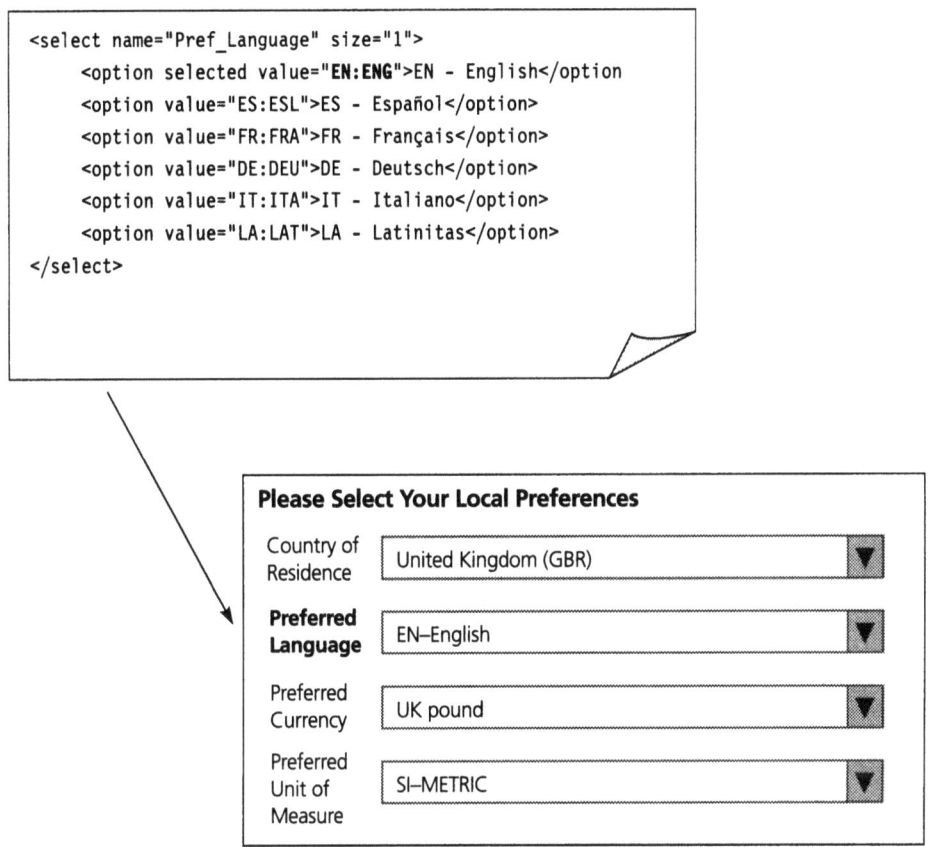

Figure 3.8 Sample design for selecting a preferred language, allowing the user to select preferences as part of locale identification

gallons, miles, etc.) is a critical error. In some cases, the inability to provide tangible measurement in metric units will offend some potential customers. Alternatively, there are many other countries where English units of measurement are readily accepted.

It is suggested that the two basic options are sufficient to address most international user preferences. Similar to the design techniques described for country, currency, and language, unit of measure can be defined by a drop-down list that allows the Web user to select their preference (see Figure 3.9).

The two most recognized unit of measure systems include English and International System of Units (also known as SI). The English unit of measure system is most common in the United States and comprises combinations of length, distance,

Chapter 3 Global Standards

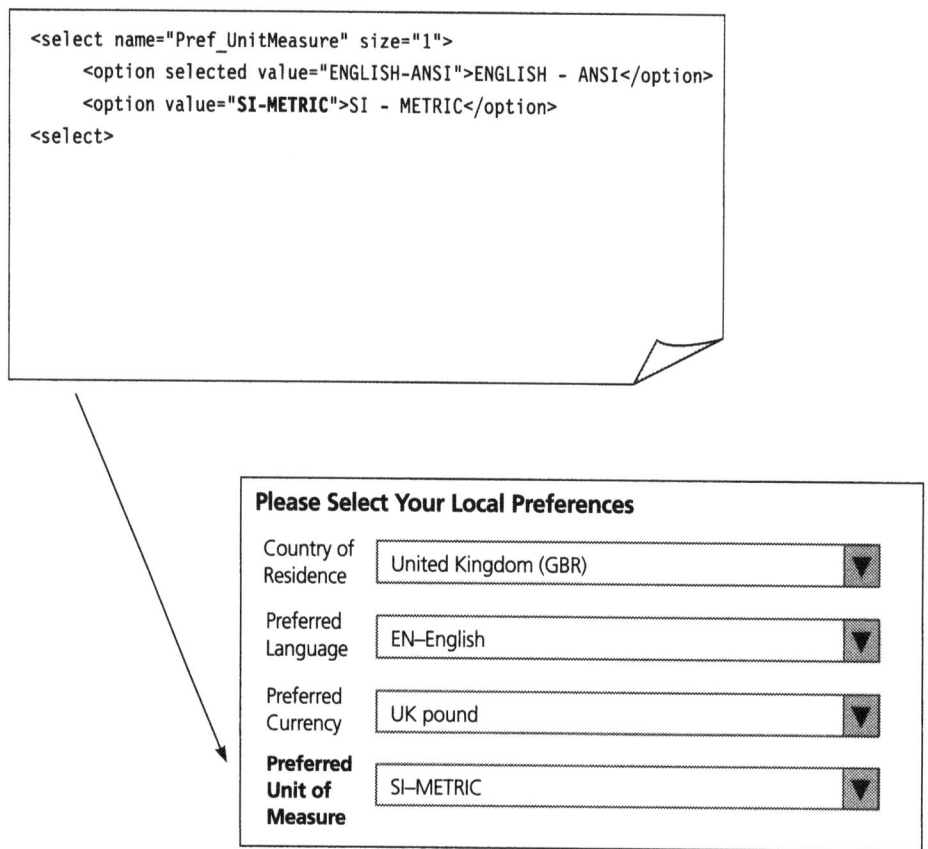

Figure 3.9 Sample design for selecting a preferred unit of measure, allowing the user to select preferences as part of locale identification

mass, and time. Although somewhat inaccurate, the International System of Units is often referred to as the metric system (see *www.bipm.fr/*). It also comprises combinations of length, distance, mass, and date. However, the units used to describe length and distance are derived from the Millimeter Kilogram Seconds (MKS) system and the Centimeter Kilogram Seconds system. Common to all of the noted units of measure are dates.

Date

The date is often mistakenly used as an identifying characteristic of locale. However, the concept of date (both inclusive and exclusive of time) is common to most

Common Consumer-Oriented Data Concepts

all cultures and locales. Variations are primarily in format and the method of presentation. Other more infrequently observed variations may be evident as a result of historic or cultural calendars. In the context of B2C Web content, it is more important to focus on the format of date information as a form of presentation and the capture of important dates in transaction-oriented forms.

The most common standard for representation of date and time is defined and maintained by the ISO. The ISO 8601 Representation of Dates and Times standard describes methods for presentation of date, time, and date and time.[8] Consideration is given to time zone as aligned with Universal Time or Universal Time Coordinated (UTC) or as a declared offset to UTC. Additionally, when considering the ISO 8601 extended format of "YYYY-MM-DD," left-to-right, and high-order collation sequences, the format described by ISO presents an efficient format for automated processing and sequencing of dates.

Other than the ISO 8601 date presentation format (YYYY-MM-DD), many locales and cultures have alternative formats. While it is recommended that adoption of the ISO 8601 format would resolve numerous examples of locale-specific disparity, there are implications to many Web-based applications and supporting technologies. Examples of varying date formats are often addressed as installation parameters or application-level options for database and computing languages (see Table 3.2). Interestingly, the default format for date data types that is implemented by some database platforms does not follow the ISO standard. In fact, there are examples where the default format does conform to the basic YYYY model invoked to resolve the well-known Y2K problem, although these technologies provide alternative formats and intrinsic functions to convert from one format to another.

As evidenced by the common date and time formats, there is a potential for interpretive error. When a standard format for presentation is not used by the Web designer or is not understood by the Web user, the sequence of day and month within a formatted date can be mistakenly swapped. Compare the common European format to the U.S. format: a U.S. formatted date of "07012002" (July 1, 2002) uses the same digits as the European formatted date for 7 January 2002.

A basic localization activity is to present dates using the appropriate format for the identified locale. From the perspective of underlying e-commerce transactions and data integration, it is recommended that transaction-oriented date content should conform to the ISO 8601 standard. It is also recommended that the ISO

---

8 International Organization for Standardization (ISO); *www.iso.org/*.
   ISO 8601, Date and Time, TC154 Technical Committee; *www.iso.ch/iso/en/stdsdevelopment/tc/tclist/ TechnicalCommittee DetailPage.TechnicalCommitteeDetail?COMMID=3827.*

Table 3.2 Common date and date–time formats

Standard or locale	Format
ISO 8601 "extended" format*	YYYY-MM-DD YYYY-MM-DDTHH:MM:SS YYYY-MM-DDTHH:MM:SSZ YYYY-MM-DD-THH:MM:SS + / -HH:MM)
U.S. format (common)	MM/DD/YYYY Month DD, YYYY MM/DD/YYYY @ HH:MM:SS (AM/PM)
European format (common)	DD.MM.YYYY DD Month YYYY
Japanese and Asian format (common)	YYYY-MM-DD
Abbreviations	*YYYY—Four-digit year* (e.g., 2003) *MM—Two-digit month* (e.g., 01 through 12) *DD—Two-digit day* (e.g., 01 through 31) *HH—Two-digit hour* *MM—Two-digit minute* *SS—Two-digit second* *Z—Literal denoting UTC time zone*

Note: The examples found in this table are abbreviated. There may be other forms and formats for date, time, and date and time.
*World Wide Web Consortium (W3C); *www.w3c.org/*. XML Schema, Part 2, Datatypes; *www.w3.org/TR/xmlschema-2/*.

8601 extended date format should be evaluated for presentation purposes. However, where the potential for misinterpretation is evident, localization personnel should carefully evaluate alternative formats.

In addition to the presentation of dates, many localization experts contend that date formats are one of several identifying characteristics of a locale. There may be examples where this approach can be effective. However, it is suggested that a date format should be derived from the identified locale rather than as a method for identifying a locale. This alternative technique can help to avoid overengineering customer preference and locale-identification schemes.

Gender

For some industries and business transactions, gender is often a required data concept (e.g., in the medical, insurance, and apparel industries). However, gender is also a highly sensitive piece of information. Some countries regulate whether gender information may be requested of an individual and if it is allowed, how it may be

Common Business-Oriented Data Concepts

used or disclosed. For some industries gender is fundamental. In the case of the medical industry, it is an extremely important characteristic of an individual that may be used to guide professional specialization, diagnosis, procedures, medication, and general care. It is also an important piece of information for residual or dependent industries such as insurance.

As simple as the topic may first appear, the concept of gender and supporting standards are mired in complexity and controversy. Web applications that are allowed by law to request, capture, and use gender information will most often rely on the traditional types of "male" and "female." The international standard for gender code recognizes these two values as well as two others for "unspecified" and "unknown."[9] While there is no specific societal or political intent of the author, it is interesting that the ISO 5218 standard does not currently define codes specific to transgender or genetic anomalies. The inability to address these gender-related conditions limits the use of gender coding to traditional applications, and may prohibit other uses such as within the medical industry without some form of extension.

As previously implied, gender or classification of sex can be highly controversial. Depending upon the country of the individual and the intended purpose, context, use, and disclosure of such information, there may be potential claims of discrimination, bias, or violation of personal privacy. If a business enterprise is considering the request and capture of gender-related information, care should be taken to validate such use with appropriate legal professionals.

Common Business-Oriented Data Concepts

In addition to the information and data that are common among most types of customers, there are also many data concepts associated with business and industry. For some Web applications, these additional data concepts may be combined with consumer-oriented data concepts for the assembly of transactions. For other Web applications, these data concepts can be critical to facilitating B2B e-commerce.

Consumer-oriented data concepts describe characteristics and context of a customer. Similarly, business-oriented data concepts describe characteristics and context for a business or industry. Many business-oriented data concepts originate from government agencies to support financial aspects of business (e.g., revenue and tax

---

9   International Organization for Standardization (ISO); *www.iso.org/*.
    ISO 5218, Representation of Human Sexes, JTC1, SC32 Technical Committee; *www.iso.ch/iso/en/ stdsdevelopment/tc/tclist/TechnicalCommitteeDetailPage.TechnicalCommitteeDetail?COMMID=160*.

reporting), while others originate from collaborative groups or business trading partner groups. Other uses of business-oriented data concepts may be in support of B2B applications and for marketing analysis. Some of the more common business-oriented data concepts include the following:

- Business identifier
- Industry code
- Bank account number or other financial account number

Identifier for a Business

For the purposes of financial and tax reporting, a business must have some form of identification. As might be imagined, relying on a business name is not sufficient. In the United States, a business may be classified as any of several types: proprietorship, partnership, limited liability company, and corporation (Chapter S, Chapter C, nonprofit, etc.). In the United States (as with most other countries) one or more identifying numbers are used for tax reporting. If the business is a proprietorship, the identifying number may be the Social Security number (SSN) of the owner, or it may be a Federal Employee Identification number (FEIN). The other business types will most often use the FEIN. The format and length of a business identifier can vary. Many are sequences of numeric digits. The identifiers of some countries may include alpha characters and may also include forms of intelligence (e.g., the identifying number including a set of codes to classify the type of business).

To further identify the business, one or more names may be used. When the business is registered, a name must be provided. In some cases, a "doing business as" (DBA) name may be used as long as a reference to the formal business name is also provided. The notion of a DBA name will often introduce controversy since it can be misunderstood and in some cases has been used to mask or hide the actual business. Although not as complex as the name of an individual (person), a business name can also be somewhat abstract. The business name may consist of several words or phrases, may be of varying length, and may have restrictions on the use of certain "reserved" words and phrases. The assignment of a business name will generally also require some form of uniqueness check to insure that it has not been previously assigned or is in use by another business. The format, length, and allowable content is generally governed by the laws and regulatory acts of the assigning entity (e.g., country, state, province, etc.).

It is important to note that there is no single overriding global standard or format for a business name or business identifier. It is suggested that additional information regarding the metadata characteristics and standards for a business identifier or name should be acquired directly from the tax, revenue, or similar government body where the business enterprise originates.

Industry Code

Most businesses are classified within an industry. A frequently used classification scheme is that of the North American Industry Classification System (NAICS), which was developed by the United States Office of Management and Budget (OMB); *www.whitehouse.gov/omb/inforeg/statpolicy.html#NAICS*. The NAICS is partly derived from and extends the context of a previous standard known as Standard Industry Classification (SIC), which has been widely used in the United States as well as by several other countries. The NAICS standard has been adopted by the United States, Canada, and Mexico, and in fact has been used to classify industries that participate in the North American Free Trade Agreement (NAFTA).

Like the data concept of a business identifier, a frequent use of industry classification is to classify an establishment for revenue and tax reporting (i.e., government or regulatory agencies). Although the base classification types are in English and the name implies "North America," the coding scheme defined by NAICS is powerful for identifying like establishments and similar groups of business enterprises. The NAICS coding scheme is six numeric digits in length and is comprised of four levels:

1. Major industry sector (first two digits, e.g., 11—Agriculture, Forestry, Fishing, and Hunting)

2. Subsector (first three digits, e.g., 111—Crop production)

3. Industry group (first four digits, e.g., 1111—Oil seed and grain farming)

4. NAICS number (five to six digits, e.g., 11111—Soybean farming and 111199—All other grain farming)

From a more international perspective, the United Nations adopted a somewhat different industry coding scheme known as the International Standard Industry Classification (ISIC), which has evolved through several revisions and enhancements (*http://unstats.un.org/unsd/class/family/famlist1.htm*). The ISIC industry coding standard is similar in concept to the NAICS industry coding standard, and although there has been some effort to align the two, there are differences evident in the summary levels and detail coding. Another somewhat less common international standard for industry coding is the Australian and New Zealand Standard Industry Classification (ANZSIC). As with ISIC, additional information can be acquired from the United Nations (see the Web site above).

Chapter 3 Global Standards

Bank Account Number

Although bank account numbers are of significant interest to a business enterprise (e.g., for payments, receipts, interest, fees, expenses, revenue, etc.), they are also of significant importance to consumer-oriented information. This is especially true of Web-based electronic financial transactions such as consumer payment using a personal checking account. In the United States, account-related transactions are routed according to an American Bankers Association routing number that is prefixed to the identifying account number for a bank account (or similar financial account). The 9-digit number is used for several purposes, including by the federal reserve to route checks (and other encoded financial instruments) from one financial institution to another. Often such routing and the resolution of transactions will utilize an automated clearing house. In addition to the routing number, the bank account number uniquely identifies an account where a transaction originates and where it may be applied. A typical U.S. bank account is 12 digits in length.

Many European bank account numbers will generally follow the International Bank Account Number standard (IBAN), which combines international routing with a basic bank account number (BBAN). The international bank account number was developed by the European Committee for Banking Standards (ECBS) and the International Organization for Standardization (ISO).[10] The IBAN standard was developed to facilitate cross-border payments and similar financial transactions. As a simple explanation, the IBAN standard prefixes international routing and classification information to country-specific bank account numbering schemes. The advantage to this approach is that each country can to some degree retain its own defined standard for internal routing and bank account identification, while leveraging the IBAN standard. To allow for exceptions, the Bank Identifier Code (BIC) is used in conjunction with IBAN.

The basic format of IBAN is as follows:

- Country code (ISO 3166, two-character alpha code)
- Check digits (two check digits, using MOD 97-10)
- Basic bank account number (maximum of 34 digits)

It is important to note that IBAN does allow for intrinsic alpha characters, although any use of alpha characters must be uppercase. Also, no separators or spaces between any digits are allowed.

---

10 European Committee for Banking Standards (ECBS); *www.ecbs.org/*.
International Organization for Standardization (ISO), ISO 13616 International Bank Account Number; *www.iso.org/*.

Customer Preferences, Locale, and Market Affinities

As previously described, an initial design challenge for global B2C e-commerce sites is identifying the locale of the Web user. The locale not only identifies important language and presentation characteristics of global Web content, but also helps to identify the necessary data concepts and supporting standards required to accurately capture globally diverse data. Acknowledging that the Web is global also introduces the notion that there are an almost unlimited number of combinations of location, language, and culture that may need to be supported. When extending the vast number of diverse possibilities, the Web site design must include some form of locale identification.

Some Web designers suggest that a locale (or a subset of identifying locale characteristics) can be implied or assumed from the method by which the user enters the site, the type of browser session, or the manner in which the user navigates the site. As an example, it might be implied that a user who accesses a site with a domain name of *www.nosuchdomain.fr* is a resident of France and speaks French as their primary language. Design and engineering for this domain would most likely include French language content, currency defined in French francs (or euros), along with other French presentation characteristics. While this approach may appear to simplify the identification of the Web user's locale, it can be highly ineffective. In this example, the Web user might be a resident of a different French-speaking country (that has adopted a currency other than French francs or the euro), or alternatively may be a resident of France who speaks German rather than French as their primary language.

There are a number of locale-identification design techniques for Web sites that may be employed. Some provide graphic symbols or icons (such as a national flag) and allow the user to click through, resulting in country- and language-specific content being presented. Other techniques provide for a list of supported languages presented in the appropriate character sets, symbols, and direction (left-to-right, right-to-left). With this technique, each supported language is a link (using an underlying HTML anchor tag - <a href=""/>) that either redirects the user to a language-specific site or presents language-specific Web page content. It is suggested that a more effective approach is to allow the Web user to identify their locale by selecting preferences. This technique allows the user to identify several predefined locale-specific characteristics that in combination are then used by the Web application to accurately identify the locale.

Of considerable controversy is the formal definition of a locale. Some experts propose that a locale can be determined from the combination of country of residence and language. Others suggest that locale is identified by country of residence, language, and currency. Still others prescribe that a locale can only be determined from language, currency, and date format. While there appear to be a number of common dimensions (country, language, currency), there is also the need to describe products and services being offered. Even though a Web site may have been engineered to present content in the language of the customer and aligned with the cultural characteristics of their country, if descriptive information for the product or service requires some system of measure, potential for misinterpretation remains.

There may be many exceptions to the definition of a locale. Rather than rely on a very narrow definition, it is suggested that the identification of a Web user's locale should be based upon some combination of the following four characteristics:

1. Geographic location (generally country of residence or delivery)
2. Language (an additional dialect being optional)
3. Currency
4. Unit of measure

Regardless of how a locale is determined, providing multilingual support and localized content for every possible locale of the globe is not only unreasonable, but most likely not feasible. Rather than attempting to design a Web site for every locale, the most effective globalization efforts will focus on desirable or target markets, and within those markets, locales of opportunity. Even within these select markets, the cost of supporting all possible locales can be prohibitive. Most globalization efforts will therefore align business goals and sales estimates with the characteristics of each market and locales within each market.

When the target markets and locales of opportunity have been determined, each locale must be defined by its characteristics. When implemented as user-selectable preferences and options, the locale can then be easily derived. Using this technique, the Web user specifies their locale by selecting preferences and options from drop-down lists (see Figure 3.10). The selectable preferences shown in this figure are primarily targeted toward English-speaking users. Language- and character set–specific versions would be required to support other international users. Also, for some locales and cultures, the perceived simplicity of multiple drop-down lists may in fact be a deterrent. Therefore, culture-specific simplification and usability are also critical design components.

Once determined through user selection, the combination of locale components are used as affinity drivers. Following selection of preferences and depending upon the underlying technology architecture, the Web user could then be redirected to a locale-specific version of the site, or localized Web page content could then be returned and presented. In addition to the traditional use of locale to identify

Please Select Your Local Preferences	
Country of Residence	United Kingdom (GBR)
Preferred Language	EN–English
Preferred Currency	UK pound
Preferred Unit of Measure	SI–METRIC

Figure 3.10 Sample design for selecting locale-specific preferences

language and content presentation requirements, identifying locale characteristics can also be used to determine the necessary data concepts and supporting data standards.

SLKD Auto Rental Example—Locale

As a fictitious example, consider a traditional North American–based business that has historically provided auto rental services for U.S. citizens. In order to expand the business, the enterprise has elected to target international visitors and vacationers to the United States. The sample business (SLKD Auto Rental) has determined that it can attract additional international customers by designing, developing, and deploying a globalized Web site. Given that the target audience is international, it becomes obvious that multilingual support is required. However, in order to keep the example simple and brief, the target markets will include a limited number of primarily English-speaking locales. Other than the obvious functionality required for an auto rental business, there are several other global Web site features and capabilities that would be required in order to attract an international visitor. This highly simplified Web site example will be used throughout the rest of the book to help describe globalization complexity and to present techniques that can be applied in some form to other global Web site efforts.

As an introduction to the SLKD Auto Rental Web site, the first challenge is to identify the locale of the Web user. As previously suggested, the locale can be derived from the combination of geography, language, currency, and unit of measure.

The design principle used is a set of drop-down lists as user-selectable preferences. In combination, these characteristics can be used to identify the Web user's locale and will drive the necessary presentation as well as the data requirements to transact business from the online Web session. Depending upon the architecture implementation and supporting technologies, they can also be used to guide language-specific navigation or redirection through the Web site (see Figure 3.11). There are many other effective locale-identification design techniques. However, a basic premise of the SLKD example is simplicity. Where required by the target market, other language- and culture-specific methods for identifying a locale should be implemented.

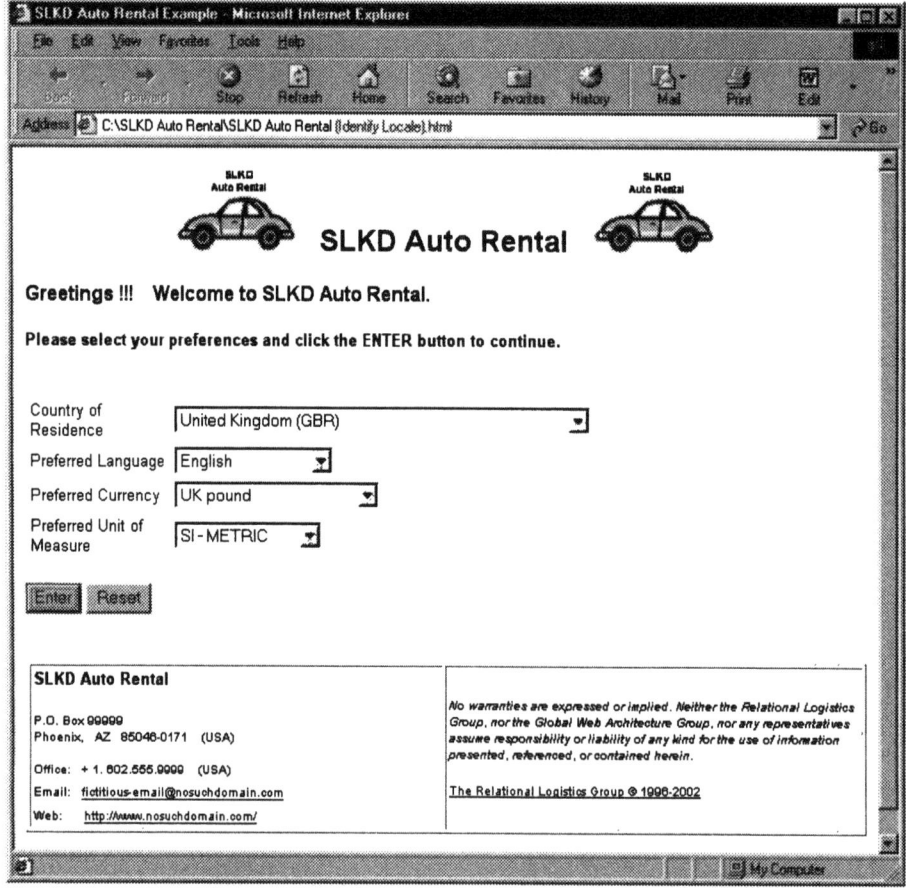

Figure 3.11 SLKD Auto Rental example, identifying the locale of a global customer

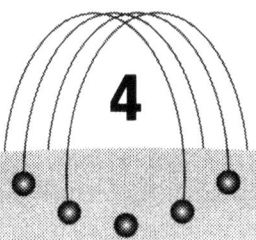

Globalized Data and Transactions

To attract and capture a Web consumer, a number of design and engineering techniques can be employed. In the case of a global Web application, identifying the locale and preferences of the customer is required in order to provide content that is tailored to their language and culture. The traditional approach to Web globalization uses the identified locale and customer preferences to present and express information in a personalized manner. Personalization and usability enable customers to feel almost as if they are interacting directly with representatives of the business during Web site visits. However, attracting and capturing an international customer are not the only challenges of Web site globalization. Of equal importance is the ability to obtain globally diverse customer data, process global business transactions, and integrate global business data with more traditional enterprise data. Addressing these additional data-oriented challenges requires a conceptual separation of presentation from data.

Presentation and Capture of Global Data

When considering consumer-oriented Web applications, presentation is a combination of visual and audio content, along with navigation and usability characteristics. Presentation of information will most often originate from the business enterprise, and will be expressed using the Web site. Presentation content will generally include product and service descriptions, marketing information, advertising, business enterprise information, company contact information, reference and informational data, and recreational data. In a B2C application, presentation is aligned with the identified locale and customer preferences of the target audience. Presented content is generally for use and consumption by the Web user or customer.

Alternatively, the capture of global data includes consumer-oriented information (descriptive, identifying, demographic, locale, and preferences) and transaction content (inquiry, quotation, pricing, purchase, payment, shipping, delivery). To accurately capture globalized data requires that HTML form fields designed to capture customer information be aligned with the data concepts and standards for that locale. Similarly, transaction content must align with the locale and preferences of the consumer, but should also conform to standards that support enterprise application and data integration. Again, the identification of the customer's locale is critical.

Descriptive and identifying information will originate with the customer and will include data concepts such as customer name, residence address, delivery address, telephone number, payment information, and preferences. Transaction content may partly originate from the customer or will be derived from consumer interaction with the Web site (e.g., site navigation, click-stream, product selection, and shopping cart data). The customer's descriptive information and transaction data are generally captured, used, and consumed by (automated applications of) the business enterprise. Exceptions to this consumer-oriented scenario are business-oriented Web sites (B2B), and interactive customer service applications and communities, where the presentation and capture of global data is more of a direct conversational exchange and may include communication with other humans.

As part of global Web site design, defining a method for identification of locale is fundamental but only one of several steps. For each of the supported locales within a target market, the Web site designer or architect must also define the functionality and data necessary to resolve overall business requirements, as well as to support global customer relationship management.

Global Customer Relationship Management (G-CRM)

Customer relationship management combines the business functions of marketing, sales, personalization, customer service, customer retention, and analysis. The ability to identify, target, attract, service, capture, grow, and retain customers are the basic objectives of customer relationship management. The concept of a relationship can take many forms, although the more common B2C Web relationship is specific to an individual customer or consumer.

Global Customer Relationship Management (G-CRM)

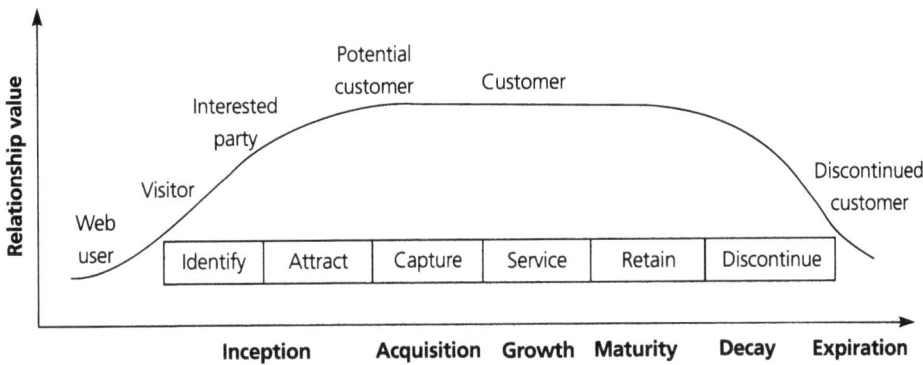

Figure 4.1 Common consumer-oriented relationship states

A relationship can evolve and mature through several states (see Figure 4.1). The most common states of a Web-based consumer relationship include the following:

- Web user (anonymous or identified)
- Visitor (solicited, unsolicited, or referred)
- Interested party
- Potential customer (or "prospect")
- Customer (or "consumer"), including ratings, classes, or categories of customer
- Discontinued relationship (due to attrition, cancellation, or discontinuation)

In a traditional Web-based B2C relationship, the various states will often occur sequentially, in a sort of life cycle. As the relationship evolves and matures, different states are assigned. Exhibiting synergy with Web globalization, global customer relationship management (G-CRM) extends the customer relationship paradigm to consider locale-specific characteristics as well as the capture of globally diverse data. There may also be scenarios where relationship states are iterative (e.g., a previous customer again becomes an interested party and then a potential customer, etc.).

Like the globalization and localization processes, G-CRM techniques used to attract, capture, service, and retain an international customer rely upon accurate identification of the customer's locale and preferences. Basically, a relationship begins with a visit to the Web site. Assuming the Web site visitor is international, the ability to attract and retain the visitor as an interested party relies upon identification of the visitor's locale and the alignment of content to the visitor's preferences.

Typical Global B2C, Web-Based Customer Relationship

The development of a customer relationship using the Web begins with identification of a site of interest by the Web user and progresses through an initial site visit, navigation of the site, selection of products or services of interest, and the transaction of business (see Figure 4.2). Each of the noted activities aligns with a typical life cycle or maturity curve. While the example portrays a typical life cycle, a more optimistic and desirable example would also include growth and propagation of customer relationships, and when the relationship approached "decay," the customer would be shifted to other relationships.

The initiation of a simple Web-based customer relationship typically begins with a Web site visit. Most likely the Web user will have found a reference to the Web site by

- Entering keywords and using a search engine
- Following a link from another Web site or Web page
- Click-through redirection from a portal
- Direct URL entry in a browser (potentially from printed advertising or referral from another user)
- URL entry error or site misdirection

Initially, the state of the relationship is "Web user." If the Web user visits the site, the state of the relationship changes to "visitor." At a minimum, the visitor should be able to understand the content that is presented (e.g., content from the home page, welcome page, or similar). In order to further advance the relationship, it is critical that the locale of the visitor has been identified and any additional Web site content is localized according to the visitor's preferences.

At this point the session should begin to be personalized. That is, the customer should have the impression that Web page content and additional interaction with the site are customized or tailored toward their preferences rather than appearing as if the Web site is directed at a broad, nonspecific audience. Assuming the products or services promoted on the site are of interest, as the Web site visitor navigates the site, they would develop an elevated level of interest. The state of the relationship then becomes that of "interested party." The underlying premise is that the locale and preferences have been leveraged to present product and service information using the customer's preferred language, product and service pricing using the preferred currency, and product dimensions and packaging in the customer's preferred unit of measure.

If the interested party continues by initiating an order for the selected products and services (e.g., initiating an engagement, purchase, request for quotation, request

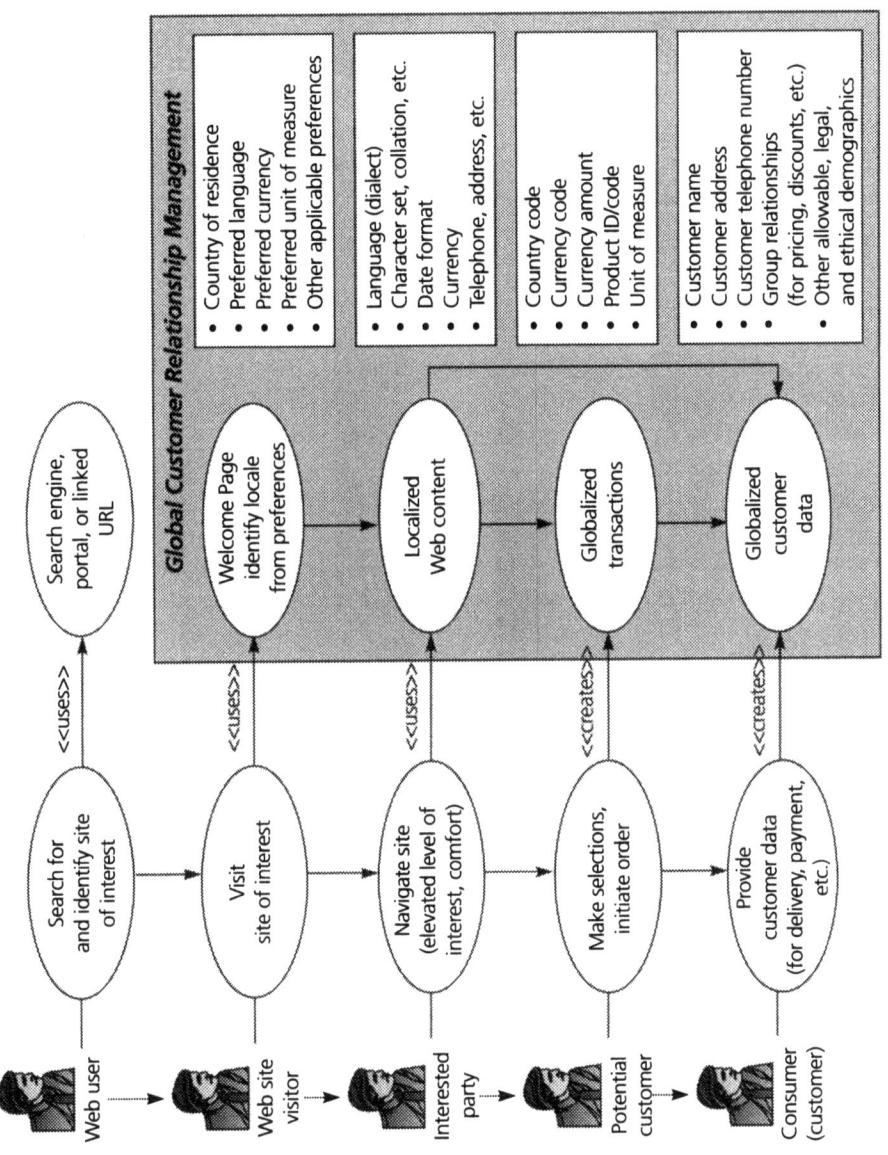

Figure 4.2 Typical global B2C, Web-based relationship

for additional product information, etc.), the state of the relationship is further elevated to "potential customer." These activities and interactions begin the creation of underlying e-commerce transactions. Information required to populate the transactions can originate from several sources. If the engagement is a product purchase, product and pricing information can be acquired from the shopping cart (or similar method of Web purchase). However, unless the customer has previously developed a relationship and the necessary information has been retained, contact, delivery, and payment information must be acquired.

The acquisition of customer information can take several forms. In the case of a B2C Web application, the most common information will include the following:

- Customer name
- Customer addresses (e.g., residence, delivery, billing, postal)
- Customer telephone numbers
- Customer identification (as appropriate)

Continuing with the order process, the customer will need to specify a form of payment and the payment medium or instrument (e.g., credit, charge, or debit card number, expiration dates, EFT account information, or third-party payer). The entry and validation of customer and payment information completes the customer side of the order process, and the relationship is then elevated to "customer."

Although in previous chapters considerable emphasis has been placed on locale identification and presentation of localized content, of equal importance is the ability to accurately and effectively capture globally diverse data. The value of the locale components is that they present a general set of criteria that can be used to identify affinities with the data that must be captured, as well as the corresponding standards that must be applied.

Typical Global B2C Technology Cycle

Taking a more technical "conversation" perspective of the global B2C, Web-based customer relationship, each step of the B2C order cycle can be defined as the result of an event (see Table 4.1). An event is initiated by an actor and prompts one or more actions. Actions produce a result, and the result is described or defined by facts (data). Most events will follow a sequential path, although shifts in site functionality, level of visitor interest, and continued visitor navigation can introduce expanded or iterative steps.

The sample set of events described in Table 4.1 is highly summarized and proposes that the technology architecture for the site includes serving localized content to the Web user. More granular events and activities would be evident,

Table 4.1 Summarized global B2C technology cycle

Event	Actor	Relationship state	Action	Result	Facts
Search for Web site	Web user	Web user	Provide keywords, use search engine	Acquire link to site of interest	Keywords used, URL of identified site
Visit site of interest	Web user	Visitor	Enter URL, download page content to browser	View content of page	Welcome (or home) page content, selectable preferences, locale characteristics
Select and submit preferences	Web user	Visitor	Select or enter preferences and locale characteristics	Preferences and locale characteristics are submitted	Country of residence, language, currency, unit of measure
Receive preferences	Web application		Map preferences to locale	Locale and standardized data concepts are identified and assembled into page content	Language, character set, date, currency, address, telephone, etc.
Localized page content is returned	Web application		Return localized page content to visitor throughout session	Localized page content is served as response to preferences	Localized page content
Navigate site further	Web user	Interested party	Navigate site, identify content, topics, products of interest	Elevated level of interest	Localized page content
Make selections, initiate order	Web user	Potential customer	Select products, initiate purchase transaction	Order process initiated	Selected products

(*continued*)

Table 4.1 (continued)

Event	Actor	Relationship state	Action	Result	Facts
Capture order information	Web application		Capture selected product information	Order and product transactions populated	Order number, order items, product number, quantity, pricing, packaging
Verify inventory	Web or application server		Check inventory with enterprise systems	Inventory reserved pending order completion	Inventory positions
Confirm availability for customer	Web server		Serve confirmation of product availability to Web user	Confirmation page content is served as response to select products, initiate order	Product availability, inventory positions, future availability
Provide customer, delivery, payment information	Web user	Customer (consumer)	Provide customer, delivery, payment information	Completes customer entry of the order process	Name, address, telephone, payment medium, payment instrument
Capture customer information	Web application		Capture customer, delivery, and payment information	Customer identification, delivery address, contact information, payment information	Name, address, telephone, payment medium, payment instrument

Table 4.1 (continued)

Event	Actor	Relationship state	Action	Result	Facts
Validate and authenticate	Web or application server		Verify customer information, authenticate payment information	Updated customer data, updated order data, complete order transactions	Payment method approval
Confirmation of order and payment acceptance	Web server		Serve order confirmation to Web user	Order complete	Updated order
Formalize customer relationship characteristics	Application server or enterprise G-CRM application		Capture, formalize, store customer relationship data	Updated customer relationship data	Customer data, customer preferences, order data, relationship state

depending upon the Web architecture and enterprise applications in use. As examples, the verification of inventory and validation of payment might be enabled through several layers of application servers and more traditional enterprise applications. Alternative designs could result in predefined content that exists as resources under different Web domains. Rather than serving localized content from a globalization Web server, the Web user would be redirected to a locale-specific domain and browser content as resources under that domain would then be served according to further navigation of the site. Both designs are similar in that the Web user is unaware of the technology solution, and the site content is localized according to their preferences and locale.

From the perspective of the enterprise, there are several important events that take place. The most obvious are a combination of traditional consumer-oriented business transactions, order servicing, and order fulfillment. These events are fundamental to revenue generation and considered "mission critical" by the enterprise. In addition, the ability to capture data about the customer, the customer's preferences, locale, and order history provides valuable information for developing the global customer relationship and personalizing future sessions.

When considering order servicing, order fulfillment, and payment, being able to integrate and exchange customer, order, and product data among traditional enterprise applications is mandatory. However, if the business is a traditional North American company, there is a high probability that globally diverse data such as customer names, addresses, and telephone numbers will vary significantly from other enterprise data. The globally diverse information will introduce variations in format, structure, length, allowable content, and potentially context. Although the example highlights the complexities of a global analogy, the problem of enterprise application integration is not revolutionary. As will be described in Chapter 7, potential solutions and challenges are many.

SLKD Auto Rental Example—Global Data

The SLKD Auto Rental Web site is designed to represent a highly simplified analogy of a globalized B2C Web site. Although the sample site is limited to a narrow, primarily English-speaking market, it does follow the basic paradigm of identification of the Web site visitor's locale, localization of additional content to support the visitor's preferences, and alignment of HTML form input fields to align with locale characteristics. Although the techniques that have been applied to the identification of locale and the presentation of content can be effective, the sample Web site is not intended to address cultural interfaces and usability. Those activities are

SLKD Auto Rental Example—Global Data

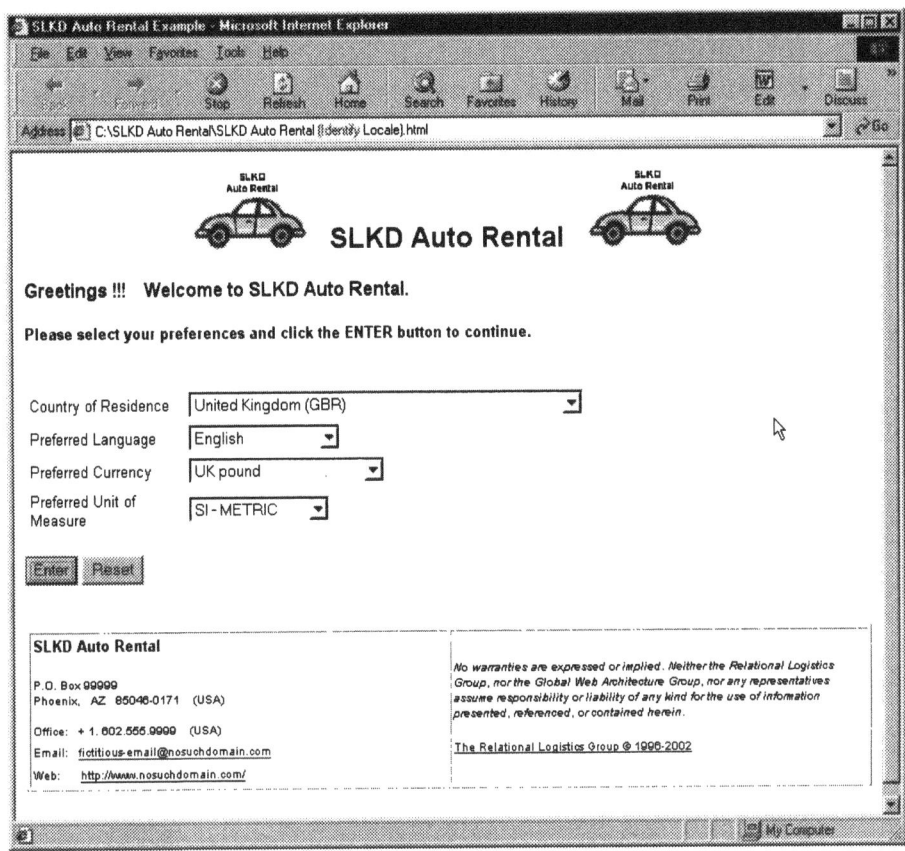

Figure 4.3 SLKD Auto Rental example—welcome page (to identify locale)

fundamental to internationalization and localization. However, the sample site is intended to portray the important and critical nature of globally diverse data. Web page examples of the fictitious SLKD Auto Rental Web site (see Figures 4.3, 4.4, and 4.7) represent a simple global customer relationship between an international Web visitor and the enterprise.

Locale Identification

To begin the sample scenario, it is assumed that an anonymous Web user has searched for and found the SLKD Auto Rental Web site or has followed a link to the site from another page. The initial content that is presented to the Web user is a type of welcome page (see Figure 4.3). The content of this page assumes that the audience either speaks English as their primary language or is reasonably English literate. It presents a simple welcome to the visitor and allows for identification of the visitor's locale. If the Web site were to target a broader global audience (e.g., users of many international markets), the technique for welcoming the user and method of locale identification would potentially require extensive multilingual support.

If the target market(s) are to include multilingual support, four common architectural approaches are often used:

- A single welcome page in a base language that is assumed to be understood by a large percentage of the target market
- A single welcome page with multiple sections of language-specific welcome content and descriptive site information
- Separate and individual welcome pages that are translated to target languages, with each identified by a unique domain (e.g., *www.abcde.co.uk*, *www.abcde.fr*, *www.abcde.au*, etc.)
- Separate and individual welcome pages that are translated to target languages, with each identified as linked or redirected resources under a single site domain

Each of these architectural approaches has advantages and disadvantages. The SLKD Auto Rental Web site example is engineered using the first architectural approach. The assumption is that the target audience for the example will primarily speak a single base language (in this case, English). It is important to note that this approach can be cost effective (due to limited translation effort and development time). However, it may also be less than effective at attracting and acquiring international customers when there are large population segments of the target market that are not literate with or do not speak the language used on the welcome page.

The sample welcome page allows the visitor to select preferences from dropdown lists for

- Country of residence
- Preferred language
- Preferred currency
- Preferred unit of measure

Given the context of an auto rental site that targets an international, English-speaking audience, the combination of the previous four characteristics can be used to identify the locale of a visitor and to present additional Web page content that is tailored accordingly. The method used to identify and capture the visitor's locale includes an underlying HTML "form" with selectable content that will be returned to the Web server when the visitor clicks the enter button. Upon receiving the content of the form (including the user-selected preferences), the Web server or application server, depending upon the architectural layers, would interpret the preferences and map them to a defined locale.

By visiting the Web site, the state of the relationship with the Web user has evolved to become "visitor." The visitor may be an anonymous individual or person. However, important information regarding their preferences and continued interaction have been identified. As determined by the locale, further Web page content will be served to the visitor's Web browser (returned to the Web visitor) in their preferred language, using their preferred currency and unit of measure, as appropriate. Additionally, localized content would include other supporting presentation and culture-specific characteristics. A few of the more important characteristics include appropriate character set, collation sequence, and date format.

The SLKD Auto Rental example is engineered with additional content pages having been previously localized and mapped to target locales. When the locale is identified from the welcome page selections and returned to the Web server, mapping to the necessary localized Web pages would be resolved. The process of localizing the Web page content to address all of the supported locales of the target market would have been accomplished during the design and engineering phases of Web site development.

Product Selection

Following the SLKD Auto Rental welcome page, selection of user preferences, and a valid submit from the browser (i.e., the visitor selected their preferences and clicked the enter button), the sample site is designed and engineered to return a content page describing available products and allowing the user to enter their desired reservation dates and select the item of interest (e.g., presenting the various available automobiles). As previously described, the content of this page would have been translated to the preferred language of the visitor and localized to their preferences.

As shown in the example (see Figure 4.4), the content of the Web page is presented using English as the preferred language. Additionally, all product dimensions and measurements are presented in both a base unit (English ANSI) and the visitor's preferred unit of measure (SI—metric). Similarly, product pricing is presented in a base currency (U.S. dollar), as well as the visitor's preferred currency (U.K. pound). It is important to note that a comprehensive internationalization and localization effort may have included "dialect" as an extension of language. Although imperfect, the identification of dialect is most often determined by the combination of country of residence and preferred language. If dialect support were a functional requirement of the internationalization and localization efforts, the

Chapter 4 Globalized Data and Transactions

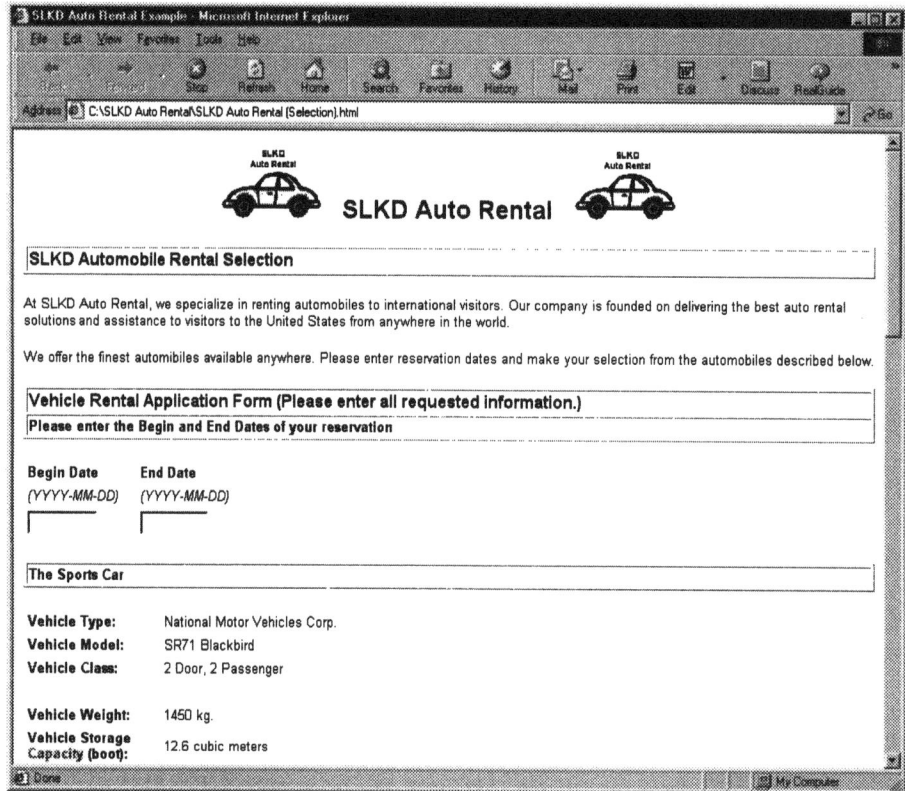

Figure 4.4 SLKD Auto Rental example—vehicle selection

example of English as the primary language would also have included colloquialisms and spelling that differs by locale (e.g., U.S. English, U.K. English, Australian English, etc.).

By continuing to navigate the Web site and viewing product- or service-oriented content, the visitor has evolved to become an "interested party."

Customer and Order Data Capture

Assuming the Web visitor (now an interested party) makes a selection from among the offered rental automobiles, the state of the relationship would become that of a "potential customer." The relationship classification "potential" is maintained until an order transaction has been completed and confirmed. Upon submission of a vehicle selection, a confirmation page is returned to the Web user (potential customer). The content of the confirmation page includes the selected vehicle, including pricing and any applicable legal disclosures, and continues with a rental application

Please Enter Your Address	
Address to	Dr. John Quincy Adams von Doe Sr.
Address	Jones Medical Complex
Address	123456 S.E. Broadwind Blvd.
Address	Building 6, Suite 9-B
Address	Phoenix, AZ 85000
Address	USA

Figure 4.5 Example of unformatted, abstract address fields

form. The purpose of the application form is to capture information about the customer (name, telephone number, address, automobile operator's license, insurance information, and driving experience) as data concepts.

During the early design phase for the Web site, functional business requirements aligned with the target market determine the data concepts that need to be captured by the application form. Similarly, affinity and mapping of target markets to supported locales and then to data concepts identifies the data standards that must be applied. Again, the example of a postal or delivery address is appropriate. If the target markets were North America, Europe, and the Pacific Rim, and supported locales were identified as primarily English speaking, a postal address formatted for the United States would be largely ineffective. The architect would need to identify the postal address formats of the supported locales and, if possible, derive a common address format that would suffice for all. If a common format were not possible, the architect would need to identify individual postal address formats mapped to each locale.

The ability to derive and use a single common postal address format presents a solution that is effective from an initial development cost and delivery perspective. As an example, the architect could design the HTML form to accept and submit five or six unformatted address lines. A set of highly abstract or free-form HTML input fields provides almost unbounded flexibility. With this technique, almost any address from any locale could be captured. However, the captured and submitted address data would exist in such an abstract form as to prohibit any use, purpose, sharing, or integration of the data for other than simple mailing labels and form letters (see Figure 4.5).

Chapter 4 Globalized Data and Transactions

The underlying HTML form would include input elements for each unformatted and abstract address line (see Listing 4.1). However, these elements could only be defined with a minimum of validation and constraint (for the most part, a maximum length for each address line). Unless some other form of validation such as client-side JavaScript or server-side logic were used, the user could enter text of any type (including valid, invalid, or even nonsensical) and in any order.

Listing 4.1 Sample listing aligned with Figure 4.5 (abstract HTML form input elements)

```
<!-- **************************************************** -->
<!-- *** Address *** -->
<!-- **************************************************** -->
<p><table cellpadding="1" border="0" width="100%">
<tr>
<td width="100%">
<font size="2" face="Arial"><strong>Please enter your Address</strong></font>
</td>
</tr>
</table></p>

<p><table cellpadding="1" border="0" width="50%">

<tr>
<td width="20%"><font size="2" face="Arial">Address To</font></td>
<td width="80%"><font size="2" face="Arial"><input type="text" name="Addr_Line_1" size="40" maxlength="40"></input></font></td>
</tr>
<tr>
<td width="20%"><font size="2" face="Arial">Address</font></td>
<td width="80%"><font size="2" face="Arial"><input type="text" name="Addr_Line_2" size="40" maxlength="40"></input></font></td>
</tr>
<tr>
<td width="20%"><font size="2" face="Arial">Address</font></td>
<td width="80%"><font size="2" face="Arial"><input type="text" name="Addr_Line_3" size="40" maxlength="40"></input></font></td>
</tr>
```

```html
<tr>
<td width="20%"><font size="2" face="Arial">Address</font></td>
<td width="80%"><font size="2" face="Arial"><input type="text" name="Addr_Line_4" size="40" maxlength="40"></input></font></td>
</tr>
<tr>
<td width="20%"><font size="2" face="Arial">Address</font></td>
<td width="80%"><font size="2" face="Arial"><input type="text" name="Addr_Line_5" size="40" maxlength="40"></input></font></td>
</tr>
<tr>
<td width="20%"><font size="2" face="Arial">Address</font></td>
<td width="80%"><font size="2" face="Arial"><input type="text" name="Addr_Line_6" size="40" maxlength="40"></input></font></td>
</tr>
</table>
```

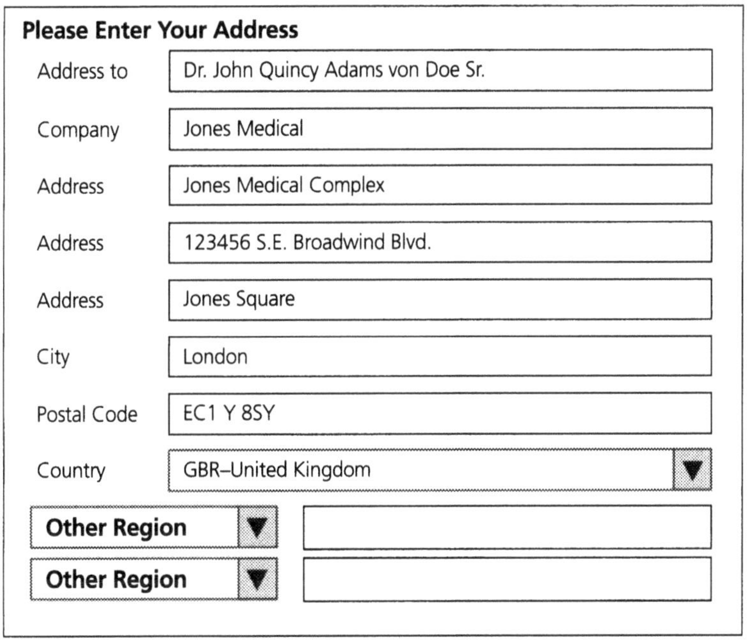

Figure 4.6 Example of formatted address (supporting multiple locales)

Chapter 4 Globalized Data and Transactions

A more effective solution would be to align the postal address formats of each locale and to develop a common format that can accept locale-specific elements, as well as common address formats (see Figure 4.6). While this approach is far more effective and would provide far more support for enterprise application and data integration, the functional use and purpose of the captured address information might require additional decomposition and formatting. As an example, the proposed technique facilitates broad operational use of the captured and submitted address information. However, it does not provide the granularity that would be required to support analytical processing, such as for a data warehouse.

The underlying HTML form for this example would include input elements for each granular address data particle that supports one or more locales (see Listing 4.2). With this example the HTML is still somewhat weak in the area of validation. Allowable content for each element is either specified as predefined selectable elements or contextually implied from the descriptive label that is rendered next to each input element. It would be desirable to incorporate server-side logic to perform additional validation.

Listing 4.2 Example listing aligned with Figure 4.6 (formatted HTML form input elements)

```
<!-- **************************************************** -->
<!-- *** Address *** -->
<!-- **************************************************** -->
<p>
<table cellpadding="1" border="1" width="100%">
<tr>
<td width="100%"><font size="2" face="Arial"><strong>Please enter your Residence (Home) Address</strong></font></td>
</tr>
</table></p>

<p><table cellpadding="1" border="0" width="86%">
<tr>
<td width="15%"><font size="2" face="Arial">Address To</font></td>
<td width="25%"><font size="2" face="Arial"><input type="text" name="Addr_To_Name" size="40" maxlength="40"></input></font></td>
<td width="12%"><font color="#FF0000" size="2" face="Arial"><em>(required)</em></font></td>
<td width="2%"><font size="2" face="Arial"> </font></td>
```

SLKD Auto Rental Example—Global Data

```
<td width="15%"><font size="2" face="Arial"> </font></td>
<td width="20%"><font size="2" face="Arial"> </font></td>
</tr>
<tr>
<td width="15%"><font size="2" face="Arial">Company</font></td>
<td width="25%"><font size="2" face="Arial"><input type="text"
name="Addr_Company" size="40" maxlength="40"></input></font></td>
<td width="12%"><font size="2" face="Arial"> </font></td>
<td width="2%"><font size="2" face="Arial"> </font></td>
<td width="15%"><font size="2" face="Arial"> </font></td>
<td width="20%"><font size="2" face="Arial"> </font></td>
</tr>
<tr>
<td width="15%"><font size="2" face="Arial">Address</font></td>
<td width="25%"><font size="2" face="Arial"><input type="text"
name="Addr_Street_1" size="40" maxlength="40"></input></font></td>
<td width="12%"><font size="2" face="Arial"> </font></td>
<td width="2%"><font size="2" face="Arial"> </font></td>
<td width="15%"><font size="2" face="Arial"> </font></td>
<td width="20%"><font size="2" face="Arial"> </font></td>
</tr>
<tr>
<td width="15%"><font size="2" face="Arial">Address</font></td>
<td width="25%"><font size="2" face="Arial"><input type="text"
name="Addr_Street_2" size="40" maxlength="40"></input></font></td>
<td width="12%"><font size="2" face="Arial"> </font></td>
<td width="2%"><font size="2" face="Arial"> </font></td>
<td width="15%"><font size="2" face="Arial"> </font></td>
<td width="20%"><font size="2" face="Arial"> </font></td>
</tr>
<tr>
<td width="15%"><font size="2" face="Arial">Address</font></td>
<td width="25%"><font size="2" face="Arial"><input type="text"
name="Addr_Street_3" size="40" maxlength="40"></input></font></td>
<td width="12%"><font size="2" face="Arial"> </font></td>
<td width="2%"><font size="2" face="Arial"> </font></td>
<td width="15%"><font size="2" face="Arial"> </font></td>
<td width="20%"><font size="2" face="Arial"> </font></td>
</tr>
```

Chapter 4 Globalized Data and Transactions

```html
<tr>
<td width="15%"><font size="2" face="Arial">City</font></td>
<td width="25%"><font size="2" face="Arial"><input type="text"
name="Addr_City" size="20" maxlength="20"></input></font></td>
<td width="12%"><font size="2" face="Arial"> </font></td>
<td width="2%"><font size="2" face="Arial"> </font></td>
<td width="15%"><font size="2" face="Arial"> </font></td>
<td width="20%"><font size="2" face="Arial"> </font></td>
</tr>
<tr>
<td width="15%"><font size="2" face="Arial">Postal Code</font></td>
<td width="25%"><font size="2" face="Arial"><input type="text"
name="Addr_Post_Code" size="15" maxlength="15"></font></td>
<td width="12%"><font size="2" face="Arial"> </font></td>
<td width="2%"><font size="2" face="Arial"> </font></td>
<td width="15%"><font size="2" face="Arial"> </font></td>
<td width="20%"><font size="2" face="Arial"> </font></td>
</tr>
<tr>
<td width="15%"><font size="2" face="Arial">Country</font></td>
<td width="25%"><font size="2" face="Arial">
<select name="Addr_Country" size="1">
<option selected value="GBR:826 (United Kingdom - England)">GBR-United
Kingdom</option>
<option value="USA:840 (United States)">USA-United States </option>
<option value="AUS:036 (Australia)">AUS-Australia </option>
<option value="NZL:554 (New Zealand)">NZL-New Zealand </option>
<option value="CAN:124 (Canada)">CAN-Canada </option>

<!-- - Other country selections removed from the sample source code for
brevity - -->

</select>
</font></td>
<td width="12%"><font size="2" face="Arial"> </font></td>
<td width="2%"><font size="2" face="Arial"> </font></td>
<td width="15%"><font size="2" face="Arial"> </font></td>
<td width="20%"><font size="2" face="Arial"> </font></td>
```

SLKD Auto Rental Example—Global Data

```
</tr>
</table><br>

<table cellpadding="2" border="0" size="70%">
<tr>
<td><font size="2" face="Arial">
<select name="Addr_Reg_1_Type" size="1">
<option value="Canton">Canton</option>
<option value="County">County</option>
<option value="Department">Department</option>
<option value="District">District</option>
<option value="Emirate">Emirate</option>
<option value="Governorate">Governorate</option>
<option value="Island">Island</option>
<option value="Jurisdiction">Jurisdiction</option>
<option value="Municipality">Municipality</option>
<option value="Parish">Parish</option>
<option value="Prefecture">Prefecture</option>
<option value="Province">Province</option>
<option value="Rayon">Rayon</option>
<option value="Region">Region</option>
<option value="Regional Centre">Regional Centre</option>
<option value="Shire">Shire</option>
<option value="State">State</option>
<option value="Territory">Territory</option>
<option value="Township">Township</option>
<option value="Zone">Zone</option>
<option selected value="Other Region">Other Region</option>
</select>
</font></td>
<td><font size="2" face="Arial">
<input type="text" size="30" maxlength="30" name="Addr_Reg_1"></ input>
</font></td>
<td> </td>
<td> </td>
</tr>
<tr>
```

Chapter 4 Globalized Data and Transactions

```
<td><font size="2" face="Arial">
<select name="Addr_Reg_2_Type" size="1">
<option value="Canton">Canton</option>
<option value="County">County</option>
<option value="Department">Department</option>
<option value="District">District</option>
<option value="Emirate">Emirate</option>
<option value="Governorate">Governorate</option>
<option value="Island">Island</option>
<option value="Jurisdiction">Jurisdiction</option>
<option value="Municipality">Municipality</option>
<option value="Parish">Parish</option>
<option value="Prefecture">Prefecture</option>
<option value="Province">Province</option>
<option value="Rayon">Rayon</option>
<option value="Region">Region</option>
<option value="Regional Centre">Regional Centre</option>
<option value="Shire">Shire</option>
<option value="State">State</option>
<option value="Territory">Territory</option>
<option value="Township">Township</option>
<option value="Zone">Zone</option>
<option selected value="Other Region">Other Region </option>
</select>
</font></td>
<td><font size="2" face="Arial">
<input type="text" size="30" maxlength="30" name="Addr_Reg_2"></
input>
</font></td>
<td> </td>
<td> </td>
</tr>
</table><br></br>
```

The primary function of the sample application form is to collect customer information that is required to facilitate the reservation of a rental automobile. Some customer information is specifically for identification of the customer, other information is intended to validate vehicle operation experience and to assess insurability and risk. When combined with the selected product (vehicle), the collected and submitted data will constitute completion of an automobile rental reservation transaction.

Before collecting customer information, the sample Web site has been engineered to confirm the product selection from the previous Web page (see Figure 4.7). The premise is that the potential customer should have the opportunity to review and modify (or potentially abandon) their selection. In addition to presenting selected product information, this section of the application page allows the enterprise to present and reconfirm pricing, terms of agreement, and a legal disclaimer.

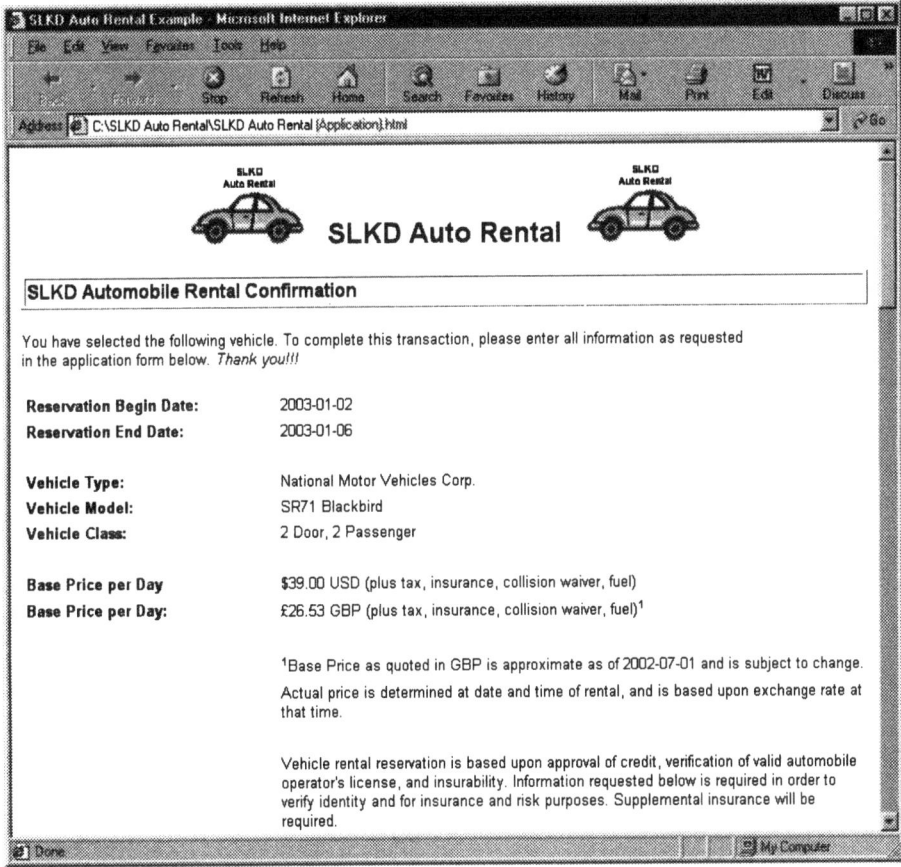

Figure 4.7 SLKD Auto Rental example—confirmation of selected product

Chapter 4 Globalized Data and Transactions

Following the confirmation of the selected automobile, the application form prompts the potential customer to enter data into the application form. The first section of the form is designed to collect identifying customer information. The customer is prompted to enter a preferred salutation, their name, and preferred titles (see Figure 4.8). The form elements defined to capture this information are designed to allow for highly diverse name formats. As previously noted, the structure and format of a person's name can be highly variable when considering multiple cultures and locales. The sample form has also adopted the technique of allowing for multiple name particles. Default name particle types are provided. However, the user will have the opportunity to select other types from predefined drop-down lists, as appropriate. It is also important to note that top-to-bottom user entry implies the preferred order of name particles, regardless of type.

When combined with the form fields that define essential global data concepts and standards, interface design and usability are critical to acquiring the necessary information and completing the transaction. Interface design is the result of functional requirements (rather than data requirements) and is a key activity of both internationalization and localization. The intent of the SLKD Auto Rental example is to present the critical data-oriented concepts of global Web site engineering. There are other alternatives to cultural- and locale-specific interface design that would be completed as part of the localization process.

In addition to the customer's name, residential and business telephone numbers are required. A telephone number is another globally diverse data concept. Standards defined by the International Telecommunications Union (ITU) have been minimally applied. The sample Web site defines a telephone number by

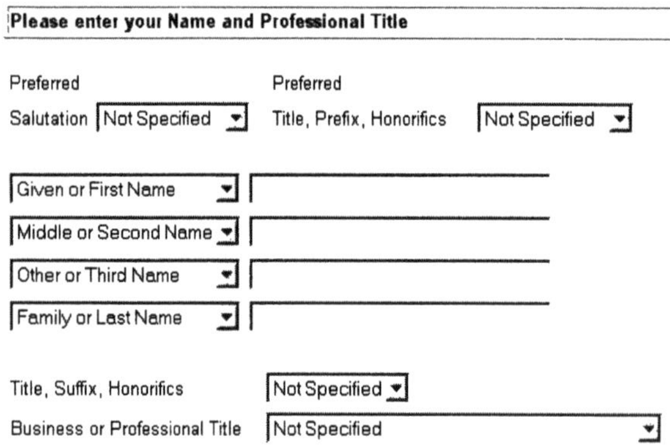

Figure 4.8 SLKD Auto Rental example—capture of customer name

individual segment and also predefines the country code prefixes as drop-down selection lists (see Figure 4.9). The initial impression of telephone number data is that it is solely for the purpose of describing a method for contacting the customer. However, telephone number segments such as country code can help to ease integration of telephone numbers with traditional enterprise data as well as to support analytical processing such as alignment of outbound customer service and sales calls by region.

The form elements for address have been derived as common to a number of locales (see Figure 4.10). This technique allows for simplification of form design and content, as well as for a level of granularity that would be acceptable to the enterprise in order to facilitate integration. It is important to note that integration of globally diverse data with traditional enterprise data is not a simple task. Even when a common format has been engineered for input and capture of global data, enterprise integration may require additional restructuring, transformation, and application of metadata rules. The value and complexities of enterprise integration are described further in Chapter 7.

Following the capture of the customer's address, the trailing portion of the SLKD Auto Rental example application form includes information that is considered necessary in the automobile rental business (see Figure 4.11). Information captured by the application form such as automobile operator's license number, insurance, and driving experience information may be considered by some to be intrusive or even a violation of personal privacy. There may be locales where such information cannot be legally requested. Regulatory and legal issues present daunting challenges to the design and engineering of global Web sites. There are numerous issues to consider in the protection of both the enterprise and the potential customer. Insuring proper disclosure and compliance with national, regional, and local law

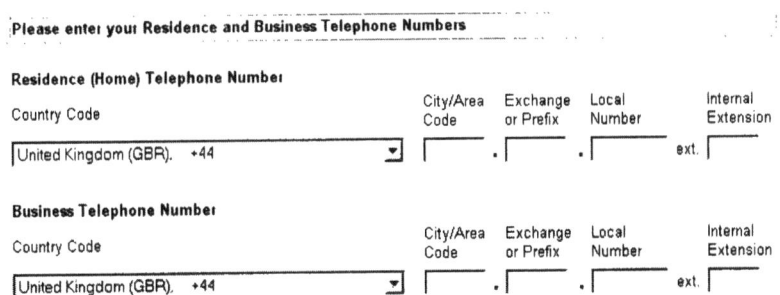

Figure 4.9 SLKD Auto Rental example—capture of customer telephone numbers

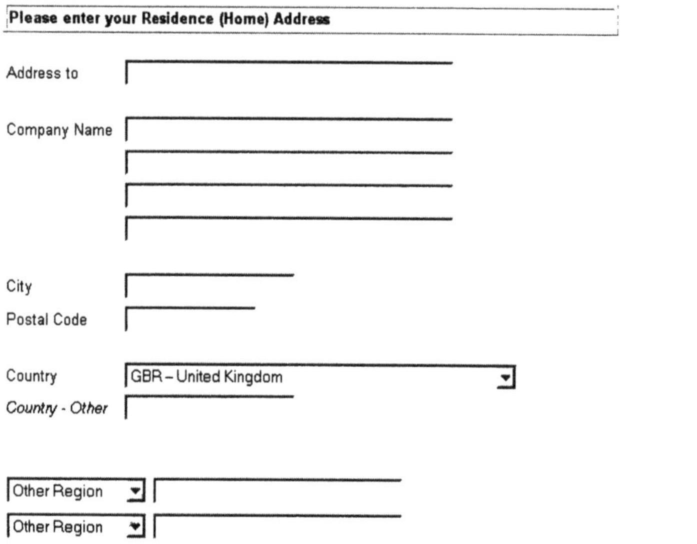

Chapter 4 Globalized Data and Transactions

Figure 4.10 SLKD Auto Rental example—capture of customer address

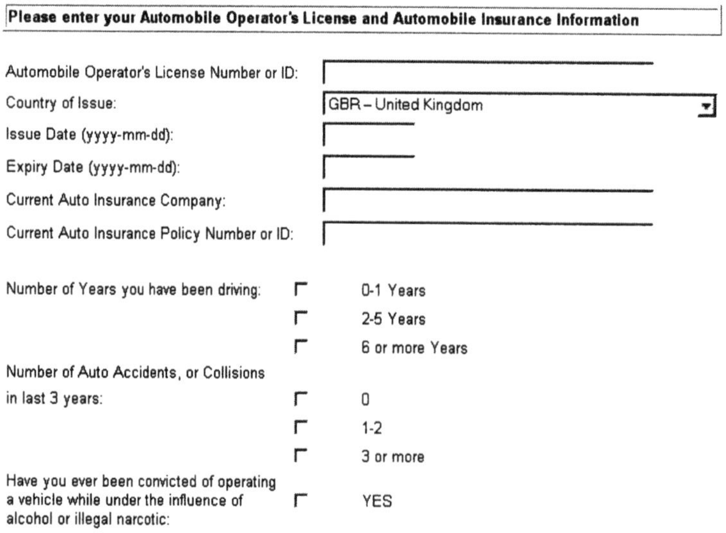

Figure 4.11 SLKD Auto Rental example—capture of critical business data

presents the need for research of legal issues and consultation with attorneys experienced with the target markets.

As implied by the intended content of the sample application form, there is considerable potential for inaccurate entry by the user. The assumption is that upon submission, the server will invoke validation logic to insure an acceptable degree of accuracy. Once it has been determined that the necessary customer data has been collected and is deemed accurate, the server will return a confirmation to the customer.

Confirmation

At acceptance of the automobile rental reservation, the Web user is presented with a confirmation page. In addition to the selected vehicle and pricing information, the confirmation page may include the specified rental dates, legal disclosure, and in this example a confirmation number (see Figure 4.12). The sample confir-

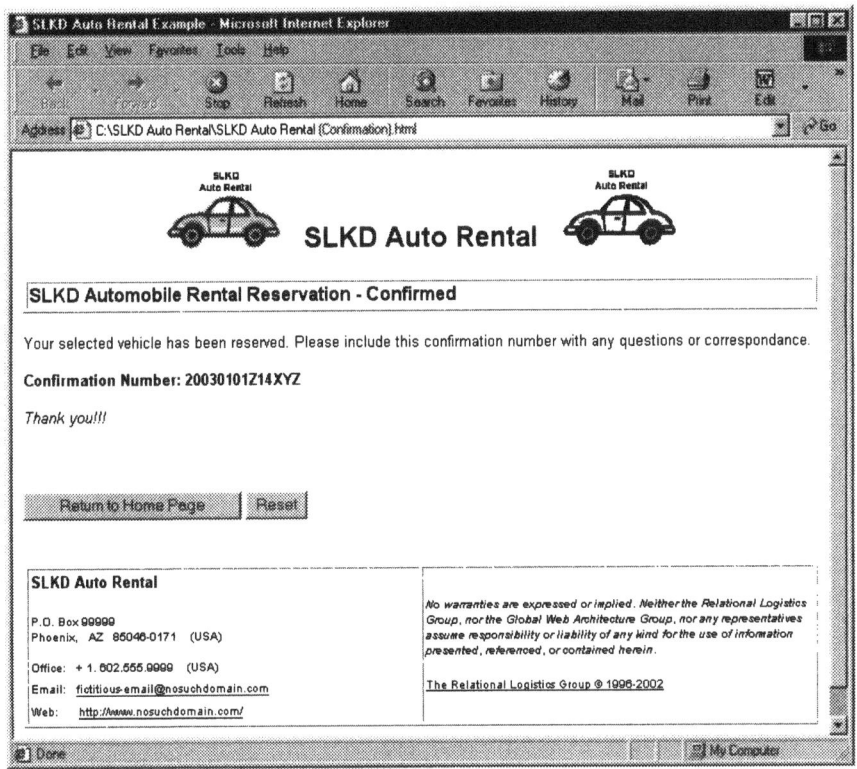

Figure 4.12 SLKD Auto Rental example—confirmation of rental reservation

mation completes the customer transaction, and the state of the relationship with the Web user (potential customer) has now matured to that of "customer." However, there may be many other non-Web processes that result (e.g., scheduling and logistics for selected inventory, verification of insurability, adjustment of forecasted revenue, etc.).

It becomes obvious that designing and engineering a Web site that targets a globally diverse audience presents daunting challenges. The complexities of language, presentation, culture, usability, and especially the capture and integration of globally diverse data are critical success factors. Solutions are not limited to internationalization, localization, or tactical deployment of Web applications. To deploy a global Web site successfully, an enterprise must recognize and embrace the global nature of the Web and begin by following a Web site globalization process.

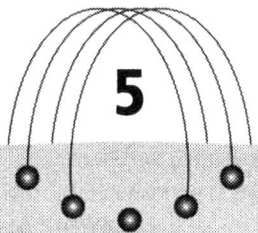

Globalization Process and Techniques

Web site globalization is first and foremost a process. The term *globalization* is far broader in context than the terms *regional*, *international*, or *local*. The scope of a globalization effort includes, extends, and complements internationalization and localization activities to also address the data- and transaction-oriented requirements of a Web site. Even when the site has been engineered to address the language and presentation characteristics of an international audience, the ability to capture globally diverse data, process transactions, and service an international customer requires alignment with and support for data standards. Without the ability to accurately and effectively capture globally diverse information, a Web site will not be able to process, integrate, and exchange the necessary operational data with traditional enterprise applications.

Internationalization, localization, and globally diverse data are critical to Web site globalization. However, jumping to Web site design and engineering without a defined strategy and process would be a critical error. Before engaging tactical language translation and Web site development activities, the business should have adopted a Web site globalization process that further supports an overall globalization strategy.

A successful Web site globalization process will include the following activities:

- Formalization of business requirements
- Identification of candidate markets
- Development of market profiles

- Validation of candidate markets
- Decomposition of business requirements
  - Functional requirements (internationalization, localization)
  - Data requirements (dimensional affinity, data concepts, data standards)
- Web site engineering
  - Development
  - Testing
  - Documentation
  - Implementation

The integration of a globalization process with technology development methodologies may take several forms. One of the more common is to define a set of activities that are both sequential and iterative. From a conceptual perspective, the process initiates with business activities and follows with more traditional design and development activities (see Figure 5.1).

Defining Global Business Requirements

The first activity of the globalization process is the definition of business requirements. As defined, the Web is by default global, without boundaries. Web users and Web sites may be located anywhere in the world. Conceptually, this provides unbounded marketing opportunities. Traditional North American businesses now have the potential to market products and services to a vast international audience. However, most likely a truly global Web site approach will not be viable. Alternatively, these businesses will focus on potential markets that represent a target audience, rather than an all-encompassing global approach. The first challenge is being able to define the general business goals that can then be used to identify these potential markets.

Market analysis will consider traditional business goals, complexities, and threats. However, these same business characteristics will be extended to consider a global marketplace:

- Scope and objectives
  - Proposed product and service offerings
  - Desired and potential goals (e.g., items and/or units sold, revenue, market share, etc.)
- Complexities and challenges
  - Global diversity of the target audience (i.e., market interest and acceptance)

Defining Global Business Requirements

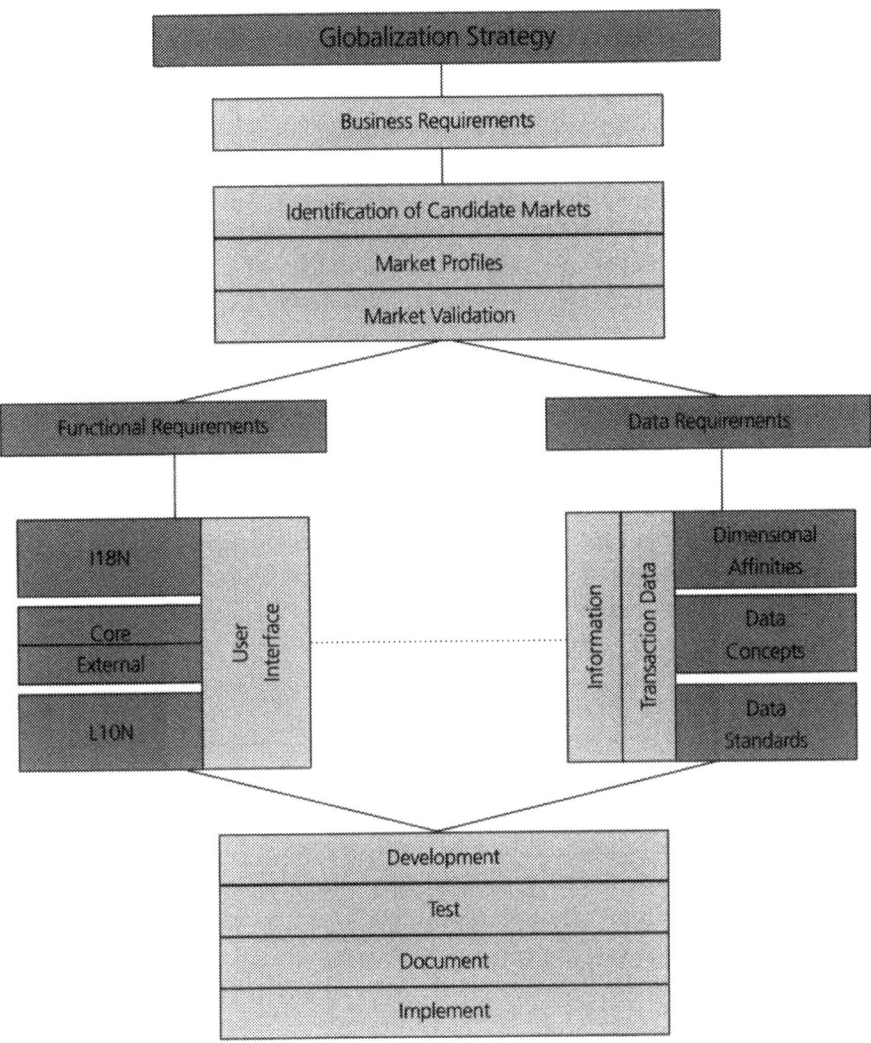

Figure 5.1 Globalization strategy—following the process (© 1996–2002 by James Bean)

- Enterprise support infrastructure (i.e., technology, customer service, fulfillment, logistics, etc.)
- Target market support infrastructure (i.e., workforce, logistics, environment)
- Legal and regulatory acts (e.g., liability, copyright/patent, privacy, etc.)
- Financial issues (e.g., currency exchange, tax and tariff, payment medium, etc.)

Chapter 5   Globalization Process and Techniques

- Threats
  - Competition
  - Social, political, and economic influences

The outcome of this activity is a set of business requirements defined to a degree of granularity that is understood by the business participants and intended to address a global audience. Business requirements should be formalized and documented as a necessary deliverable of the effort. Additionally, the requirements should be classified according to globalization dimensions.[1] Globalization dimensions are a method of classification for requirements, data concepts, and data standards as they apply to a global audience. Given the level of granularity and the context of business requirements, examples of globalization dimensions might include the following:

- Geographic (proposed markets)
- Economic (financial goals and relationship to proposed markets)
- Cultural and demographic (characteristics of the target audience)
- Functional (infrastructure, transportation, logistics, workforce)
- Regulatory (import/export, liability, copyright/patent, privacy, etc.)

From the perspective of business requirements, the ability to group and classify requirements by globalization dimensions allows for affinity and decomposition of business requirements to represent candidate markets, functional requirements, and data requirements. Considering the earlier SLKD Auto Rental example, business leadership would have identified the overall objective of the Web site globalization effort as the ability to provide automobile rental services to international visitors to the United States. More specifically, sample business requirements for SLKD Auto Rental would include the following:

- Geographic
  - Defining context of a "target market"—residents of one or more countries
  - Proposed target markets
    - England
    - Canada
    - Australia
- Economic
  - Increase in gross units rented of 20% annually

---

1   Globalization Strategy, Web Globalization Guide Framework, Relational Logistics Group, James Bean © 1996–2002, *www.globalwebarch.com/*.

- Increase in gross sales revenue of 15% annually (measured in U.S. dollars)
- Support for preferred currencies of proposed markets
- Cultural
  - Target market audience will be computer literate and have access to the Web.
  - Target market audience will be primarily English speaking.
  - Target market audience will be licensed drivers in their country of residence.
- Functional
  - Primary sales channel for the proposed markets will be the Web.
  - Offered products will include rental vehicles (Sports and Family models).
  - Support will be provided for alternate unit of measure systems.
  - Target market audience data will be captured and integrated with existing enterprise applications.
    - Reservation processing
    - Inventory allocation
    - Fulfillment
    - Sales analysis
    - Marketing
- Regulatory
  - Target markets must have unrestricted trade agreements with the United States.
  - Target market audience must have valid automobile operator's license.
  - Target market audience must be insurable under U.S. law and under applicable U.S. state law where vehicle will be delivered.
  - Business enterprise must identify and determine risks associated with liability (both in the United States and the proposed markets).
  - Web site must align with applicable privacy acts (both in the United States and the proposed markets).

As evidenced by the business requirements, additional definition and decomposition will be required before tactical design and engineering activities can be initiated. However, before engaging Web site design, a prerequisite is the identification of potential markets.

Identifying Potential Markets

Potential markets are defined in the context of the business requirements. Some businesses will have previously defined regional markets that are not strictly aligned with geographic boundaries or political borders. In other scenarios, a potential market might be defined in the context of a cultural population. In still others, potential markets are defined specifically by recognized countries. The definition of a "market" is fundamental to the identification activity, but is dependent upon enterprise business processes, business vocabulary, and context.

The premise of this activity (identifying potential markets) is to narrow or expand the number of proposed target markets to include those that align with and support all of the documented business requirements. Initially, this may appear to be a simple task. However, some business requirements may imply indirect support or restrictions for a target market—for example, 1) the cultural business requirement noting that the target market audience must be primarily English speaking, and 2) the regulatory business requirement that the target market audience must have valid automobile operator's licenses. Both requirements provide baseline characteristics that support the target markets.

The SLKD Auto Rental business has elected to define markets by country. The target markets proposed by the business requirements include Canada, England, and Australia. Through simple and subjective validation, these proposed target markets qualify as potential markets (based upon common knowledge and subjective experience of SLKD business leadership, each has a significant English-speaking population and regulatory requirements regarding automobile operation).

Also of importance are subtle or hidden markets, also known as markets of opportunity. The concept is that there may be additional markets not identified during initial development of business requirements that can be addressed by the Web site globalization with a minimum of additional development effort. Taking as an example the market of Australia, it can be noted that nearby New Zealand also has a significant English-speaking population, as well as regulatory acts in support of automobile operation. In addition, New Zealand is in proximity to Australia, and the population represents a reasonable source for visitors to the United States. For these reasons, New Zealand will be added to SLKD Auto Rental's list of potential markets. The revised list now includes the following:

- Canada
- England
- Australia
- New Zealand

Market identification does not end with a list of potential markets. At this point in the process, potential markets may have been selected based upon common knowledge and subjective assessment. Continuing with this activity, the next step is the validation of each market in support of the business requirements. Market profiles must be developed in preparation for market validation.

Developing Market Profiles

Market profiles characterize each potential market. A market profile serves several purposes. The first is to describe a market by the criteria that will help to validate the market as a candidate. Prior to this point of the process, the identification of target markets has been primarily a summary-level activity that may have included subjective judgment. Each market profile should include basic geographic and economic information. In order to map potential markets to business requirements, each market must also include characteristics that describe functional infrastructure, political and regulatory issues, and primary cultures.

A second purpose for market profiles is to perform affinity analysis with business requirements that will be used to describe supported locales. As previously noted, the identification of a Web visitor's locale is critical to providing language- and culture-specific content. The SLKD Auto Rental example defines locale as the combination of country of residence, preferred language, preferred currency, and preferred unit of measure. When a market is defined as a country, the country of residence is implied. The market profile can also identify the nationally recognized (official) language, as well as additional common languages. The market profile will also describe nationally recognized currencies. Unit of measure systems tend to be selected by the Web visitor, although many countries have official unit of measure systems. If such information is not readily available, the unit of measure system would remain a selectable preference.

A third purpose for market profiles is to identify important global data concepts and supporting data standards. A core set of data concepts and data standards can be identified through affinity and mapping of characteristics for each country (e.g., country-specific postal address formats, international telephone number format, etc.). Variations can be derived from locale components (e.g., multicurrency support).

Development of market profiles is largely a result of research, reference, analysis, synthesis, and documentation activities. The market analyst or globalization architect can acquire a vast amount of characteristic information from the combination of publicly available Web sites and commercial publications. Recommended reference sources include the following:

Recommended Web Site References

- The World Factbook Web site (CIA), *www.cia.gov/cia/publications/factbook/index.html*
- International Trade Administration Web site, *www.ita.doc.gov/*

- U.S. Census Bureau Web site, *www.census.gov*
- United Nations Web site, *www.un.org*
- World Trade Organization Web site, *www.wto.int*

Recommended Commercial Publications

- *Financial Times World Desk Reference* (D&K; ISBN: 0-7894-4894-7)
- *Essential World Atlas* (D&K; ISBN: 0-7894-7989-3)
- *Book of the World Atlas and Factfile* (D&K; ISBN: 0-7894-3623-X)
- *The World Almanac* (World Almanac Books; ISBN: 0-88687-872-1)
- *Pocket World in Figures* (The Economist; ISBN: 0-471-24838-X)

There are many other reference sources that may be used to supplement the development of market profiles. Some are available from various economic and trade organizations, while others are available directly from representative governmental and institutional sources for each market. The specific content and characteristics of a market profile can vary depending upon the definition of a market as determined by the type of business being conducted, requirements, and Web globalization goals of the business enterprise.

In addition to statistical and demographic research, the specific characteristics of a market profile should be grouped or classified according to globalization dimensions. This technique will help to perform affinity analysis and to map markets to business requirements. The market profiles developed for SLKD Auto Rental include the following characteristics:

- Geographic
  - Country name(s)
  - Capital city
  - Recognized regional subdivisions
  - Geographic area
  - Geographic terrain
  - Climate and weather conditions
  - Largest cities
  - Bordering countries
- Economic
  - Currency
  - Inflation rate
  - Gross domestic product (GDP)
  - Travel and tourism

- Cultural and demographic
  - Primary languages
  - Cultures and ethnicities
  - Population
  - Education and literacy
  - Automobiles per capita
  - Computers per capita
  - Number of Internet users
- Functional
  - Surface roadways
  - Internet service providers
- Regulatory
  - Personal privacy
  - Vehicle licensing

Of the market characteristics described by the sample list, those classified under the "regulatory" globalization dimension can present the greatest challenge and complexity. Regulatory information may not be easily accessible, and the ability to identify and interpret applicable laws and acts can be difficult. Being unable to describe these characteristics without a significant degree of accuracy can pose a risk or threat to the business. Professional legal expertise is therefore recommended.

Market Validation

Although business leadership has already targeted specific markets, it is important that these markets be validated. Market profiles are critical to the validation of potential markets. In this context, market validation is a broad comparison of business requirements to supporting market characteristics. If it is expected that the potential markets can present sufficient opportunity to achieve the business requirements, they would be considered valid. At that point, the market profiles play an important role in identifying locale-specific presentation and content characteristics, necessary global data concepts, and supporting data standards. As a caveat, it is important to note that potential exposure to risks as implied or identified by a market profile can invalidate a previously targeted potential market.

Comparison of business requirements to market profile characteristics can take several forms. In some cases a comparison can be directly identified and assessed as the result of a documented metric. In other cases, comparisons may require combinations of characteristics and metrics, with a degree of subjective analysis and assessment.

The SLKD Auto Rental example was developed under the assumption that potential markets include Canada, the United Kingdom, and Australia. New Zealand was added as a potential market due to its synergies with the characteristics of the other markets (e.g., language, culture, and location). However, the identification of these markets was primarily subjective. In order to validate whether these markets can help to achieve the business goals and requirements of the Web globalization effort, the characteristics of each market should be mapped and compared to those requirements. The grouping of business requirements and of market profile information can help to simplify the mapping process.

Geographic business requirements presented a simple definition for the market: "The defining context of a target market will be residents of one or more countries." Supporting this definition, SLKD business leadership identified England, Canada, and Australia as proposed markets. The corresponding market profiles are representative of each market as a country, and market profiles are developed for the proposed markets, as well as New Zealand. The market profiles include other basic geographic information as general background and to further describe each country (see Table 5.1).

Economic business requirements are more focused on sales and revenue goals. Specific SLKD Auto Rental requirements targeted annual increases of 20% in gross units sold (rented) and 15% in gross revenue. Both requirements imply the need to compare previous and current sales and revenue to potential revenue of the markets. Obviously, a market profile will not identify specific mapping to these types of requirements. However, in the case of auto rentals, subjective assertions can be made by comparing the population, purchasing power, and travel frequency to the United States (see Table 5.2).

Cultural and demographic business requirements include general characteristics of the target Web audience, as well as constraints or restrictions that may not be directly described by the market profiles. As examples, SLKD business requirements noted that the target market audience will be computer literate, will have access to the Web, and will be primarily English speaking. The importance of the technology-related requirements should be obvious given that the Web is the primary communication channel for attracting and capturing an international audience. Validation of this requirement can be implied by the estimated per capita ownership of computers and the number of Internet users. Additional support may be derived by the number of Internet service providers (ISPs), which is a characteristic of the functional dimension.

Also of importance is the business requirement that the target audience speaks English as their primary language. The market profiles note that English is a primary and common language for resident populations. For the sake of simplicity, the SLKD

Table 5.1 Market profiles—geographic dimension

Geographic dimension	Canada	United Kingdom	Australia	New Zealand
Country				
Official name	Canada	United Kingdom of Great Britain	Commonwealth of Australia	The Dominion of New Zealand
Common name(s)	Canada	U.K., Great Britain, England	Australia	New Zealand
Capital city	Ottawa	London	Canberra	Wellington
Regional subdivisions	10 provinces 3 territories	47 counties 7 metro counties 26 districts 9 regions	6 states 2 territories	4 major islands
Geographic area				
Land	9,220,970 sq. km.	241,590 sq. km.	7,617,930 sq. km.	268,670 sq. km.
Water	755,150 sq. km.	3,230 sq. km.	68,920 sq. km.	10 sq. km.
Total	9,976,140 sq. km.	244,820 sq. km.	7,686,850 sq. km.	268,680 sq. km.
Geographic terrain	Plains Mountains Lowlands	Rugged hills Low mountains Rolling plains	Low plateau Deserts Fertile plains	Mountains Coastal plains

(continued)

Table 5.1 (continued)

Geographic dimension	Canada	United Kingdom	Australia	New Zealand
Climate and weather conditions	Temperate to subarctic	Temperate	Arid to semiarid Tropical	Temperate
Three largest cities				
#1	4.7 million (Toronto)	7.6 million (London)	3.6 million (Sydney)	1.1 million (Auckland)
#2	3.4 million (Montreal)	2.2 million (Birmingham)	3.1 million (Melbourne)	0.3 million (Wellington)
#3	2.0 million (Vancouver)	1.4 million (Leeds)	1.5 million (Brisbane)	0.3 million (Christchurch)
Bordering countries				
#1	United States	Republic of Ireland		
#2				
#3				

Table 5.2 Market profiles—economic dimension

Economic dimension	Canada	United Kingdom	Australia	New Zealand
Currency	Canadian Dollar	British Pound	Australian Dollar	New Zealand Dollar
Inflation rate	1.8% (est. 1997)	3.1% (est. 1997)	1% (est. 1997)	2% (est. 1997)
Gross domestic product (GDP)				
% real growth	3.5% (est. 1997)	3.5% (est. 1997)	3.3% (est. 1997)	2.5% (est. 1997)
Per capita	21,700 (USD)	21,200 (USD)	21,400 (USD)	17,700 (USD)
Travel				
Visitors to the United States	14.5 million	4.7 million		
Percentage of all tourist arrivals to the US	33%	6%		
Average tourist spending in the US (USD)	1,975	440		
Total tourist spending in the US (USD)	6,206 million	8,398 million		
Total tourist spending (USD)	10,220 million	24,815 million	4,604 million	
Average number of vacation days/year	26	28		

Auto Rental example is intentionally limited to an English-speaking audience. Obviously, targeting a broader international audience would result in requirements for multilingual support and translated Web page content. Exclusively targeting English speakers will limit the potential audience. However, the sample Web site SLKD Auto Rental has accepted these limitations and constraints.

Cultural and demographic market profile characteristics also provide additional information regarding each population's ethnicity, literacy, and automobile ownership (see Table 5.3). Population data can be used to derive a number of supporting metrics. Ethnicity and literacy are more subtle characteristics to provide additional indirect support for language. Although somewhat abstract, automobile ownership provides indirect metrics for licensed drivers.

Functional business requirements support the general premise of a Web globalization effort, as well as describe functional needs that can be translated into application logic, interface, and data requirements. The first business requirement notes that the primary sales channel for the proposed markets will be the Web. This requirement is supported by the number of Internet service providers, as well as similar technology characteristics from the cultural/demographic dimension. The balance of the requirements are focused on the processes and activities that are fundamental to business operations. In many cases, these business requirements are not directly supported by market profile data, but must be addressed by the formalization of technology requirements. However, the market profiles do provide additional information, such as driving direction, in support of general auto rental processes (see Table 5.4).

One business requirement of interest is support for multiple unit of measure systems. The premise of this requirement is that the traditional U.S. (English or ANSI) system may not be recognized by an international audience. Given an automobile-related business scenario, the ability to describe vehicle size, capacity, and fuel consumption in alternate units of measure can be invaluable to an international audience. Additionally, the requirement suggests that preferred unit of measure should be user selectable rather than mandated by the market. This would allow for Web site visitors that are familiar with the U.S. and English systems as well as the International System.

Regulatory business requirements imply the need for international legal and regulatory expertise. Some international regulatory information can be acquired from readily available sources and should be included as supporting market profile characteristics. Indirect support for the automobile operator's licensing requirement may be implied by the vehicle licensing characteristic. Privacy issues may also be implied by the proper application of privacy acts and practices (see Table 5.5). However, beware that the level of detail, interpretation, and application of such information is subject to risk: professional, legal, and regulatory expertise is recommended.

Table 5.3 Market profiles—cultural/demographic dimension

Cultural/demographic dimension	Canada	United Kingdom	Australia	New Zealand
Languages	English, French	English, Welsh, Gaelic	English, Aboriginal	English, Maori
Highest population cultures and ethnicities				
#1	44% (British Isles origin)	81.5% (English)	92% (Caucasian)	74.5% (European)
#2	25% (French origin)	9.6% (Scottish)	7% (Asian)	9.7% (Maori)
#3	20% (other European origin)	1.9% (Welsh)	1% (Aboriginal and other)	4.6% (other European)
Population	30,675,398 (est. July 1998)	58,970,119 (est. July 1998)	18,613,087 (est. July 1998)	3,625,388 (est. July 1998)
Education and Literacy	15+ years, 97%	15+ years, 99%	15+ years, 100%	15+ years, 99%
Automobiles				
Automobiles per capita	467 per 1,000	366 per 1,000	465 per 1,000	463 per 1,000
Extended by population	14,325,225	21,583,020	8,655,045	1,678,375
Computers				
Computers per capita	25 per 100	20 per 100	27 per 100	23 per 100
Extended by population	7,668,825	11,794,020	5,025,510	833,819
Internet users	13.2 million	19.4 million	7.7 million	1.3 million

Table 5.4 Market profiles—functional dimension

Functional dimension	Canada	United Kingdom	Australia	New Zealand
Surface roadways				
Driving direction	Drive on the right	Drive on the left	Drive on the left	Drive on the left
Paved	358,371 km	372,000 km	353,331 km	53,568 km
Unpaved	662,629 km	0 km	559,669 km	38,632 km
Internet service providers	599,213	733,538	509,360	84,075

Table 5.5 Market profiles—regulatory dimension

Regulatory dimension	Canada	United Kingdom	Australia	New Zealand
Personal privacy (suggested practices)	W3C-P3P	ITA Safe Harbor	W3C-P3P	W3C-P3P
Vehicle licensing	Plate (CDN)	Plate (GB)	Plate (AUS)	Plate (NZ)

The result of the SLKD market validation activity is the validation of Canada, the United Kingdom, Australia, and New Zealand as target markets. When combined with business requirements, market profiles become the foundation for the design approach.

Formalizing the Design Approach

Following market validation, a key activity takes place where the business requirements and market profiles are combined and extended to identify both functional requirements and data requirements. Functional requirements drive the internationalization and localization processes and, more specifically, interface design. Data requirements identify necessary global data concepts and applicable data standards. As these activities progress toward Web site engineering activities, the globalization process will align and integrate the different designs (see Figure 5.2).

Formalizing the Design Approach

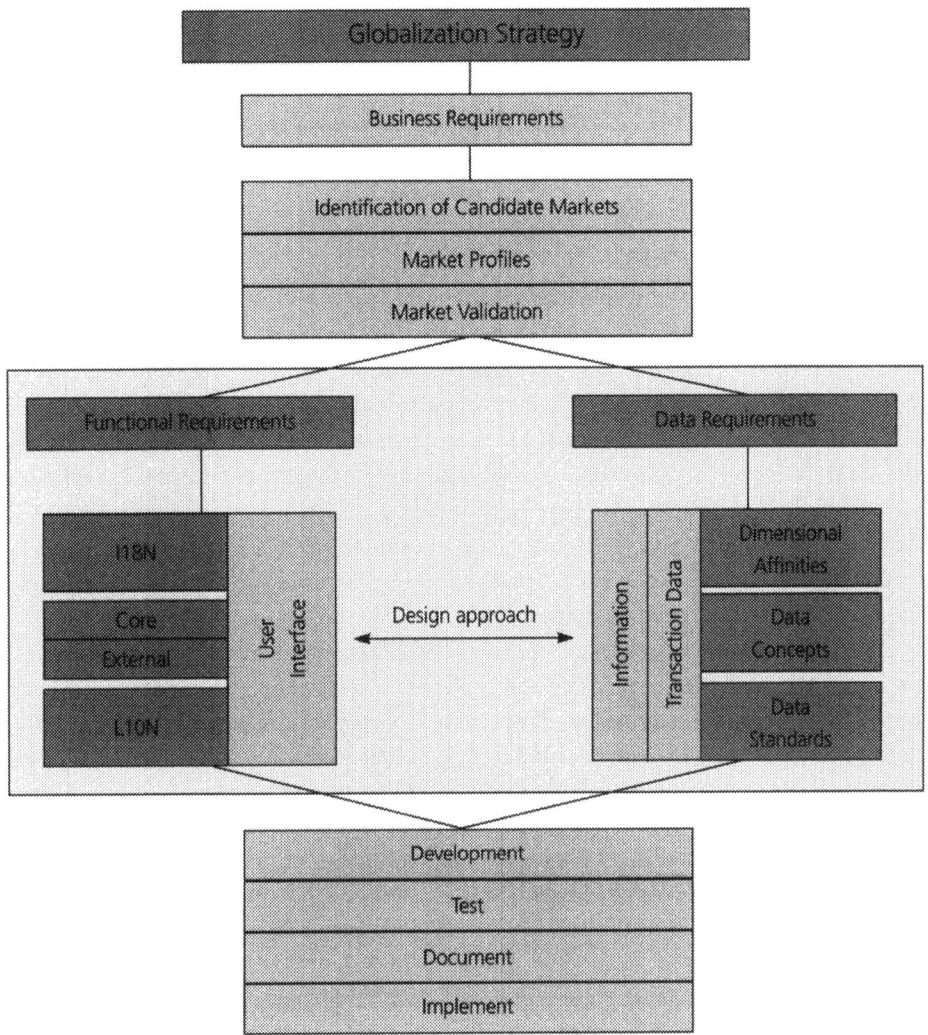

Figure 5.2 Globalization strategy—design approach (© 1996–2002 by James Bean)

Rather than focus exclusively on presentation, language, and cultural personalization, or on data and transaction structures, the globalization process will combine the designs. A Web site that has been engineered using a combined design approach will be more apt to attract and capture customers from the international target markets, facilitate the development of global customer relationships, and integrate data in order to fulfill orders and service customers.

Initially, functional requirements and data requirements will tend to diverge. To split the functional requirements from the data requirements, the project team must consider the fundamental purpose behind the two activities. Functional requirements are primarily focused on attracting and capturing the target audience. Data requirements are focused on the effective capture, processing, and integration of globally diverse data and e-commerce transactions.

Functional Requirements

As previously described, internationalization and localization tend to focus on cultural and language presentation characteristics. Internationalization takes into account the Web site processes, navigation, flow, and content that are common to all supported markets. Project team members responsible for internationalization will also identify the baseline language, culture, and presentation characteristics of each individual market. For those requirements that are unique to each market, the design will include externalized logic and content to allow for ease of extension, if other markets are added in the future. The combination of all functional requirements will result in a design that targets the user interface, navigation, and Web page content that is aligned to language and culture (see Figure 5.3).

The internationalization team members will also need to plan and estimate both internationalization and localization efforts. Internationalization planning activities must consider a number of complexities that go well beyond language translation. The processes of internationalization and localization must consider the technology that is generally available to each of the supported markets. As an example, current versions of some Web browsers are not readily supported or available in some areas. Additionally, in some markets, Internet connection speeds may be far slower than that available in the United States. As a result, the design approach must consider limiting the amount of content and the resolution of graphic images.

Also important are the characteristics of each language such as reading left to right or right to left, special characters, and language variants such as dialect and colloquialisms. Similarly, Web page "real estate" is a consideration. Depending upon the source or base language from which translated content will be derived, designing translated Web page content may result in the need for increased or decreased space. The more traditional technology development activities that follow the development of requirements must also consider quality issues. Language translation requires not only traditional peer review and testing activities, but also review by a sampling of the target audience.

Functional requirements and data requirements are reintegrated prior to technology engineering. The method of integration is primarily through alignment of

Formalizing the Design Approach

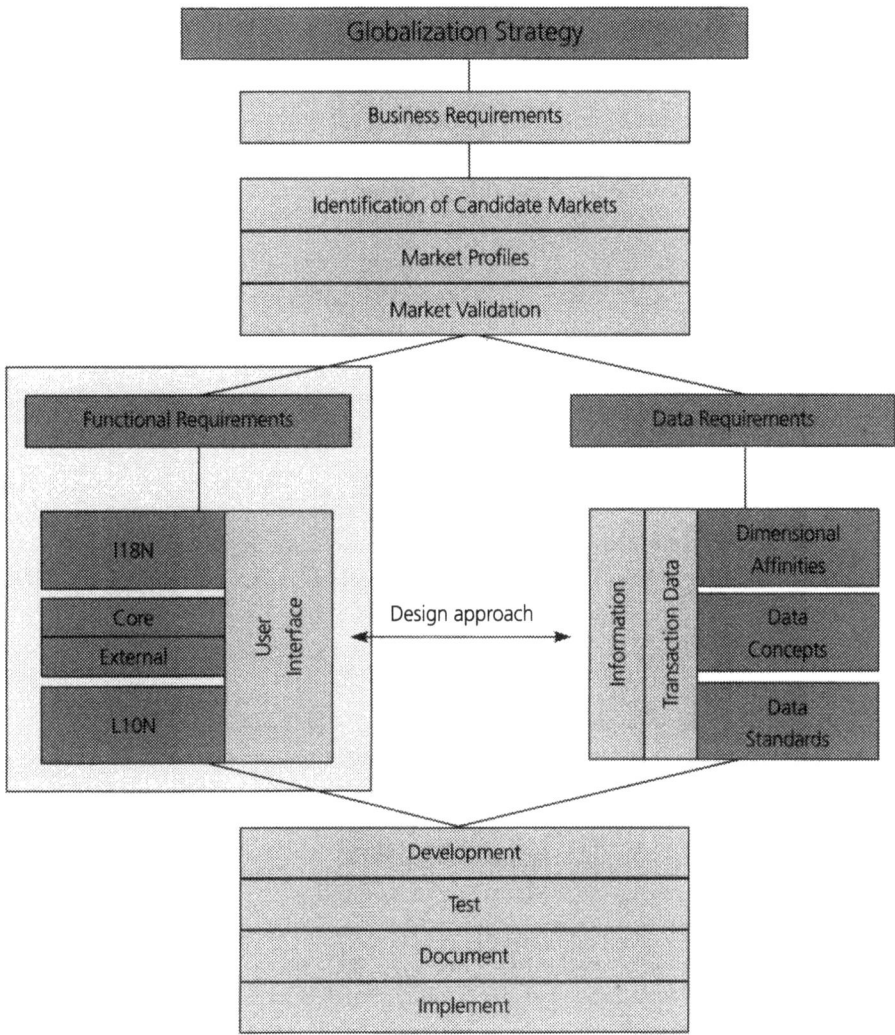

Figure 5.3 Globalization strategy—functional requirements (© 1996–2002 by James Bean)

the user interface and requisite global data concepts. Globalization dimensions help to support alignment by grouping like or similar requirements.

Geographic business requirements for the SLKD Auto Rental Web site describe the need to support auto rental reservations for international visitors and in particular those from the markets of Canada, the United Kingdom, Australia, and New Zealand. Other than obvious geographic characteristics, this implies the need to capture globally diverse address and telephone number information. The number and organization of form fields for capturing this information can vary between each of the supported markets. To help describe geographic functional requirements for the user interface, the geographic requirements must address potentially different address and telephone number formats (see Table 5.6).

In addition to revenue- and sales-related requirements, economic SLKD business requirements describe the need to support multiple currencies. The SLKD Web site presents pricing information, and the base currency used to facilitate business in the United States is the U.S. dollar. However, in order to present amounts in the Web visitor's preferred currency, all rental quotations and pricing must support multiple currencies, currency symbols, decimalization, and decimal punctuation (see Table 5.7).

Cultural and demographic requirements include fundamental characteristics of language, character set, character order, collation sequence, and date format (see Table 5.8). Most cultural and demographic requirements are presentation oriented. Language drives multilingual support, context, colloquialisms, and in some cases spelling. The SLKD Web site has targeted primarily an English-speaking audience, which simplifies the language-related activities. If the Web site were to target a broader international market, multilingual support and translation would be of greater significance.

Date format presents a dilemma for most Web site designers. Internationalization and localization practitioners will often emphasize the importance of using culturally recognized date formats. However, these formats may vary and can introduce the potential for error or misinterpretation. This is especially true when the date format is limited to numeric digits rather than spelled-out days and months. Additionally, some common date formats are not Y2K compliant (e.g., year data is represented as two low-order digits, rather than complete, four-digit century and year combined). The recent implications of Y2K have introduced a movement to standardize the format, presentation, and processing of dates to follow the ISO 8601 date and time standard (see *www.iso.int*). Although local date formats for the target markets may vary, the SLKD Web site designers have elected to adhere to ISO 8601.

The format, structure, and sequence of a person's name also presents a design challenge. From the perspective of functional requirements and the user interface, it is more important to specify whether a name will be captured as a single concatenated string or as individual name particles, and the descriptive text that guides the Web visitor as to intended entry. The SLKD Web site design allows for four name particles, prefixed by a preferred salutation, preferred title, and suffixed by a preferred title, and a business or professional title. Although this design technique allows for multiple name particles, some cultures may have a preferred sequence (e.g.,

Table 5.6 Functional requirements (user interface)—geographic dimension

Geographic dimension	Canada	United Kingdom	Australia	New Zealand
Country				
Official name	Canada	United Kingdom of Great Britain	Commonwealth of Australia	The Dominion of New Zealand
Common name(s)	Canada	U.K., Great Britain, England	Australia	New Zealand
Address				
Address delivery format	Address to (person's name)	Address to (person's name)	Address to (person's name)	Address to (person's name)
	Company name	Company name	Company name	Company name
	Address line 1	Address line 1	Address line 1	Address line 1
	Address line 2	Address line 2	Address line 2	Address line 2 (private bag)
	City, province/territory, postal code	Address line 3	Address line 3	City, postal code
	Country	City	City, state, postal code	Country
		Country	Country	
		Postal Code		

(continued)

Table 5.6 (continued)

Geographic dimension	Canada	United Kingdom	Australia	New Zealand
Regional subdivisions	*Provinces/Territories*		*States/Territories*	*Islands*
	Alberta	England	Australian Capital Territory	North Island
	British Columbia	Ireland	New South Wales	South Island
	Manitoba	Scotland	Northern Territory	Stewart Island
	New Brunswick	Wales	Queensland	Campbell Island
	Newfoundland		South Australia	
	Nova Scotia		Tasmania	
	Northwest Territories		Victoria	
	Ontario		Western Australia	
	Prince Edward Island			
	Québec			
	Saskatchewan			
	Yukon			
Telephone number				
International dialing prefix	+	+	+	+
Separator	Period (.)	Period (.)	Period (.)	Period (.)
Country code	1	44	61	64
City/area code	999	9999	9	9
Local exchange/prefix	999		9999	999
Local number	9999	99999	9999	9999

Table 5.7 Functional requirements (user interface)—economic dimension

Economic dimension	Canada	United Kingdom	Australia	New Zealand
Currency	Canadian Dollar	British Pound	Australian Dollar	New Zealand Dollar
Symbol	$	£	$	$
Decimal units	2	2	2	2
Decimal separator	Period (.)	Period (.)	Period (.)	Period (.)

family, or last, name preceding the given, or first, name). Since the order of name particles can vary widely by culture, a more effective technique allows the user to specify the order of name particles upon entry. Although this technique can resolve the more structural aspects of a person's name, caution is advised when considering usability.

The preferred unit of measure can in some cases be used to extend the definition of a locale. Although most countries of the world have adopted or plan to adopt the SI (International System of Units)[2] as their standard, visitors to the United States will by default be exposed to the English system of units. The SLKD Web site allows the user to select a preferred unit of measure system, which will be used to provide alternate measurements, such as storage capacity and fuel efficiency of a rental vehicle.

Requirements classified by the functional dimension are specific to the functional navigation and interaction of the Web user with the Web site (see Table 5.9). Functional requirements will reference information that is intended to be captured, as well as how such information is allocated to specific Web pages, and whether specific formatting or standards may apply. At this point the Web site designer should have determined how the interaction, or "conversation," between the Web user and the Web site will occur. The sequence of each Web page and navigation between pages are also defined. Also of importance is the "state" of the relationship between the Web visitor and the Web site as the visitor navigates and interacts.

Depending upon the intended functionality of the Web site, requirements classified as "functional" may also be specified to a greater degree of granularity. The sample Web site has a fairly simple architecture and is divided into four primary functions (each represented by a Web page):

---

[2] Bureau International des Poids et Mesures (BIPM), SI International System of Units, *www.bipm.fr.*

Table 5.8 Functional requirements (user interface)—cultural/demographic dimension

Cultural/demographic dimension	Canada	United Kingdom	Australia	New Zealand
Person's name				
Salutation	Dear, Esteemed, Greetings…	Dear, Esteemed, Greetings…	Dear, Esteemed, Greetings…	Dear Esteemed, Greetings…
Prefix, title, honorific	Dr., Mr., Ms., Sir…	Dr., Mr., Ms., Sir…	Dr., Mr., Ms., Sir…	Dr., Mr., Ms., Sir…
Name 1	First	Given	First	First
Name 2	Middle	Second	Second	Second
Name 3	Other	Third	Third	Third
Name 4	Last	Family	Last	Last
Suffix, title, honorific	M.D., Ph.D. II, III…	M.D., Ph.D. II, III…	M.D., Ph.D. II, III…	M.D., Ph.D. II, III…
Business or professional title	President, Director, CEO…	President, Director, CEO…	President, Director, CEO…	President, Director, CEO…
Primary languages	English	English	English	English
Extended code	ENG.CA	ENG.GB	ENG.AU	ENG.NZ
Unicode character set	UTF-8	UTF-8	UTF-8	UTF-8
HTML entity set	ISO-8859-1	ISO-8859-1	ISO-8859-1	ISO-8859-1
Character order	Left to right	Left to right	Left to right	Left to right
Collation sequence	ASCII low order to high order	ASCII low order to high order	ASCII low order to high order	ASCII low order to high order
Data format				
Descriptive	Day, Month, Year	Day, Month, Year	Day, Month, Year	Day, Month, Year
Shorthand (non-Y2K)	DD-Month-YY	DD-Month-YY	Day, DD Month YYYY	Day, DD Month YYYY
ISO 8601	YYYY-MM-DD	YYYY-MM-DD	YYYY-MM-DD	YYYY-MM-DD

Table 5.9 Functional requirements (user interface)—functional dimension

Functional dimension	Canada	United Kingdom	Australia	New Zealand
Unit of Measure systems				
Metric	SI-metric	SI-metric	SI-metric	SI-metric
English	English-ANSI			
Identify locale				
Country of residence	Drop-down list (ISO 3166)	Drop-down list (ISO 3166)	Drop-down list (ISO 3166)	Drop-down list (ISO 3166)
Preferred language	Drop-down list (ISO 639)	Drop-down list (ISO 639)	Drop-down list (ISO 639)	Drop-down list (ISO 639)
Preferred currency	Drop-down list (ISO 4217)	Drop-down list (ISO 4217)	Drop-down list (ISO 4217)	Drop-down list (ISO 4217)
Preferred unit of measure system	Drop-down list (English, SI)	Drop-down list (English, SI)	Drop-down list (English, SI)	Drop-down list (English, SI)
Selection				
Reservation dates	Begin date (ISO 8601) End date (ISO 8601)	Begin date (ISO 8601) End date (ISO 8601)	Begin date (ISO 8601) End date (ISO 8601)	Begin date (ISO 8601) End date (ISO 8601)
Vehicle selection (sports car)	Check box (SC-1)	Check box (SC-1)	Check box (SC-1)	Check box (SC-1)
Vehicle selection (family car)	Check box (FC-1)	Check box (FC-1)	Check box (FC-1)	Check box (FC-1)
Application				
Vehicle selection	Present vehicle selection	Present vehicle selection	Present vehicle selection	Present vehicle selection

(continued)

Table 5.9 (continued)

Functional dimension	Canada	United Kingdom	Australia	New Zealand
Customer data	Name (four-part)	Name (four-part)	Name (four-part)	Name (four-part)
	Telephone numbers (ITU E.123)	Telephone numbers (ITU E.123)	Telephone numbers (ITU E.123)	Telephone numbers (ITU E.123)
	Address (UPU)	Address (UPU)	Address (UPU)	Address (UPU)
	Auto operators license	Auto operator's license	Auto operator's license	Auto operator's license
	Automobile insurance	Automobile insurance	Automobile insurance	Automobile insurance
	Driving record	Driving record	Driving record	Driving record
Confirmation (rental reservation)				
Confirmation of rental reservation	Confirmation number	Confirmation number	Confirmation number	Confirmation number

- Identification of locale
- Selection
- Application
- Confirmation

Identification of locale allows the user to select the necessary preferences that will be used to identify localized Web page content. *Selection* allows the user to view product information (vehicle specifications) and make a desired selection. *Application* presents information for the selected vehicle and captures customer information that would be required to process a rental reservation and to verify insurability. *Confirmation* is a response to the customer indicating acceptance of the vehicle reservation. A more granular example would include additional user interface and interaction components, as well as the identification of business logic (e.g., validation of entered data).

Requirements of the regulatory dimension may need to address a vast number of issues and characteristics. Due to the diversity of regulatory acts, the potential for misinterpretation, and risk of noncompliance, international legal and regulatory expertise is strongly advised. The SLKD regulatory requirements are intentionally limited to privacy and the collection of related identification, licensing, and insurance data (see Table 5.10). In the case of privacy, general suggestions have been made to both the Platform for Privacy Preferences (P3P) recommendations of the W3C (see *www.w3c.org*) and to Safe Harbor Privacy Principles as defined by the U.S. International Trade Administration (ITA; see *www.ita.doc.gov*). While these recommendations may not fully define all necessary privacy characteristics, they do provide general guidance.

As described, functional requirements are generally focused on presentation, user interface, and application logic. The examples noted by the figures are representative of the SLKD sample Web site and are intentionally simplified. A greater level of granularity and definition would be required to support a more complex Web site globalization effort.

Functional requirements represent half of the globalization equation. To complete the globalization design activities in preparation for development and engineering, data requirements are also required. For many Web site globalization efforts, the design of the user interface (primarily for the entry and capture of data) and the design of e-commerce transactions are the two facets where the globalization activities are again combined.

Global Data Requirements

As previously described, internationalization and localization tend to focus on cultural and language presentation characteristics. Alternatively, globalization of data

Table 5.10 Functional requirements (user interface)—regulatory dimension

Regulatory dimension	Canada	United Kingdom	Australia	New Zealand
Personal privacy				
Suggested privacy practices	W3C-P3P	ITA Safe Harbor	W3C-P3P	W3C-P3P
Security	SSL, encryption on data entry	SSL, encryption on data entry	SSL, encryption on data entry	SSL, encryption on data entry
Vehicle licensing	Plate (CDN)	Plate (GB)	Plate (AUS)	Plate (NZ)
Automobile operator's license				
Automobile operator's license or ID	X(20)	X(20)	X(20)	X(20)
Country of issue	Drop-down list (ISO 3166)	Drop-down list (ISO 3166)	Drop-down list (ISO 3166)	Drop-down list (ISO 3166)
Effective date	YYYY-MM-DD	YYYY-MM-DD	YYYY-MM-DD	YYYY-MM-DD
Expiration date	YYYY-MM-DD	YYYY-MM-DD	YYYY-MM-DD	YYYY-MM-DD
Automobile insurance				
Automobile insurance company (issuer)	X(30)	X(30)	X(30)	X(30)
Automobile insurance policy ID	X(20)	X(20)	X(20)	X(20)
Number of years driving	99	99	99	99
Number of accidents	99	99	99	99
Driving while under the influence	Yes (1) No (0)	Yes (1) No (0)	Yes (1) No (0)	Yes (1) No (0)

Formalizing the Design Approach 121

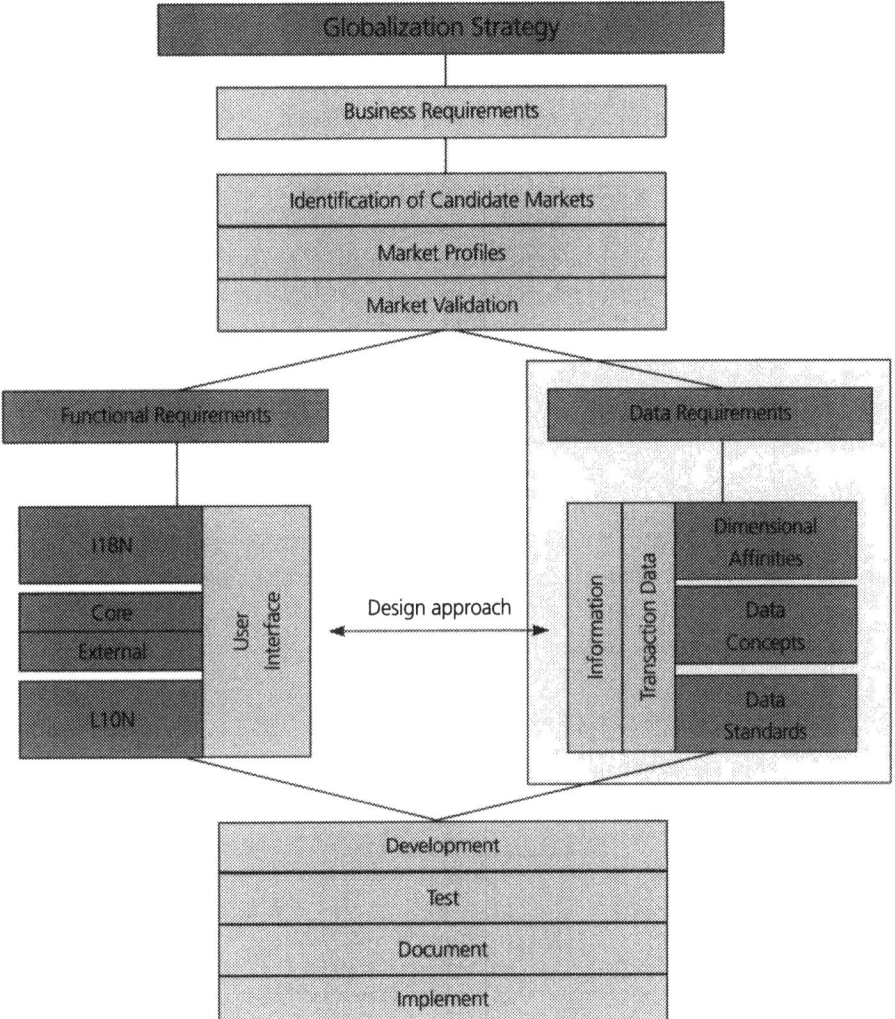

Figure 5.4 Globalization strategy—data requirements

will focus on the formalization, capture, processing, and integration of globally diverse data. Initially, these activities split, and practitioners skilled in each discipline will take responsibility for developing what appear to be separate designs (see Figure 5.4).

The importance of identifying and formalizing data concepts and then aligning them with supporting data standards is obvious. Without these activities, validation,

Chapter 5 Globalization Process and Techniques

processing, and integration of globally diverse data captured from the Web site is highly complex and potentially impossible. Data that are captured in the abstract, or in many different formats, are also prone to quality errors. The ability to process e-commerce transactions, perform order fulfillment, and advance the state of the customer relationship will suffer. A proper globalization approach will consider data requirements to be of importance equal to that of functional requirements.

Globalization dimensions and affinity analysis activities are used to drive the data requirements efforts. Unlike the functional requirements, where multiple user interfaces may be designed and developed to facilitate differing locales, global data solutions focus on standardized, common, and flexible data formats. The development of data requirements will also prepare for the complexities of integration of global Web site data with other traditional enterprise data, as well as providing methods of identification to recognize the importance of autonomy.

Business requirements combined with functional and user interface requirements are primary sources of information for the development of data requirements. As individual requirements for locale-specific data concepts are identified, they are classified by globalization dimensions. Affinities between like concepts should also be identified and architectural solutions developed. Using the example of geographic data requirements, address formats, structures, and allowable content can vary widely from locale to locale. However, there are obvious affinities. Each address of the target markets requires the following:

- Address to (person's name)
- Address lines
- City
- Regional subdivisions (state, province, territory, etc.)
- Country
- Postal code

The sequence of these address components varies both by locale and intended purpose. If the address information is used for postal or product delivery, sequence and line position of each address component is important for each locale. However, if the address data are intended for marketing analysis or other decision support–type processing, delivery-specific formats may not be of significance.

The first activity is to identify the address standards for each supported locale. In this case, the Universal Postal Union (UPU) is an excellent source of postal address standards and related information (see *www.upu.int*). The decomposition of address data into individual address components follows. Once decomposed, the Web designer or architect can then identify affinities between components. The end result is a set of address components that can be populated according to any of the supported locales. The level of granularity allows for alignment with the corresponding functional requirements (e.g., user interface and Web forms for data capture), as well as later integration with enterprise data.

In addition to address information, geographic data requirements also include telephone numbers and time zones (see Table 5.11). Given the functionality of the SLKD Web site, time zones will not be directly captured from the Web page, but will be important as part of the time-stamp process for underlying transactions. Also, time zones represented as an offset to UTC are described by the ISO 8601 standard for dates and times.

From a locale perspective, international telephone numbers also present globalization complexities. The country code for each of the four locales is a different value. Also, the format of a telephone number for each locale is different (differing components as well as the number of allowable digits). Similar to address, the first activity is to identify applicable telephone number formats for each locale. The next activity is to identify applicable data standards. In this case, the best source of telephone number data standards information is the International Telecommunications Union (ITU), and more specifically the E.123 and E.164 standards.[3] Following the identification of applicable standards, the architect must decompose the different telephone number formats. By aligning the different components of each locale-specific telephone number, a common format can then be formalized that would consider any of the four.

Also of value is the classification of telephone number. The SLKD Web site requires that both residential and business telephone numbers be captured. The corresponding user interface defines HTML form entry fields for both types of telephone numbers. However, the underlying transaction data could use a single common format and allow for multiple types to be applied.

The SLKD economic data requirements are primarily focused on providing multiple-currency support, the intent being to provide quotations and pricing in both a base currency unit (U.S. dollar) and the preferred currency of the Web visitor. As defined earlier, preferred currency is one of the locale characteristics that is user selectable. Providing multiple-currency support also presents several challenges. The most important is making sure that the base currency is used by all enterprise applications for processing monetary amounts. Conversion to alternate

---

[3] International Telecommunications Union (ITU); E.123—Notation for national and international telephone numbers, email addresses, and Web addresses; E.164—The international public telecommunication numbering plan; *www.itu.org*.

Table 5.11 Data requirements—geographic dimension

Geographic dimension	Canada	United Kingdom	Australia	New Zealand
Country				
Official name	Canada	United Kingdom of Great Britain	Commonwealth of Australia	The Dominion of New Zealand
Common name(s)	Canada	U.K., Great Britain, England	Australia	New Zealand
ISO Code 3166 (A-3)	CAN	GBR	AUS	NZL
ISO Code 3166 (N-3)	124	826	036	554
Address				
Address to	Address to (person's name)	Address to (person's name)	Address to (person's name)	Address to (person's name)
Company name	Company name	Company name	Company name	Company name
Address line 1	Address line 1	Address line 1	Address line 1	Address line 1
Address line 2	Address line 2	Address line 2	Address line 2	Address line 2 (Private bag)
Address line 3		Address line 3	Address line 3	
City	City	City	City	City
Region (type)	Province/territory	County	State	
Postal code	Postal code (A9A-9A9)	Postal code (AA9A 9AA)	Postal code (9999)	Postal code (9999)

Table 5.11 (continued)

Geographic dimension	Canada	United Kingdom	Australia	New Zealand
Country	Country	Country	Country	Country
Telephone number				
International dialing prefix	+	+	+	+
Separator	Period (.)	Period (.)	Period (.)	Period (.)
Country code	1	44	61	64
City/area code	999		9	9
Local exchange/prefix	999	9999	9999	999
Local number	9999	999999	9999	9999
Time zones (with offset to UTC)	−3.5 UTC, −8 UTC	0, UTC	+8 UTC, +10 UTC	+11 UTC, +12 UTC

currency units should be done from rationalized base currency amounts. If not, there is the potential for error.

Also of importance is the exchange rate at which alternate currency amounts are derived from base currency amounts. This issue also introduces potential challenges as to an official or recognized source for exchange rates and in the area of legal disclosure. Although quotations and pricing may be provided using the preferred currency of the user, the annotation of these amounts should include some form of disclosure to advise the user that all business is transacted in U.S. dollars as the base currency unit and that exchange rates can fluctuate. The user should not misinterpret monetary amounts as being fixed in their preferred currency unless that it is the intention of the enterprise.

Last is the format and classification of currency amounts as defined for e-commerce transactions. Each monetary amount should include the numeric value without punctuation. In addition, monetary amounts should be classified by standard encoding. The International Organization for Standardization (ISO) has developed a code set to represent monetary currencies, specifically, ISO 4217 Currency and Funds Code List (see *www.iso.int*). As a point of integration with the user interface design, consideration should also be given to the number of supported fractional currency digits, the currency symbol, and any punctuation used to delimit whole amounts from fractional amounts (see Table 5.12). Currency symbols can be expressed using Unicode sets,[4] which is generally supported by Web technologies such as XML and HTML.

Cultural and demographic data requirements primarily support data concepts such as a person's name, identification of applied language, and date formats (see Table 5.13). Names are highly complex, globally diverse, and not defined by any single recognized data standard. In addition to identifying and supporting a set of name particles, support for other name information is important. As examples, salutation, prefixed titles, suffixed titles, and business or professional titles may be necessary. When possible, this additional name information should be defined as a structured list and used as an internal enterprise standard.

Developing a formalized and structured list that allows the user to determine the value of a name element and a preferred sequence is the best approach. This technique requires an underlying set of name particles with each having a selected type and order. This approach has been adopted by the SLKD Web site but also introduces potential challenges in the area of usability and simplicity. While this technique provides the most flexible solution, caution is advised in that pushing entry

---

[4] Unicode Consortium, Currency Symbols Range: 20A0–20CF; *www.unicode.org*.

Table 5.12 Data requirements—economic dimension

Economic dimension	Canada	United Kingdom	Australia	New Zealand
Currency	Canadian Dollar	British Pound	Australian Dollar	New Zealand Dollar
ISO Code 4217 (A-3)	CAD	GBP	AUD	NZD
ISO Code 4217 (N-3)	124	826	036	554
Symbol	$	£	$	$
Unicode value	&#36;	&#163;	&#36;	&#36;
Decimal units	2	2	2	2
Decimal separator	Period (.)	Period (.)	Period (.)	Period (.)

Table 5.13 Data requirements—cultural/demographic dimension

Cultural/demographic dimension	Canada	United Kingdom	Australia	New Zealand
Person's name				
Salutation	Dear, Esteemed, Greetings...	Dear, Esteemed, Greetings...	Dear, Esteemed, Greetings...	Dear, Esteemed, Greetings...
Prefix, title, honorific	Dr., Mr., Ms., Sir...	Dr., Mr., Ms., Sir...	Dr., Mr., Ms., Sir...	Dr., Mr., Ms., Sir...
Name 1	First	Given	First	First
Name 2	Middle	Second	Second	Second
Name 3	Other	Third	Third	Third
Name 4	Last	Family	Last	Last
Suffix, title, honorific	M.D, Ph.D, II, III...	M.D, Ph.D, II, III...	M.D, Ph.D, II, III...	M.D, Ph.D, II, III...
Business or professional title	President, Director, CEO...	President, Director, CEO...	President, Director, CEO...	President, Director, CEO...
Languages	English, French	English, Welsh, Gaelic	English, Aboriginal	English, Maori
ISO Code 639 (A-2)	EN	EN	EN	EN
ISO Code 639 (A-3)	ENG	ENG	ENG	ENG
Extended code	ENG.CA	ENG.GB	ENG.AU	ENG.NZ
Unicode character set	UTF-8	UTF-8	UTF-8	UTF-8
HTML entity set	ISO-8859-1	ISO-8859-1	ISO-8859-1	ISO-8859-1
Date format				
Descriptive	Day, Month, Year	Day, Month, Year	Day, Month, Year	Day, Month, Year
Shorthand (non-Y2K)	DD-Month-YY	DD-Month-YY	Day, DD Month YYYY	Day, DD Month YYYY
ISO 8601	YYYY-MM-DD	YYYY-MM-DD	YYYY-MM-DD	YYYY-MM-DD

complexity out to the Web user may result in frustration and termination of the Web browser session.

Language is primarily a function of internationalization and localization and is another important characteristic of a locale. However, rather than relying on a textual description of language, it is important that a method of standardized encoding is used to identify the preferred language of the Web user. The ISO has engineered a code set that is used by a number of other similar standards and recommendations. The ISO 639 code for the representation of names of languages (see *www.iso.int*) is widely recognized and is also supported by the XML language attribute.

Date formats are also a focus of internationalization and localization. Traditionally, when presented in or captured by a Web page, date information is generally formatted according to the accepted format of the identified locale. However, this also introduces the potential for misinterpretation and data entry error. This is especially true when the date format is entirely numeric digits, where the day, month, and year may be sequenced according to the locale. Additionally, some locales do not yet fully recognize a four-digit year. The ISO has developed a standard format for representing date and time, as well as offsets to UTC and some support for duration (see *www.iso.int*). Although a localized date format may be better received by the international Web user, the SLKD requirement has adopted the ISO 8601 date format of YYYY-MM-DD.

Functional data requirements are primarily focused on data concepts and data standards that support the basic operation of the Web site and data capture from HTML Web forms. The SLKD Auto Rental site was designed to provide four basic operations, each supported by a corresponding Web page (see Table 5.14). The first of the SLKD Web pages is a "welcome," or home, page. It is intended as the first point of contact with a new Web site visitor and allows the selection of preferences that will identify the visitor's locale. Selectable preferences are predefined to the HTML form as drop-down lists. The four preferences defined to this page include the following:

- Country of residence
- Preferred language
- Preferred currency
- Preferred unit of measure

Using predefined drop-down selections helps to simplify the user interface. In addition, each of the locale characteristics must be supported by a defined data standard. The ISO has defined an encoding standard for the identification of countries, ISO 3166. Entries from this standard are used to describe the code values that

Table 5.14 Data requirements—functional dimension

Functional	Canada	United Kingdom	Australia	New Zealand
Identify locale				
Country of residence	ISO 3166: Canada (CAN:124)	United Kingdom (GBR:826)	Australia (AUS:036)	New Zealand (NZL:554)
Preferred language	ISO 639: English (ENG.CA)	English (ENG.UK)	English (ENG.AU)	English ENG.NZ)
Currency	ISO 4217: Canadian Dollar (CAD:124)	U.K. Pound (GBP:826)	Australian Dollar (AUD:036)	New Zealand Dollar (NZD:554)
Preferred unit of measure	English, SI	SI	SI	SI
Selection				
Begin date	ISO 8601: YYYY-MM-DD	ISO 8601: YYYY-MM-DD	ISO 8601: YYYY-MM-DD	ISO 8601: YYYY-MM-DD
End date	ISO 8601: YYYY-MM-DD	ISO 8601: YYYY-MM-DD	ISO 8601: YYYY-MM-DD	ISO 8601: YYYY-MM-DD
Sports car	Internal product ID (SC-1)	Internal product ID (SC-1)	Internal product ID (SC-1)	Internal product ID (SC-1)
Family car	Internal product ID (FC-1)	Internal product ID (FC-1)	Internal product ID (FC-1)	Internal product ID (FC-1)
Application				
Name	Extended name data—four particles	Extended name data—four particles	Extended name data—four particles	Extended name data—four particles
Telephone number	ITU E.123, E.163, E.164	ITU E.123, E.163, E.164	ITU E.123, E.163, E.164	ITU E.123, E.163, E.164
Address	UPU address format (common)	UPU address format (common)	UPU address format (common)	UPU address format (common)

Table 5.14 (continued)

Functional	Canada	United Kingdom	Australia	New Zealand
Automobile operator's license or ID	X(20)	X(20)	X(20)	X(20)
Country of issue	ISO 3166: A-3, N-3	ISO 3166: A-3, N-3	ISO 3166: A-3, N-3	ISO 3166: A-3, N-3
Effective date	ISO 8601: YYYY-MM-DD	ISO 8601: YYYY-MM-DD	ISO 8601: YYYY-MM-DD	ISO 8601: YYYY-MM-DD
Expiration date	ISO 8601: YYYY-MM-DD	ISO 8601: YYYY-MM-DD	ISO 8601: YYYY-MM-DD	ISO 8601: YYYY-MM-DD
Automobile insurance company (issuer)	X(30)	X(30)	X(30)	X(30)
Automobile insurance policy ID	X(20)	X(20)	X(20)	X(20)
Numbers of years driving	99	99	99	99
Number of accidents	99	99	99	99
Driving while under the influence	Yes (1) No (0)	Yes (1) No (0)	Yes (1) No (0)	Yes (1) No (0)
Confirmation (rental reservation)				
Confirmation number	System auto generate	System auto generate	System auto generate	System auto generate

underlie each of the predefined country-of-residence selections. Following the country is the preferred language of the Web site visitor. The ISO has defined an encoding standard to identify primary languages, ISO 639. Similarly, the ISO has also defined an encoding standard for the identification of currencies ISO 4217. When the content of the Web form is submitted to the server for validation and processing, standard codes from each of the noted encoding standards would be defined as underlying attribute values for each of the predefined drop-down selections.

In addition to the three locale selections, the Web visitor is also prompted to select a preferred unit of measure system. This additional characteristic can be used to narrow similar locales, as well as to guide the presentation of supplemental content. The SLKD Auto Rental enterprise is a traditional North American (U.S.) organization that uses the English system of units (inches, feet, miles, gallons, etc.) to describe quantity or similar measurement. Web site visitors from other countries and locales may prefer to view measurements using the International System of units (a.k.a., SI or metric). When a Web site visitor selects a preferred unit of measure other than the English system, tangible measurements will be converted and presented using the SI system in addition to the English system (see *www.bipm.fr*).

Once the Web visitor has selected from the available locale characteristics and submitted the form for processing, Web navigation will continue to the product-selection page. SLKD Auto Rental product selection allows for the entry of rental reservation dates and the selection of available rental vehicles. Although some localization experts may argue that dates should be localized, the SLKD Auto Rental example has proposed that the ISO 8601 standard for presentation of date and time will be used. This standard proposes an ordinal left-to-right format for date information (i.e., YYYY-MM-DD). Although locale variations may exist, adhering to the ISO 8601 standard will help to promote global standardization, avoid complex validation, and reduce potential entry anomalies.

The SLKD Auto Rental business provides a very limited number of products for rental. This limitation helps to simplify the entry logic for the selection Web page, and an internal product identification scheme is used to identify each possible vehicle selection. Other businesses may allow for extensive product and service catalogs. In this case, the combination of Uniform Code Council (UCC) and EAN International numbering systems provide two possible standards for the standard identification of products. The Universal Product Code (UPC) from the UCC is primarily a North American product identification system (see *www.uc-council.org*). The Global Trade Item Number (GTIN) system from EAN is used internationally (see *www.ean-int.org*).

Following the entry of rental dates and selection of an automobile, the form content is submitted to the server for validation and processing. The SLKD sample

Formalizing the Design Approach 133

enterprise systems support scheduled inventory management, and the server application can determine if the selected vehicle is available for the desired rental dates. Using data standards for date and for product identification simplify the backend enterprise systems application logic. Assuming the selected vehicle is available, the Web user is then presented with an application Web page. This page is intended to capture general customer data as well as information required to determine if the customer can be insured in the United States.

Name, telephone number, and address are defined according to one or more standards. Name data are highly diverse and no single standard exists. In this case, the cultural characteristics of each locale play an important role, and the allowable components of a person's name can be described by a common data structure. This structure is defined to capture up to four name particles in addition to a preferred salutation or greeting, prefixed title, suffixed title, and a business or professional title. The localization process would still require descriptive text labeling for each of the name fields as entered on the Web forms that is unique to each of the supported locales. This would allow for culturally aligned entry forms specific to each supported locale, yet provide a reasonably common and standardized name structure. For other locales or cultures, additional name elements of the same design could be added as necessary.

Telephone numbers are also variable, but would be based upon the International Telecommunications Union (ITU) standards for the representation and structuring of international telephone numbers. These standards describe the allowable length of a telephone number as dialable digits and suggest a format for presentation. Rather than allow for the entry of a single text field to contain a telephone number string, the SLKD Web architect has determined that segmentation is of value, so a format to allow for the entry of three telephone number components has been defined. In addition, the country code of the telephone number is of importance and has been predefined as a drop-down list to simplify entry for the Web visitor. The Web architect has also determined that two telephone numbers should be captured. From a data architecture perspective, a single common format for telephone number should be defined. Each of the captured telephone numbers would then be classified by a type (e.g., residence and business). The user interface is designed to allow for entry of both types of telephone numbers, with the underlying transaction content classified by type based upon which form entry fields were populated.

Similar to a person's name, address formats may vary widely. The Universal Postal Union (UPU) provides excellent resources and numerous examples of international postal address formats (see *www.upu.int*). The Web architect could have engineered separate address structures and form fields for each of the supported locales, but this would have required the development of separate HTML Web forms or dynamically generated entry panels. There are many common address particles between the different formats, and in this case a common address structure can be defined to support each of the locale-specific address formats. The address format would be derived from each of the locale-specific address formats and would include the following:

- Address to (person's name)
- Company name
- Street address lines (up to three)
- City
- Postal code
- Country
- Regional subdivisions (as necessary)

To simplify entry, the corresponding user interface would include predefined drop-down lists of countries and of regional subdivision types. Underlying the list of countries are the ISO 3166 country codes for the supported locales. Similarly, regional subdivision types are also defined by drop-down lists and are aligned to UPU regional subdivision sample values.

In addition to basic customer information of name, telephone number, and address, the application form also captures automobile license, driver history, and insurance data. There are a number of complexities exhibited by this information. Driver license number formats vary by locale. Additionally, information required to determine insurability may be considered personal or confidential. In this case, the license number is allocated as a free-form text field with effective and expiration dates entered following the ISO 8601 date format. As with several other data concepts, country of issue is supported by the ISO 3166 country code standard. Other insurance and driver history information is acquired as text data and converted by backend enterprise systems for applicable processing. The capture of personal and confidential information may be subject to associated regulatory acts.

The SLKD Auto Rental confirmation Web page is self-explanatory and assumes that all previous selections and entered data are valid, and the selected vehicle is available from inventory during the desired dates. At that point the customer is presented with a confirmation number that can be used to track the rental reservation at a later date.

In order to avoid potential noncompliance or legal action, all regulatory data requirements should be subject to review and advice of licensed international attorneys (see Table 5.15). The SLKD Auto Rental example assumes that appropriate legal expertise has been acquired and that the capture of automobile operator's

Table 5.15 Data requirements—regulatory dimension

Regulatory dimension	Canada	United Kingdom	Australia	New Zealand
Personal privacy (suggested practices)	W3C-P3P	ITA Safe Harbor	W3C-P3P	W3C-P3P
Automobile operator's license				
Automobile operator's license or ID	X(20)	X(20)	X(20)	X(20)
Country of issue	ISO 3166: A-3, N-3	ISO 3166: A-3, N-3	ISO 3166: A-3, N-3	ISO 3166: A-3, N-3
Effective date	ISO 8601: YYYY-MM-DD	ISO 8601: YYYY-MM-DD	ISO 8601: YYYY-MM-DD	ISO 8601: YYYY-MM-DD
Expiration date	ISO 8601: YYYY-MM-DD	ISO 8601: YYYY-MM-DD	ISO 8601: YYYY-MM-DD	ISO 8601: YYYY-MM-DD
Automobile insurance				
Automobile insurance company (issuer)	X(30)	X(30)	X(30)	X(30)
Automobile insurance policy ID	X(20)	X(20)	X(20)	X(20)
Number of years driving	99	99	99	99
Number of accidents	99	99	99	99
Driving while under the influence	Yes (1) No (0)	Yes (1) No (0)	Yes (1) No (0)	Yes (1) No (0)

license, insurance data, and driving history are all acceptable practices for the business. In addition, the capture, transmission, exchange, and exposure of such information should be subject to appropriate legal and regulatory acts, and ethical practices. The World Wide Web Consortium (W3C) has developed a general guideline regarding personal privacy (see *www.w3c.org*), and the U.S. International Trade Administration (ITA) has worked with the European Union to identify similar practices (see *www.ita.doc.gov*). The combination of both specifications should be used for the sample Web site.

At a more granular level, automobile operator's effective and expiration dates should adhere to the ISO 8601 date standard, and the ISO 3166 country code standard should be applied to the supported country of issue options from the drop-down list. Other internal enterprise data standards may be applied to regulate data quality and conformance. As an example, check boxes should be characterized by boolean data types (e.g., values of Yes/No, 1/0).

Reintegration of Requirements

The identification and formalization of requirements should conclude with a comparison, alignment, and reintegration activity. The most common methods of affinity from which to perform this activity are globalization dimensions used for mapping similar requirements, the user interface (specifically, cultural characteristics and HTML form elements), and data requirements. Each entry field of the user interface should align with the metadata characteristics of the corresponding data requirements, which are all requisite to enterprise data integration, global customer relationship management, and Web site globalization success:

- Organization of elements within their associated data concept group (e.g., the number of address lines within an address, name particles within a name, etc.)
- Supported and allowable code values (e.g., country codes, currency codes, language codes, etc.)
- Capture and presentation formats (e.g., date format, etc.)
- Granularity (e.g., particles used to capture telephone numbers and a person's name)
- Length of each element
- Implied data type

Once the requirements have been realigned and all participants have agreed upon the design approach, the requirements will be extended to a greater level of detail. The detailed requirements will drive global Web site development and transaction engineering. Internationalization and localization participants will begin development of user interfaces, application logic, and presentation schemes. These activities will leverage enterprise technology standards such as HTML, XHTML, XML, and so on.

Data architecture and enterprise integration participants will model, design, and develop supporting database structures (or extensions to existing structures), will develop reference and validation structures (to contain code values for each of the encoding standards), and will engineer transaction formats for the movement and exchange of data. The ability to move, share, and exchange data between Web servers, application servers, and enterprise applications is critical to the general functionality of the Web site as well as traditional enterprise processes. Other development and engineering activities will include identification of supporting protocols and encryption methods, environment setup, DBMS infrastructures, testing, documentation, implementation, and deployment.

As previously emphasized, the ability to capture, validate, exchange, and integrate globally diverse data among traditional enterprise applications is critical to order processing, fulfillment, and global customer relationship management. A frequently used method for resolving these challenges is to develop corresponding transactions that are described by schemas (also known as vocabularies).

Global Transaction Design

The SLKD Auto Rental example relies upon HTML-based Web forms to capture data. Combinations of predefined drop-down lists, form field entry, and checkboxes are used for capturing data. The processing of an HTML Web form inserts captured content into an HTTP transaction that is submitted to the receiving Web server. Depending upon the architecture layering of the Web site, the Web server may perform minimal validation, reformat or transform the element content of the forms into a transaction, and pass the transaction on to one or more application servers. In order to address performance and volumetrics, other architecture alternatives may avoid any processing or logic by the Web server and place the reformatting of form content as transactions in an application server. If localized content will be returned to the browser, the application server may also exchange transaction data with one or more localization servers. Depending upon the purpose of the transaction and the architecture of the Web site, the application servers then pass the transactions to one or more enterprise application servers (see Figure 5.5).

Of importance is the movement and exchange of data between servers. From a global enterprise perspective, this data movement will result in processing by traditional enterprise applications and the integration of globally diverse Web data with

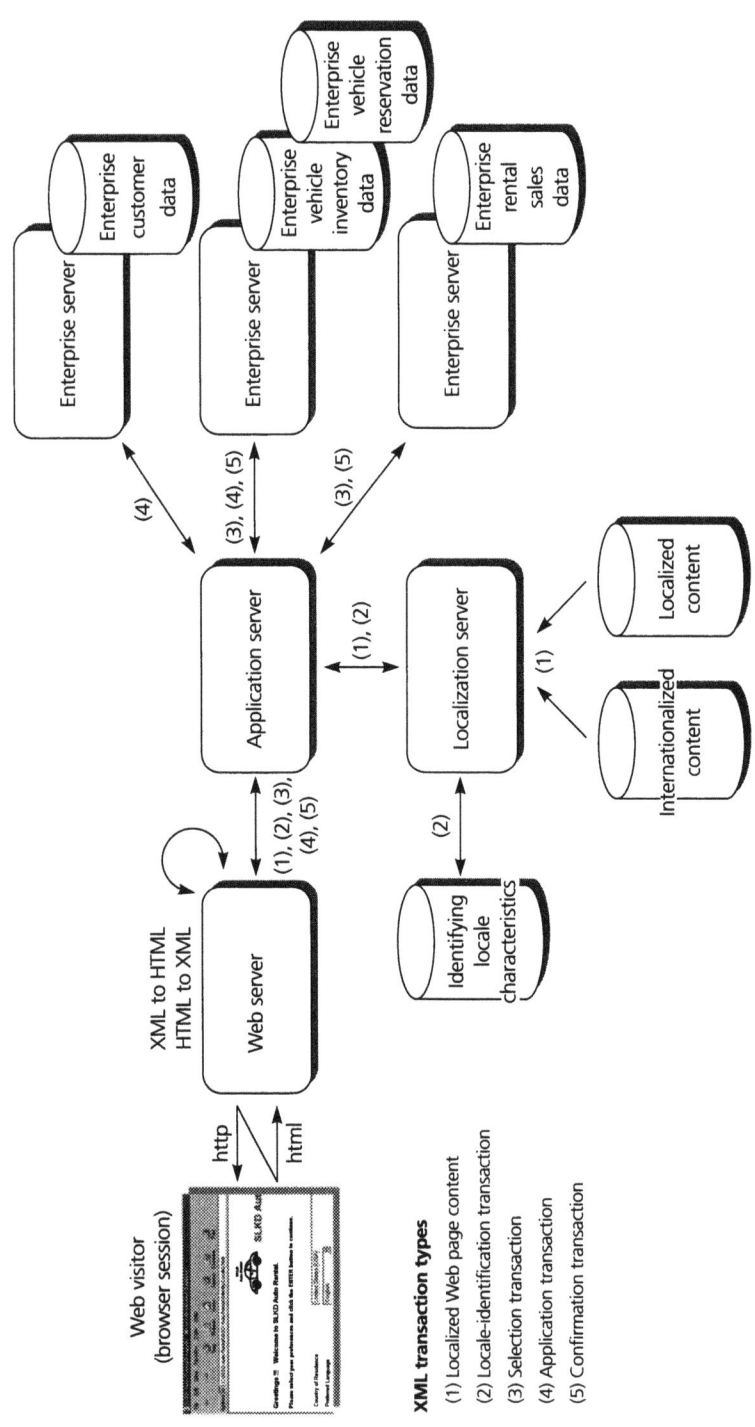

Figure 5.5 Conceptual globalized Web site architecture

traditional enterprise data. This implies the need for highly standardized, flexible, and reusable transactions that are described by enterprise transaction schemas (i.e., vocabularies). If a set of common transactions are used, the application and transformation logic applied to the data at each server is significantly reduced and simplified. Applications need only process the transaction content applicable to their function, and the transaction content is structured in a manner that promotes reuse rather than extended propagation of numerous additional and varied transactions. As part of the detailed design activities, transaction design should also consider global data capture (aligned with the user interface), global Web page content, and supporting data requirements.

The exchange of transaction data as described by the SLKD Auto Rental conceptual architecture diagram implies that application functionality is maintained within the enterprise. Alternatively, a more complex model might also include the movement and exchange of transaction data with external entities and partners. Using the example of an international auto rental Web site, such processing might include validation of automobile operator's license, automobile insurance, and driving history. Obviously, such processes are subject to appropriate regulatory compliance and secure encryption of data, as necessary.

There are several possible techniques for designing transactions. One of the more common is to align transaction content with the functionality implied by the functional interaction of each Web page. This technique describes each HTTP request (put or get) as an individual transaction, which can then be processed by the appropriate functional applications. One complexity of this technique is that some data content, such as locale characteristics, may need to be carried redundantly between multiple transactions. A Web site with more complex functionality and significantly higher transaction volumes might require alternative transaction formats and decomposition of those transactions into multiple subordinate transactions.

As described by the functional and data requirements, globally diverse data can be highly complex. The application of data standards as well as the ability to support variable data content are of fundamental importance. The exchange of transaction data between the Web server, application servers, and enterprise servers implies the need for transformation from originating HTML form content to other transaction forms. Based upon the SLKD Web site conceptual architecture diagram, HTML form field data are captured from a browser session and then passed to the Web server. The Web server performs minimal validation and then transforms the content to internal transactions. The content and structure of each transaction represents the functionality of each Web page.

The preferences and characteristics that identify the Web visitor's locale are of fundamental importance and are carried as part of each successive transaction. The technical identification of the browser session is captured in the HTTP header.

These data allow the Web server to track the source of each transaction request and to serve responses accordingly. Also, some transaction content is populated by application and enterprise functionality in preparation for the return of data back to the Web visitor (browser). The following design includes descriptive transaction content, as well as the corresponding HTML form elements (in parentheses) for the "locale-identification" Web page:

- General transaction data (extracted from the HTTP header)
- Transaction ID (system assigned)
- Locale characteristics
  - Country of residence (Locale_Country_Res)
  - Preferred language (Locale_Pref_Language)
  - Preferred currency (Locale_Pref_Currency)
  - Preferred unit of measure (Locale_Pref_UnitMeasure)

In addition to the desired rental dates, the transaction content from the "selection" Web page includes identification of the selected vehicle and descriptive characteristics of the selected vehicle derived from the vehicle selection. HTML form elements are described in parentheses.

- General transaction data (extracted from the HTTP header)
- Transaction ID (system assigned)
- Locale characteristics
  - Country of residence (Locale_Country_Res)
  - Preferred language (Locale_Pref_Language)
  - Preferred currency (Locale_Pref_Currency)
  - Preferred unit of measure (Locale_Pref_UnitMeasure)
- Requested rental dates
  - Rental from date (Res_Begin_Date)
  - Rental to date (Res_End_Date)
- Selected vehicle information
  - Vehicle ID (Rental_Vehicle)
  - Vehicle type (derived from value of Rental_Vehicle)
  - Vehicle model (derived from value of Rental_Vehicle)
  - Vehicle class (derived from value of Rental_Vehicle)
- Vehicle rental pricing
  - Daily rental price in base currency (derived from value of Rental_Vehicle)
  - Daily rental price in alternate currency (derived from value of Rental_Vehicle)

Transaction content from the "application" Web page is primarily customer oriented (name, address, telephone number), and also includes automobile operator's license and automobile insurance information, as well as driving history as it relates to insurability. Corresponding HTML form elements are described in parentheses. It is important to note that much of the information captured by the sample "application" Web page is personal and confidential. The capture and submission of these data to the Web server may introduce requirements for secure exchange and possibly some form of encryption.

- General transaction data (extracted from the HTTP header)
- Transaction ID (system assigned)
- Locale characteristics
  - Country of residence (Locale_Country_Res)
  - Preferred language (Locale_Pref_Language)
  - Preferred currency (Locale_Pref_Currency)
  - Preferred unit of measure (Locale_Pref_UnitMeasure)
- Customer name
  - Preferred salutation or greeting (Name_Salutation)
  - Prefix, title, or honorific (Name_Prefix)
  - Name 1 (Name_1_Type, Name_1)
  - Name 2 (Name_2_Type, Name_2)
  - Name 3 (Name_3_Type, Name_3)
  - Name 4 (Name_4_Type, Name_4)
  - Suffix, title, honorific (Name_Suffix)
  - Business or professional title (Name_Prof_Title)
- Customer telephone number
  - Residence telephone country (Res_Telephone_Country)
  - Residence area or city code (Res_Telephone_City_Area)
  - Residence exchange or prefix (Res_Telephone_Exch_Prefix)
  - Residence local number (Res_Telephone_Local_No)
  - Residence internal extension (Res_Telephone_Ext_No)
  - Business telephone country (Bus_Telephone_Country)
  - Business area or city code (Bus_Telephone_City_Area)
  - Business exchange or prefix (Bus_Telephone_Exch_Prefix)
  - Business local number (Bus_Telephone_Local_No)
  - Business internal extension (Bus_Telephone_Ext_No)
- Customer address
  - Address to name (Addr_To_Name)
  - Company name (Company Name)
  - Address line 1 (Addr_Street_1)
  - Address line 2 (Addr_Street_2)
  - Address line 3 (Addr_Street_3)

- City (Addr_City)
- Postal code (Addr_Post_Code)
- Country (Addr_Country)
- Country, other (Addr_Country_Other)
- Regional subdivision 1 (Addr_Reg_1_Type, Addr_Reg_1)
- Regional subdivision 2 (Addr_Reg_2_Type, Addr_Reg_2)
- Customer automobile operator's license
  - Automobile operator's license number (Auto_Lic_ID)
  - Country of issue (Auto_Lic_Country)
  - Issue date (Auto_Lic_Issue_Date)
  - Expiration date (Auto_Lic_Expire_Date)
- Customer automobile insurance
  - Auto insurance company (Auto_Ins_Company)
  - Auto insurance policy number (Auto_Ins_Policy_ID)
- Customer driving history
  - Years of driving experience (Years_Driving_Exp)
  - Number of accidents or collisions within past three years (No_Accidents)
  - Conviction for driving under the influence (Operate_Under_Influence)

The "confirmation" Web page does not capture data from the browser, but upon acceptance and validation of previously entered data, returns a system-generated confirmation number to the customer. The confirmation transaction is generated by enterprise applications and has very limited content. This transaction is intended to be returned to the Web browser.

- General transaction data (extracted from the HTTP header)
- Transaction ID (system assigned)
- Locale characteristics
  - Country of residence (Locale_Country_Res)
  - Preferred language (Locale_Pref_Language)
  - Preferred currency (Locale_Pref_Currency)
  - Preferred unit of measure (Locale_Pref_UnitMeasure)
- Rental reservation confirmation number (system assigned)

Once the transactions have been designed and the content is aligned with the source of each transaction, the next related activity is transaction engineering.

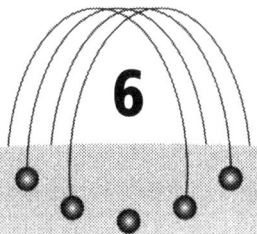

6

Transaction Engineering

The transaction engineering activity extends transaction design to technical implementation. The underlying technology may vary widely depending upon enterprise technology standards and the functionality of the Web site. Some of the more common Web technologies include HTML, XML/XSL, XHTML, WAP/WML, and ASP. The SLKD Auto Rental example relies upon HTML for presentation of Web page content, and HTML forms for the capture of data from the browser. The example also uses eXtensible Markup Language (XML) as the technology for describing transaction content that is exchanged between Web architecture layers.

Although XML is a fairly recent technology,[1] it is a subset of the well-established Standard Generalized Markup Language (SGML) technology.[2] XML is a self-describing extensible metadata language. XML can be used to describe the content of a document, file, message, or, as in the case of the SLKD Auto Rental example, a transaction. XML allows the architect to define custom transactions in order to meet specific requirements. Another advantage of XML is that it is platform agnostic. That is, XML can be exchanged with and processed on any platform that

---

1 eXtensible Markup Language (XML), World Wide Web Consortium (W3C); *www.w3c.org/XML/*.
2 Standard Generalized Markup Language (SGML, ISO 8879), International Organization for Standardization (ISO); *www.iso.org*.

accepts ASCII text and supports an XML parser. In addition, when XML transactions are architected to allow for highly variable and diverse content, they exhibit extensive support for transactions that contain globally diverse data.[3]

XML-Based Transaction Solutions

As noted previously, XML provides numerous capabilities and advantages for describing globally diverse transaction content. XML also resembles HTML in that tags are encapsulated by angle brackets (e.g., <CustomerData>). However, development with HTML code is sometimes relaxed and may include "acceptable" violations of the technology. On the other hand, XML conforms to a rigorous set of rules and constraints.

The two basic components of XML are the XML document (i.e., the content) and, optionally, a constraining schema. Given the context of data exchange between application servers and enterprise servers, the transaction can be implemented as an XML document. Similarly, there may be rules and constraints that further describe the transaction (e.g., grouping and relationship of elements within the transaction, data types, allowable values, etc.). These rules and constraints can be implemented in a referencing XML schema.

The basic premise of a transaction is that it contains data that are structured and scoped to resolve or respond to a functional request. When considering the globally diverse content of a transaction, there is an implied need and advantage to apply flexible structures and data standards. Structural definition and data standards can be applied as rules and constraints. The application of rules and constraints to an XML transaction is done using a schema and a validating XML parser. The validating parser will compare the structure and content of the XML transaction to the rules and constraints defined to the schema, and will identify violations. Schemas can be of several types. The most common XML schemas include Document Type Definitions (DTD), XML Data Reduced schemas (XDR), and XML Schemas (XSD). The capabilities afforded by an XML Schema allow the Web architect to define transaction structures and rules that will support globally diverse data, adhere to appropriate data standards, and help to simplify integration with traditional enterprise information.

The definition of a transaction structure using XML can take several forms. When transforming HTML to XML, the most simple is a direct element-to-element

---

3   *XML Globalization and Best Practices,* James Bean, Active Education, 2001; *www.activeed.com/.*

XML-Based Transaction Solutions

transformation. XML Stylesheet Transform (XSLT) can provide basic capabilities in this area. With this technique, the HTML form field elements are defined by corresponding XML element containers of the same name (see Figure 6.1). It is important to note that XSLT has some limitations with transforming complex content and mathematical derivations. In these cases, supplemental transformation logic using other languages such as Java, Visual Basic (VB), or C may be warranted.

Direct transformation of HTML form elements to corresponding XML elements is the most simple and rudimentary technique. When the content of the transaction has very limited content and is not variable as to structure or the number of elements, this technique is effective. The advantages of this technique are that transformation is intuitive and simple and the resulting structure is easily navigable. However, direct transformation of HTML elements to XML may not be as effective when the content of the transaction is variable and highly diverse.

An example of variable and globally diverse data is the data concept of a person's name. When considering the broad variations of name introduced by locale and culture, it is difficult to predefine name elements. Questions arise as to how name elements of a transaction should be described (e.g., first, given, family, last, middle, etc.), the order in which names should be assembled or presented (e.g., family before given, first before last), and which elements should always be populated. Defining all reasonable name possibilities to a transaction as elements will result in a large and complex transaction, complex and inefficient processing, and potential limitations regarding integration of name data with traditional enterprise data. When the content of a transaction is variable and highly diverse, a more effective technique is to define a flexible element structure within the transaction that includes a defined classification or type for each element, as well as a specific order or sequence (see Figure 6.2).

This technique requires that the element names be abstractly named and repeated using controlled repetition (also known as cardinality). Cardinality is the nominal measure of instances in a relationship. From the perspective of XML, cardinality is the declarative constraint between a group or parent element and the number of nested child elements. As a result of changing the HTML form element names, transformation from the originating HTML form elements may require additional mapping in order to cross-reference the XML element names. In Figure 6.2, cardinality of the name elements is defined as "1" to "4".

With repeating abstract element technique (also known as abstract containers), the content of the transaction can dynamically contract or expand as necessary to match populated name particles. When a name element is not populated, it can be eliminated from the transaction. The type attribute associated with each name particle describes the type of content held by each name container. The order attribute

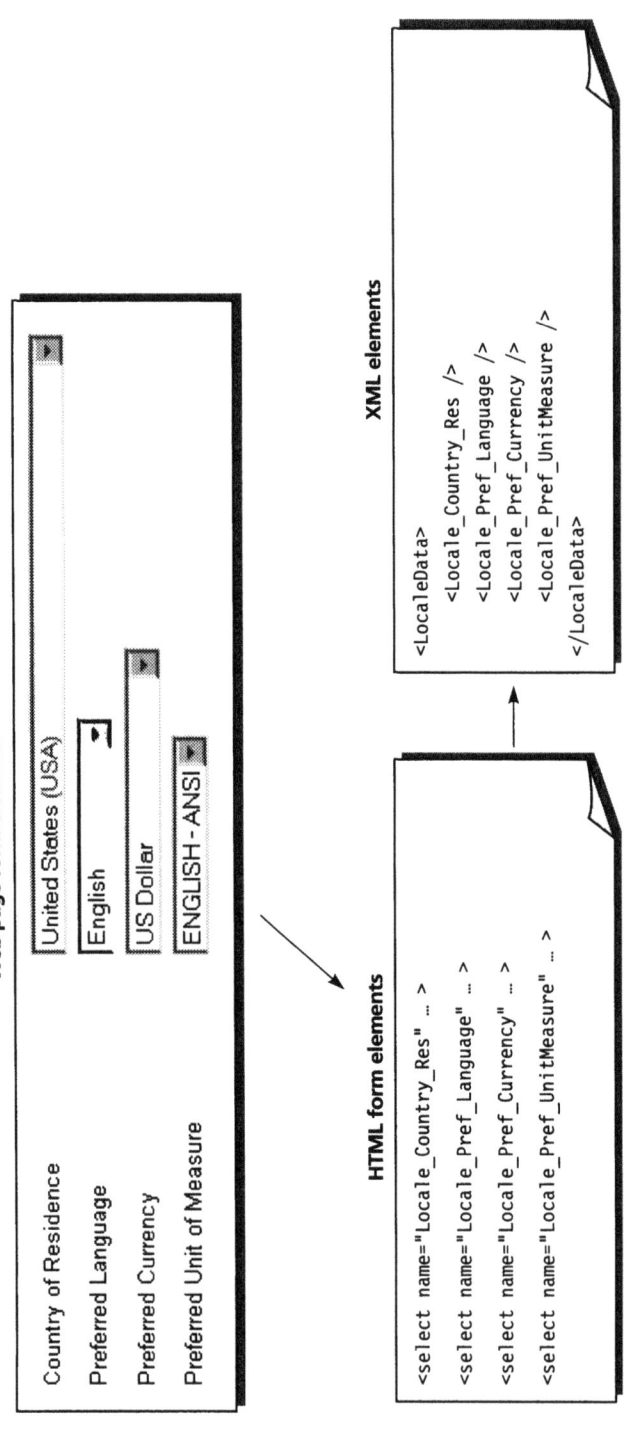

Figure 6.1 Direct HTML form element transformation to XML

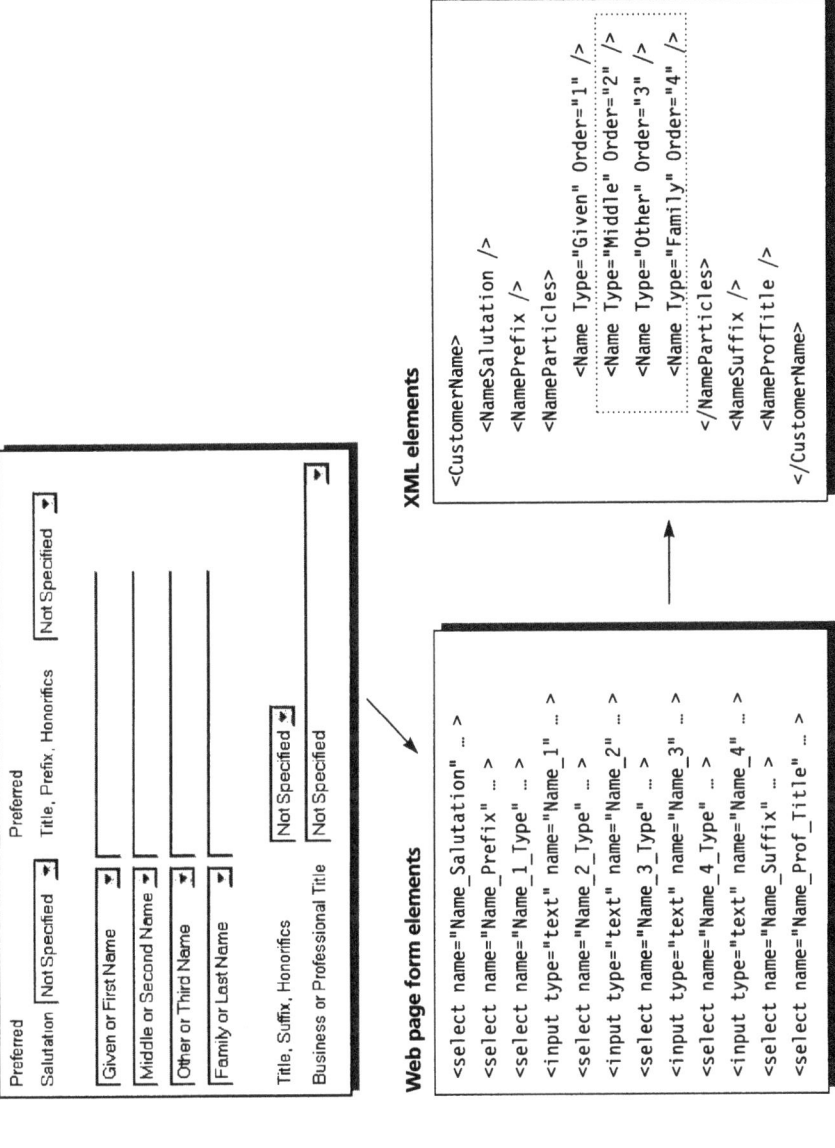

Figure 6.2 Variable transaction structure

declares the sequence of name particles as determined from the Web page form entry. Architecturally, the advantages of this technique are numerous. The transaction size can be limited since it will only contain populated elements. Also, person names that are globally diverse, complex, and variable can be defined by a single transaction definition.

The architect should also be aware of potential disadvantages when using this technique. Some developers may have difficulty interpreting and navigating the transaction structure. This complexity is a result of having multiply occurring abstractly named containers that are described by other metadata internal to the transaction. In order for the developer to determine what is contained in a name element, the type attribute must be interrogated. Similarly, in order to properly sequence the content of name elements, the order attribute must also be interrogated.

When an XML transaction structure is described by an XML Schema, other transaction engineering techniques may also be applied. As an example, there may be elements that are common to many transaction structures. Rather than redundantly defining the rules and constraints for these common elements in each XML Schema where they are applied, they can be externalized as a single standard structure and reused by other XML Schema structures by reference (see Figure 6.3).

Combinations of these and other transaction engineering techniques can be applied. Advantages and disadvantages depend upon transaction characteristics. In order to effectively apply transaction engineering techniques, the architect must evaluate the following:

- The intended purpose of the transaction
- The complexity of the transaction structure
- The size of the transaction
- The exchange and processing frequency of the transaction

In addition to the examples given for the architectural engineering of transaction data, there are other capabilities afforded by XML Schemas. As previously noted, the application of data standards provides a method for identifying, describing, and classifying globally diverse data. ISO 3166 Country Code, ISO 4217 Currency Code, and ISO 639 Language Codes are examples of well-defined and accepted encoding-type data standards. The SLKD Auto Rental example relies on these and other data standards. XML Schemas provide the ability to define allowable values for an element or attribute (see Figure 6.4). An XML Schema could be defined to include the valid or allowable values for each of the data elements that are aligned with an encoding standard. When the XML transaction is validated to a schema, this capability would allow the XML parser to validate whether valid values were found and to raise errors if not.

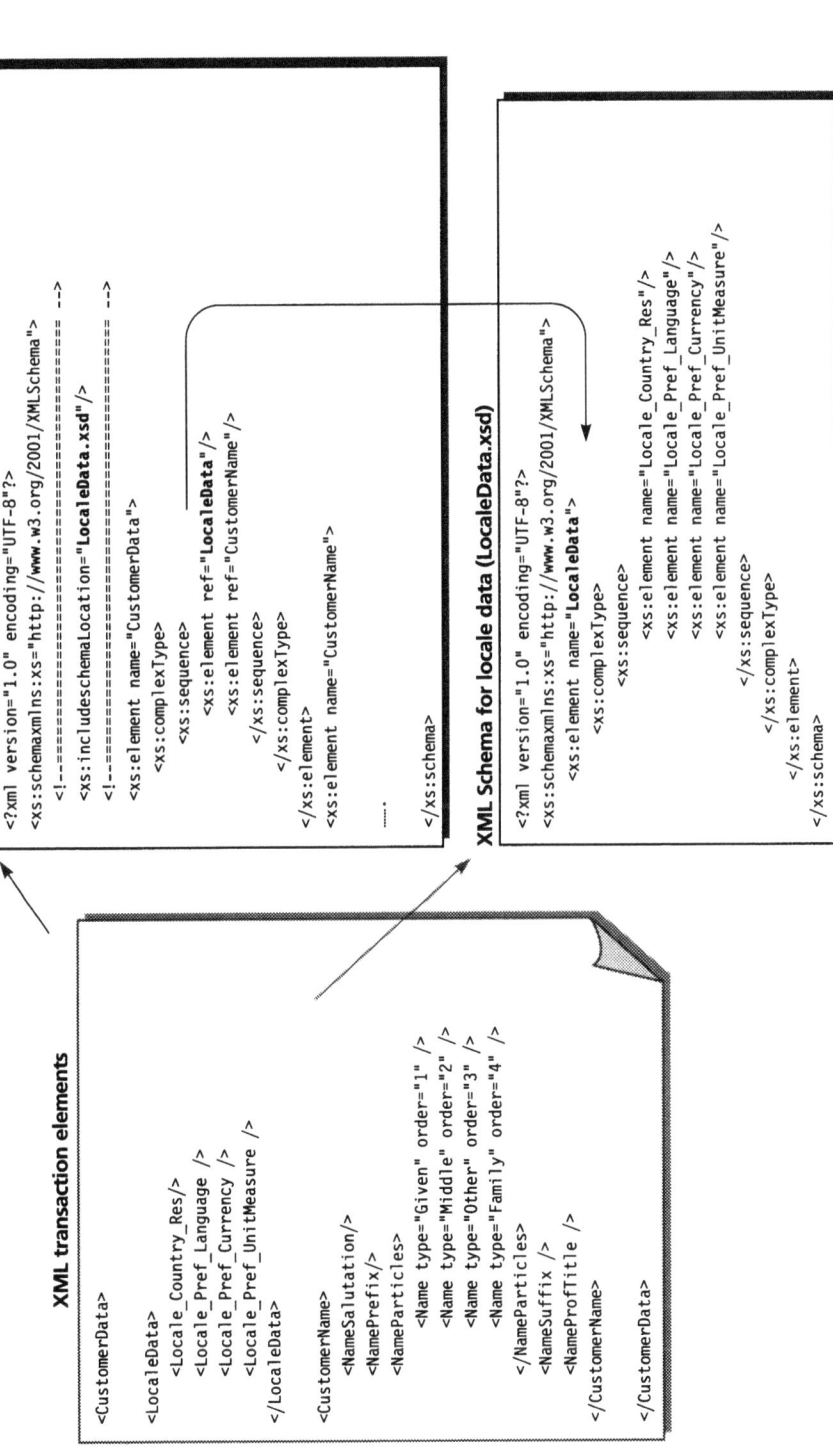

Figure 6.3 Externalized transaction schema structure

Chapter 6 Transaction Engineering

```
<xs:attribute name="Locale_Country_Res" use="required">
    <xs:simpleType>
        <xs:restriction base="xs:string">
            <xs:enumeration value="USA:840"/>
            <xs:enumeration value="GBR:826"/>
            <xs:enumeration value="AUS:036"/>
            <xs:enumeration value="CAN:124"/>
            <xs:enumeration value="NZL:554"/>
        </xs:restriction>
    </xs:simpleType>
</xs:attribute>
```

Figure 6.4 Allowable values using XML Schemas

As a method of applying rules and constraints, XML Schemas also provide extensive data type support. Individual transaction elements and attributes can be described by specific data types and their constraining facets. Facets can include constraints such as minimum length, maximum length, fractional digits, total digits, minimum value, maximum value, and so on. Additionally, XML Schemas provide the capability to define custom data types as extensions and variations of other types. When the XML transaction is validated to a defining schema, data values within the element and attribute containers must comply with the appropriate data types (see Figure 6.5).

Transaction engineering for the SLKD Auto Rental example applies all of the noted techniques in some form. Elements and attributes are defined by constraining data types and facets, encoding standards are defined by allowable values, and common elements are defined as external XML Schemas that can be reused by reference. The following examples are specific to the locale transaction and include a sample locale-identification transaction in XML format, a corresponding XML Schema, and several externalized XML Schemas that are reused by reference. The externalized schemas include allowable values that align with data standards for country, language (including the ISO standard for language and extended with regional dialect), currency, and unit of measure codes (which is an internal enterprise standard). Once the locale data is transformed into an XML transaction, it would initially be used by the localization server to identify internationalized and localized content. Following this initial interaction, the localization data would be included with all of the other functional transactions to ensure that the corresponding application and enterprise servers utilize the appropriate preferences.

XML-Based Transaction Solutions

```
<xsd:element name="decimalpositive14.4">
    <xsd:complexType>
        <xsd:simpleContent>
            <xsd:restriction base="xsd:decimal">
                <xsd:totalDigitsvalue="18"/>
                <xsd:fractionDigitsvalue="4"/>
            </xsd:restriction>
        </xsd:simpleContent>
    </xsd:complexType>
</xsd:element>
```

Figure 6.5 XML Schema data types

Locale Transaction—List of Source Code Examples

- Locale transaction (see Listing 6.1)
- Locale transaction schema (see Listing 6.2)
- Session data schema (see Listing 6.3)
- Locale data schema (see Listing 6.4)
- ISO 3166 country data values schema (see Listing 6.5)
- ISO 639 language data values schema (see Listing 6.6)
- ISO 4217 currency data values schema (see Listing 6.7)
- UM measure data values schema (see Listing 6.8)

Listing 6.1 Locale transaction (XML)

```xml
<?xml version="1.0" encoding="UTF-8"?>
<LocaleTransaction xmlns:xsi="http://www.w3.org/2001/XMLSchema-instance"
xsi:noNamespaceSchemaLocation="LocaleTransaction.xsd">
    <SessionData>
        <HTTP_Header />
        <TransactionID />
    </SessionData>
    <LocaleData>
        <Locale_Country_Res>GBR:826</Locale_Country_Res>
        <Locale_Pref_Language>ENG:GB</Locale_Pref_Language>
        <Locale_Pref_Currency>GBP:826</Locale_Pref_Currency>
```

Chapter 6 Transaction Engineering

```xml
        <Locale_Pref_UnitMeasure>SI:METRIC</Locale_Pref_UnitMeasure>
    </LocaleData>
</LocaleTransaction>
```

Listing 6.2 Locale transaction schema (XML Schema)

```xml
<?xml version="1.0" encoding="UTF-8"?>
<xs:schema xmlns:xs="http://www.w3.org/2001/XMLSchema">
    <!--=======================================-->
    <xs:include schemaLocation="SessionData.xsd"/>
    <xs:include schemaLocation="LocaleData.xsd"/>
    <!--=======================================-->
    <xs:element name="LocaleTransaction">
        <xs:complexType>
            <xs:sequence>
                <xs:element ref="SessionData"/>
                <xs:element ref="LocaleData"/>
            </xs:sequence>
        </xs:complexType>
    </xs:element>
</xs:schema>
```

Listing 6.3 Session data schema (externalized and reusable XML Schema)

```xml
<?xml version="1.0" encoding="UTF-8"?>
<xs:schema xmlns:xs="http://www.w3.org/2001/XMLSchema">
    <xs:element name="SessionData">
        <xs:complexType>
            <xs:sequence>
                <xs:element ref="HTTP_Header"/>
                <xs:element ref="TransactionID"/>
            </xs:sequence>
        </xs:complexType>
    </xs:element>
    <xs:element name="HTTP_Header" type="xs:string" />
    <xs:element name="TransactionID" type="xs:string" />
</xs:schema>
```

XML-Based Transaction Solutions

Listing 6.4 Locale data schema (externalized and reusable XML Schema)

```xml
<?xml version="1.0" encoding="UTF-8"?>
<xs:schema xmlns:xs="http://www.w3.org/2001/XMLSchema">
   <!-=======================================->
   <xs:include schemaLocation="ISO3166_Country.xsd"/>
   <xs:include schemaLocation="ISO639_Language.xsd"/>
   <xs:include schemaLocation="ISO4217_Currency.xsd"/>
   <xs:include schemaLocation="UM_Measure.xsd"/>
   <!-=======================================->
   <xs:element name="LocaleData">
      <xs:complexType>
         <xs:sequence>
            <xs:element ref="Locale_Country_Res"/>
            <xs:element ref="Locale_Pref_Language"/>
            <xs:element ref="Locale_Pref_Currency"/>
            <xs:element ref="Locale_Pref_UnitMeasure"/>
         </xs:sequence>
      </xs:complexType>
   </xs:element>
   <xs:element name="Locale_Country_Res" type="ISO3166_Country" />
   <xs:element name="Locale_Pref_Language" type="ISO639_Language" />
   <xs:element name="Locale_Pref_Currency" type="ISO4217_Currency" />
   <xs:element name="Locale_Pref_UnitMeasure" type="UM_Measure" />
</xs:schema>
```

Listing 6.5 ISO 3166 country data values schema (externalized and reusable XML Schema)

```xml
<?xml version="1.0" encoding="UTF-8"?>
<xs:schema xmlns:xs="http://www.w3.org/2001/XMLSchema">
   <xs:simpleType name="ISO3166_Country">
      <xs:restriction base="xs:string">
         <xs:enumeration value="USA:840"/>
         <xs:enumeration value="GBR:826"/>
         <xs:enumeration value="CAN:124"/>
         <xs:enumeration value="AUS:036"/>
         <xs:enumeration value="NZL:554"/>
```

Chapter 6 Transaction Engineering

```
      </xs:restriction>
    </xs:simpleType>
</xs:schema>
```

Listing 6.6 ISO 639 language data values schema (externalized and reusable XML Schema)

```xml
<?xml version="1.0" encoding="UTF-8"?>
<xs:schema xmlns:xs="http://www.w3.org/2001/XMLSchema">
    <xs:simpleType name="ISO639_Language">
      <xs:restriction base="xs:string">
        <xs:enumeration value="ENG:US"/>
        <xs:enumeration value="ENG:CA"/>
        <xs:enumeration value="ENG:GB"/>
        <xs:enumeration value="ENG:AU"/>
        <xs:enumeration value="ENG:NZ"/>
      </xs:restriction>
    </xs:simpleType>
</xs:schema>
```

Listing 6.7 ISO 4217 currency data values schema (externalized and reusable XML Schema)

```xml
<?xml version="1.0" encoding="UTF-8"?>
<xs:schema xmlns:xs="http://www.w3.org/2001/XMLSchema">
    <xs:simpleType name="ISO4217_Currency">
        <xs:restriction base="xs:string">
          <xs:enumeration value="USD:840"/>
          <xs:enumeration value="GBP:826"/>
          <xs:enumeration value="CAD:124"/>
          <xs:enumeration value="AUD:036"/>
          <xs:enumeration value="NZD:554"/>
        </xs:restriction>
    </xs:simpleType>
</xs:schema>
```

Listing 6.8 UM measure data values schema (externalized and reusable XML Schema)

```xml
<?xml version="1.0" encoding="UTF-8"?>
<xs:schema xmlns:xs="http://www.w3.org/2001/XMLSchema">
  <xs:simpleType name="UM_Measure">
    <xs:restriction base="xs:string">
      <xs:enumeration value="EN:ANSI"/>
      <xs:enumeration value="SI:METRIC"/>
    </xs:restriction>
  </xs:simpleType>
</xs:schema>
```

The following XML transaction represents content captured from the SLKD selection Web page form. The XML transaction is the result of a transformation from the originating HTML Web form content. Once transformed into XML, this transaction would be used to initiate the reservation process (e.g., requested reservation dates and selected vehicle). It would be used by application and enterprise servers to verify vehicle inventory availability and to reserve the selected vehicle. Several elements of the transaction would be unpopulated as a result of user entry, but would then be populated by the enterprise servers with descriptive vehicle information in preparation for return to the Web user's browser. The transaction would also be exchanged with the rental sales server to log a pending rental amount expressed in both the base currency of U.S. dollars and the Web user's preferred (alternate) currency. Once the entire set of Web functions are completed and the rental reservation is accepted, the rental sales data would be updated from pending to forecasted rental sales.

The XML source code includes a sample selection transaction in XML format, a corresponding XML Schema describing rules for the selection transaction, and several externalized common XML Schemas that are reused by reference. Several of these schemas include allowable values that align with data standards for vehicles (which, in the case of SLKD Auto Rental, is an internal enterprise standard), country, language, currency, and unit of measure codes.

The XML Schema for the selection transaction also incorporates data typing. Specifically, the requested rental dates (from and to) are defined as the XML "date" data type, which allows for the ISO 8601 extended date format of "YYYY-MM-DD." In addition, the rental price amounts are defined by the decimal data type, with facets for the number of fractional digits and total digits.

Chapter 6 Transaction Engineering

Selection Transaction—List of Source Code Examples

- Selection transaction (see Listing 6.9)
- Selection transaction schema (see Listing 6.10)
- Session data schema (see Listing 6.3)
- Locale data schema (see Listing 6.4)
- ISO 3166 country data values schema (see Listing 6.5)
- ISO 639 language data values schema (see Listing 6.6)
- ISO 4217 currency data values schema (see Listing 6.7)
- UM measure data values schema (see Listing 6.8)
- Vehicle data schema (see Listing 6.11)

Listing 6.9   Selection transaction (XML)

```xml
<?xml version="1.0" encoding="UTF-8"?>
<SelectionTransaction xmlns:xsi="http://www.w3.org/2001/XMLSchema-instance" xsi:noNamespaceSchemaLocation="SelectionTransaction.xsd">
  <SessionData>
    <HTTP_Header />
    <TransactionID />
  </SessionData>
  <LocaleData>
    <Locale_Country_Res>GBR:826</Locale_Country_Res>
    <Locale_Pref_Language>ENG:GB</Locale_Pref_Language>
    <Locale_Pref_Currency>GBP:826</Locale_Pref_Currency>
    <Locale_Pref_UnitMeasure>SI:METRIC</Locale_Pref_UnitMeasure>
  </LocaleData>
  <RentalDates>
    <RentalFromDate>2003-06-10</RentalFromDate>
    <RentalToDate>2003-06-12</RentalToDate>
  </RentalDates>
  <VehicleData>
    <VehicleID>SC-1</VehicleID>
    <VehicleType>National Motor Vehicles Corp</VehicleType>
    <VehicleModel>SR71 Blackbird</VehicleModel>
    <VehicleClass>2 Door, 2 Passenger</VehicleClass>
  </VehicleData>
  <VehiclePricing>
```

XML-Based Transaction Solutions

```xml
      <RentalPrice type="base" currency="USD:840">39.00</RentalPrice>
      <RentalPrice type="alternate" currency="GBP:826">26.53</RentalPrice>
   </VehiclePricing>
</SelectionTransaction>
```

Listing 6.10 Selection transaction schema (XML Schema)

```xml
<?xml version="1.0" encoding="UTF-8"?>
<xs:schema xmlns:xs="http://www.w3.org/2001/XMLSchema">
   <!--=========================================-->
   <xs:include schemaLocation="SessionData.xsd"/>
   <xs:include schemaLocation="LocaleData.xsd"/>
   <xs:include schemaLocation="VehicleData.xsd"/>
   <!--=========================================-->
   <xs:element name="SelectionTransaction">
      <xs:complexType>
         <xs:sequence>
            <xs:element ref="SessionData"/>
            <xs:element ref="LocaleData"/>
            <xs:element ref="RentalDates"/>
            <xs:element ref="VehicleData"/>
            <xs:element ref="VehiclePricing"/>
         </xs:sequence>
      </xs:complexType>
   </xs:element>
   <xs:element name="RentalDates">
      <xs:complexType>
         <xs:sequence>
            <xs:element name="RentalFromDate" type="xs:date"/>
            <xs:element name="RentalToDate" type="xs:date"/>
         </xs:sequence>
      </xs:complexType>
   </xs:element>
   <xs:element name="VehicleData">
      <xs:complexType>
         <xs:sequence>
            <xs:element name="VehicleID" type="VehicleID"/>
```

Chapter 6 Transaction Engineering

```xml
            <xs:element name="VehicleType" type="xs:string"/>
            <xs:element name="VehicleModel" type="xs:string"/>
            <xs:element name="VehicleClass" type="xs:string"/>
         </xs:sequence>
      </xs:complexType>
   </xs:element>
   <xs:element name="VehiclePricing">
      <xs:complexType>
         <xs:sequence>
            <xs:element ref="RentalPrice" minOccurs="1" maxOccurs="2"/>
         </xs:sequence>
      </xs:complexType>
   </xs:element>
   <xs:element name="RentalPrice">
      <xs:complexType>
        <xs:simpleContent>
           <xs:extension base="PriceType">
             <xs:attribute name="type">
               <xs:simpleType>
                  <xs:restriction base="xs:string">
                     <xs:enumeration value="base" />
                     <xs:enumeration value="alternate" />
                  </xs:restriction>
               </xs:simpleType>
             </xs:attribute>
             <xs:attribute name="currency" type="ISO4217_Currency"/>
           </xs:extension>
        </xs:simpleContent>
      </xs:complexType>
 </xs:element>
 <xs:simpleType name="PriceType">
     <xs:restriction base="xs:decimal">
         <xs:totalDigits value="6"/>
         <xs:fractionDigits value="2"/>
     </xs:restriction>
 </xs:simpleType>
</xs:schema>

</SelectionTransaction>
```

XML-Based Transaction Solutions

Listing 6.11 Vehicle data schema (XML Schema)

```
<?xml version="1.0" encoding="UTF-8"?>
<xs:schema xmlns:xs="http://www.w3.org/2001/XMLSchema">
  <xs:simpleType name="VehicleID">
    <xs:restriction base="xs:string">
      <xs:enumeration value="SC-1"/>
      <xs:enumeration value="FC-1"/>
    </xs:restriction>
  </xs:simpleType>
</xs:schema>
```

The following transaction represents customer application data captured from the SLKD application Web page. The data captured by this HTML Web form is the most comprehensive and complex of all the SLKD Web pages. The application transaction would serve several purposes and would be exchanged with the application and enterprise customer servers. Since the transaction includes locale information, preferences, and customer data, it would also serve as the foundation for global customer relationship management (G-CRM). Also of importance is the sensitivity of the data contained in this transaction. Since the data includes both personal and identity information, security and confidentiality are of significant importance.

Similar to the previous selection transaction, the session and locale data are included and reuse common XML Schema definitions by referencing external XML Schemas. The example assumes a single XML transaction is transformed from the originating application HTML Web form. If the data captured from the HTML Web form were more voluminous or a significant number of transactions were expected, it might be necessary to decompose this single transaction as several smaller transactions, all targeting specific servers and functions. The XML source code examples include an application transaction in XML format, a corresponding XML Schema for the application transaction, and several externalized common XML Schemas that are reused by reference. Several of these schemas include allowable values that align with data standards for country, language, currency, unit of measure codes, and postal address–region types. In the case of country codes, telephone country codes (international access codes) are different than the ISO 3166 country codes.

The application transaction has also been engineered to include abstract containers for person name and address lines. This technique allows for multiple instances of like-named elements for a person's name and for the street address lines of a postal address. In both cases an order attribute has been defined to specify the sequence in which these elements should occur. The name elements are also classified by a type attribute to specify the type of name data held by each repeating element.

Application Transaction—List of Source Code Examples

- Application transaction (see Listing 6.12)
- Application transaction schema (see Listing 6.13)
- Session data schema (see Listing 6.3)
- Locale data schema (see Listing 6.4)
- ISO 3166 country data values schema (see Listing 6.5)
- ISO 639 language data values schema (see Listing 6.6)
- ISO 4217 currency data values schema (see Listing 6.7)
- UM measure data values schema (see Listing 6.8)
- Telephone country data values schema (see Listing 6.14)

Listing 6.12 Application transaction (XML)

```xml
<?xml version="1.0" encoding="UTF-8"?>
<ApplicationTransaction xmlns:xsi="http://www.w3.org/2001/XMLSchema-instance" xsi:noNamespaceSchemaLocation="ApplicationTransaction.xsd">
  <SessionData>
    <HTTP_Header/>
    <TransactionID/>
  </SessionData>
  <LocaleData>
    <Locale_Country_Res>CAN:124</Locale_Country_Res>
    <Locale_Pref_Language>ENG:CA</Locale_Pref_Language>
    <Locale_Pref_Currency>CAD:124</Locale_Pref_Currency>
    <Locale_Pref_UnitMeasure>EN:ANSI</Locale_Pref_UnitMeasure>
  </LocaleData>
  <CustomerName>
    <Name_Salutation>Greetings</Name_Salutation>
    <Name_Prefix>Mr.</Name_Prefix>
    <Name_Particles>
      <Name type="Given" order="1">John</Name>
      <Name type="Middle" order="2">William</Name>
      <Name type="Other" order="3">Christian</Name>
      <Name type="Family" order="4">Doe</Name>
```

```xml
    </Name_Particles>
    <Name_Suffix>M.D.</Name_Suffix>
    <Name_Prof_Title>Director</Name_Prof_Title>
</CustomerName>
<CustomerTelephone>
    <Telephone type="res"
      Telephone_Country="CAN:1"
      Telephone_City_Area="999"
      Telephone_Exch_Prefix="999"
      Telephone_Local_No="9999"
      Telephone_Ext_No="">1.999.999.9999</Telephone>
    <Telephone type="bus"
      Telephone_Country="CAN:1"
      Telephone_City_Area="999"
      Telephone_Exch_Prefix="999"
      Telephone_Local_No="9999"
      Telephone_Ext_No="">1.999.999.9999</Telephone>
</CustomerTelephone>
<CustomerAddress>
    <Addr_To_Name>Dr. John William Doe, PhD.</Addr_To_Name>
    <Addr_Company>Doe and Company</Addr_Company>
    <Addr_Street_Lines>
       <Addr_Street order="1">9876 N. GlobalExample Ln.</Addr_Street>
       <Addr_Street order="2">Plaza 9</Addr_Street>
       <Addr_Street order="3">Suite B-9</Addr_Street>
    </Addr_Street_Lines>
    <Addr_City>Montreal</Addr_City>
    <Addr_Post_Code>X9X 9X9</Addr_Post_Code>
    <Addr_Country>CAN:124</Addr_Country>
    <Addr_Country_Other></Addr_Country_Other>
    <Addr_Reg Addr_Reg_Type="Province">Quebec</Addr_Reg>
    <Addr_Reg Addr_Reg_Type=""></Addr_Reg>
</CustomerAddress>
<AutomobileOperatorLicense>
    <Auto_Lic_ID>123456789012345</Auto_Lic_ID>
    <Auto_Lic_Country>CAN:124</Auto_Lic_Country>
    <Auto_Lic_Issue_Date>2000-01-01</Auto_Lic_Issue_Date>
    <Auto_Lic_Expire_Date>2004-01-01</Auto_Lic_Expire_Date>
</AutomobileOperatorLicense>
```

Chapter 6 Transaction Engineering

```xml
<AutomobileInsurance>
   <Auto_Ins_Policy_ID>123456789012345</Auto_Ins_Policy_ID>
   <Auto_Ins_Company>ABC ACME Insurance Co. Ltd.</Auto_Ins_Company>
</AutomobileInsurance>
<DrivingHistory>
   <Years_Driving_Exp>2-5</Years_Driving_Exp>
   <No_Accidents>0</No_Accidents>
   <Operator_Under_Influence>0</Operator_Under_Influence>
</DrivingHistory>
</ApplicationTransaction>
```

Listing 6.13   Application transaction schema (XML Schema)

```xml
<?xml version="1.0" encoding="UTF-8"?>
<xs:schema xmlns:xs="http://www.w3.org/2001/XMLSchema">
   <!-=======================================->
   <xs:include schemaLocation="SessionData.xsd"/>
   <xs:include schemaLocation="LocaleData.xsd"/>
   <xs:include schemaLocation="Telephone_Country.xsd"/>
   <!-=======================================->
   <xs:element name="ApplicationTransaction">
      <xs:complexType>
         <xs:sequence>
            <xs:element ref="SessionData"/>
            <xs:element ref="LocaleData"/>
            <xs:element ref="CustomerName"/>
            <xs:element ref="CustomerTelephone"/>
            <xs:element ref="CustomerAddress"/>
            <xs:element ref="AutomobileOperatorLicense"/>
            <xs:element ref="AutomobileInsurance"/>
            <xs:element ref="DrivingHistory"/>
         </xs:sequence>
      </xs:complexType>
   </xs:element>
   <xs:element name="CustomerName">
      <xs:complexType>
         <xs:sequence>
            <xs:element name="Name_Salutation"/>
```

```xml
            <xs:element name="Name_Prefix"/>
            <xs:element ref="Name_Particles"/>
            <xs:element name="Name_Suffix"/>
            <xs:element name="Name_Prof_Title"/>
        </xs:sequence>
    </xs:complexType>
</xs:element>
<xs:element name="Name_Particles">
    <xs:complexType>
        <xs:sequence>
            <xs:element ref="Name" maxOccurs="4"/>
        </xs:sequence>
    </xs:complexType>
</xs:element>
<xs:element name="Name">
    <xs:complexType>
        <xs:simpleContent>
            <xs:extension base="xs:string">
                <xs:attribute name="type" use="required">
                    <xs:simpleType>
                        <xs:restriction base="xs:string">
                            <xs:enumeration value="First"/>
                            <xs:enumeration value="Given"/>
                            <xs:enumeration value="Middle"/>
                            <xs:enumeration value="Second"/>
                            <xs:enumeration value="Other"/>
                            <xs:enumeration value="Third"/>
                            <xs:enumeration value="Last"/>
                            <xs:enumeration value="Family"/>
                        </xs:restriction>
                    </xs:simpleType>
                </xs:attribute>
                <xs:attribute name="order" type="xs:int" use="required"/>
            </xs:extension>
        </xs:simpleContent>
    </xs:complexType>
</xs:element>
<xs:element name="CustomerTelephone">
    <xs:complexType>
```

```xml
            <xs:sequence>
               <xs:element ref="Telephone" minOccurs="1" maxOccurs="2"/>
            </xs:sequence>
         </xs:complexType>
      </xs:element>
      <xs:element name="Telephone">
         <xs:complexType>
            <xs:simpleContent>
               <xs:extension base="xs:string">
                  <xs:attribute name="type" use="required">
                     <xs:simpleType>
                        <xs:restriction base="xs:string">
                           <xs:enumeration value="res"/>
                           <xs:enumeration value="bus"/>
                        </xs:restriction>
                     </xs:simpleType>
                  </xs:attribute>
                  <xs:attribute name="Telephone_Country" type=
                  "Telephone_Country" use="required"/>
                  <xs:attribute name="Telephone_City_Area" use="optional"/>
                  <xs:attribute name="Telephone_Exch_Prefix" use="optional"/>
                  <xs:attribute name="Telephone_Local_No" use="optional"/>
                  <xs:attribute name="Telephone_Ext_No" use="optional"/>
               </xs:extension>
            </xs:simpleContent>
         </xs:complexType>
      </xs:element>
      <xs:element name="CustomerAddress">
         <xs:complexType>
            <xs:sequence>
               <xs:element name="Addr_To_Name"/>
               <xs:element name="Addr_Company" minOccurs="0"/>
               <xs:element ref="Addr_Street_Lines"/>
               <xs:element name="Addr_City"/>
               <xs:element name="Addr_Post_Code"/>
               <xs:element name="Addr_Country" type="ISO3166_Country"
               minOccurs="0"/>
               <xs:element name="Addr_Country_Other" minOccurs="0"/>
               <xs:element ref="Addr_Reg" minOccurs="0" maxOccurs="2"/>
```

```xml
      </xs:sequence>
    </xs:complexType>
</xs:element>
<xs:element name="Addr_Street_Lines">
    <xs:complexType>
      <xs:sequence>
         <xs:element ref="Addr_Street" minOccurs="1" maxOccurs="3"/>
      </xs:sequence>
    </xs:complexType>
</xs:element>
<xs:element name="Addr_Street">
    <xs:complexType>
      <xs:simpleContent>
         <xs:extension base="xs:string">
           <xs:attribute name="order" type="xs:int" use="required"/>
         </xs:extension>
      </xs:simpleContent>
    </xs:complexType>
</xs:element>
<xs:element name="Addr_Reg">
    <xs:complexType>
      <xs:simpleContent>
         <xs:extension base="xs:string">
           <xs:attribute name="Addr_Reg_Type" use="required">
              <xs:simpleType>
                <xs:restriction base="xs:string">
                   <xs:enumeration value="Canton"/>
                   <xs:enumeration value="County"/>
                   <xs:enumeration value="Department"/>
                   <xs:enumeration value="District"/>
                   <xs:enumeration value="Province"/>
                   <xs:enumeration value="Region"/>
                   <xs:enumeration value="Shire"/>
                   <xs:enumeration value="State"/>
                   <xs:enumeration value="Territory"/>
                   <xs:enumeration value="Zone"/>
                   <xs:enumeration value="Other"/>
                   <xs:enumeration value=""/>
                </xs:restriction>
```

```xml
            </xs:simpleType>
          </xs:attribute>
        </xs:extension>
      </xs:simpleContent>
  </xs:complexType>
</xs:element>
<xs:element name="AutomobileOperatorLicense">
  <xs:complexType>
    <xs:sequence>
      <xs:element name="Auto_Lic_ID"/>
      <xs:element name="Auto_Lic_Country" type="ISO3166_Country"/>
      <xs:element name="Auto_Lic_Issue_Date"/>
      <xs:element name="Auto_Lic_Expire_Date"/>
    </xs:sequence>
  </xs:complexType>
</xs:element>
<xs:element name="AutomobileInsurance">
  <xs:complexType>
    <xs:sequence>
      <xs:element name="Auto_Ins_Policy_ID"/>
      <xs:element name="Auto_Ins_Company"/>
    </xs:sequence>
  </xs:complexType>
</xs:element>
<xs:element name="DrivingHistory">
  <xs:complexType>
    <xs:sequence>
      <xs:element name="Years_Driving_Exp">
        <xs:simpleType>
          <xs:restriction base="xs:string">
            <xs:enumeration value="0-1"/>
            <xs:enumeration value="2-5"/>
            <xs:enumeration value="6+"/>
          </xs:restriction>
        </xs:simpleType>
      </xs:element>
      <xs:element name="No_Accidents">
        <xs:simpleType>
```

XML-Based Transaction Solutions

```xml
            <xs:restriction base="xs:string">
              <xs:enumeration value="0"/>
              <xs:enumeration value="1-2"/>
              <xs:enumeration value="3+"/>
            </xs:restriction>
          </xs:simpleType>
        </xs:element>
        <xs:element name="Operator_Under_Influence"
        type="xs:boolean"/>
      </xs:sequence>
    </xs:complexType>
  </xs:element>
</xs:schema>
```

Listing 6.14 Telephone country data values schema (XML Schema)

```xml
<?xml version="1.0" encoding="UTF-8"?>
<xs:schema xmlns:xs="http://www.w3.org/2001/XMLSchema">
  <xs:simpleType name="Telephone_Country">
    <xs:restriction base="xs:string">
      <xs:enumeration value="USA:1"/>
      <xs:enumeration value="GBR:44"/>
      <xs:enumeration value="CAN:1"/>
      <xs:enumeration value="AUS:61"/>
      <xs:enumeration value="NZL:64"/>
    </xs:restriction>
  </xs:simpleType>
</xs:schema>
```

Each of the previous transaction examples (locale, selection, application) include data that would have originated as data captured from one of the SLKD Auto Rental Web pages, as well as populated by and returned data from application processing. After completion and acceptance of all SLKD rental reservation transactions, the enterprise rental reservation server would generate a confirmation transaction that would be returned to the customer, as well as used to complete the update of pending rental sales data. As with the other transactions, transaction identifiers and locale characteristics would be prepended to the confirmation transaction.

Chapter 6 Transaction Engineering

Confirmation Transaction—List of Source Code Examples

- Confirmation transaction (see Listing 6.15)
- Confirmation transaction schema (see Listing 6.16)
- Session data schema (see Listing 6.3)
- Locale data schema (see Listing 6.4)
- ISO 3166 country data values schema (see Listing 6.5)
- ISO 639 language data values schema (see Listing 6.6)
- ISO 4217 currency data values schema (see Listing 6.7)
- UM measure data values schema (see Listing 6.8)

Listing 6.15 Confirmation transaction (XML)

```xml
<?xml version="1.0" encoding="UTF-8"?>
<ConfirmationTransaction xmlns:xsi="http://www.w3.org/2001/XMLSchema-
instance" xsi:noNamespaceSchemaLocation="ConfirmationTransaction.xsd">
    <SessionData>
        <HTTP_Header/>
        <TransactionID/>
    </SessionData>
    <LocaleData>
        <Locale_Country_Res>GBR:826</Locale_Country_Res>
        <Locale_Pref_Language>ENG:GB</Locale_Pref_Language>
        <Locale_Pref_Currency>GBP:826</Locale_Pref_Currency>
        <Locale_Pref_UnitMeasure>SI:METRIC</Locale_Pref_UnitMeasure>
    </LocaleData>
    <Confirmation>
        <Confirmation_Number>20030101Z14XYZ</Confirmation_Number>
    </Confirmation>
</ConfirmationTransaction>
```

Listing 6.16 Confirmation transaction schema (XML Schema)

```xml
<?xml version="1.0" encoding="UTF-8"?>
<xs:schema xmlns:xs="http://www.w3.org/2001/XMLSchema">
    <!-=======================================->
    <xs:include schemaLocation="SessionData.xsd"/>
    <xs:include schemaLocation="LocaleData.xsd"/>
    <!-=======================================->
```

```
        <xs:element name="ConfirmationTransaction">
          <xs:complexType>
            <xs:sequence>
              <xs:element ref="SessionData"/>
              <xs:element ref="LocaleData"/>
              <xs:element ref="Confirmation"/>
            </xs:sequence>
          </xs:complexType>
        </xs:element>
        <xs:element name="Confirmation">
          <xs:complexType>
            <xs:sequence>
              <xs:element name="Confirmation_Number"/>
            </xs:sequence>
          </xs:complexType>
        </xs:element>
</xs:schema>
```

The SLKD Auto Rental transactions have been engineered to align with the Web site interface and functionality. However, there are other opportunities to apply architectural principles to the process of transaction engineering. Two of the most important areas to address are changes to requirements or standards and support for enterprise application and data integration.

Change Is Inevitable

XML Schemas present significant value and advantage as a method of applying rules and constraints. One of the most obvious strengths is the specification of allowable values or "enumeration." When considering encoding standards such as ISO 3166 Country Code, ISO 4217 Currency Code, or ISO 639 Language Code, a frequently observed technique is to define the code values of these standards as enumeration lists within an XML Schema. When the schema is applied to the XML transaction as part of the validation process, only those values of the enumeration list will be allowed, and violations will be raised as errors.

However, change is inevitable. Even though the standards for country, currency, and language are well defined, accepted, and pervasive, the data concepts supported by these standards are subject to change. Specifically, changes and additions to countries and currencies occur almost annually. As examples, consider changes in recent years for Rhodesia, Zimbabwe, Bosnia, and the Soviet Union. Also consider the Euro, which as of 2002 has replaced 12 European currencies. Many technologists and architects tend to forget that such changes occur and may not have provided an architecture that supports change while mitigating the impact to reengineering efforts.

Also of importance are global data concepts that are not supported by a well-defined data standard. Person name is one of the more common. When addressing a globally and culturally diverse audience, the sequence and structure of an individual's name can be of numerous forms. Acknowledging the importance of localized Web pages, incorrectly presenting or capturing the name of an international visitor can injure or prohibit a customer relationship. With examples such as a person's name, the architect should ensure that the Web interface and underlying transactions are as flexible and extensible as possible. When technologies such as HTML forms are used to capture data, this can be a challenge. When declaring HTML form fields, input elements should in most cases be uniquely named and identified. This means that unless other more dynamic technologies such as DHTML are used, HTML form fields for capturing globally diverse data such as a person's name must be uniquely named and statically defined. If a Web page includes an HTML form with elements to capture a person's name and the name is defined by three input fields, adding another name field to accommodate more culturally diverse names will result in additional modification of the application.

The technologist or architect should consider more flexible and extensible models where several HTML form field elements for name particles are defined and the user is allowed to determine what each name particle will represent. After submission to the server, transformation of the HTML form content can reapply the data as a variable XML transaction structure. As a word of caution, consideration should also be given to user interface simplicity or what is defined as usability. If the HTML form entry is too complex or the Web page is too "busy," the potential customer may abandon the session in frustration. Localization experts can assist in identifying the best combination of flexibility, extensibility, and acceptable complexity as it applies to the user interface.

Another area of potential change is with data concepts such as a postal address. Although postal address formats for most locales of the globe are reasonably well defined, attempting to develop separate HTML postal address forms for each supported locale can result in significant development cost and complexity. Also, while these address formats are well documented, there can be exceptions (e.g., designing the HTML form and resulting transaction to allow for two address lines, and then discovering that three are required). In many cases, the architect can identify affinities between address formats of supported locales and derive a common postal address format. This technique is used by the SLKD Auto Rental example. Resulting transaction and data exchange between application and enterprise servers can be accommodated by variable XML transaction structures. The critical success factor of this technique is being able to identify locale-specific address components at a granular level and allow for the greatest possible number of address street lines for all supported locales. This can be accomplished by including elements for such data particles as city, country, postal code, and regional subdivisions.

Global Transaction Engineering Principles to Avoid

Although XML and in particular XML Schemas provide extensive capabilities in the area of rules and constraints, there are some techniques that should be avoided when engineering global e-commerce transactions. First is the enumeration capability used to specify allowable values for an element or an attribute. When implemented correctly, this technique can be used to provide extensive support for encoding type data standards such as ISO 3166 Country Codes and ISO 4217 Currency Codes. As noted earlier, the problem is that the codes within these broadly recognized and accepted standards are subject to change. If the list of allowable (enumerated) values is specified within the primary XML Schema for a transaction, any changes to code values will result in similar changes to the primary XML Schema. A more effective application of XML Schema–based enumeration is to externalize encoding type data standards as enumerated values within a single standard XML Schema. The externalized schema can then be reused by reference from numerous other XML Schemas. If changes to code values occur, they can be implemented in a single XML Schema rather than many (see Figure 6.6).

Another development and engineering technique to avoid is weak taxonomy. The name applied to elements and attributes (both HTML and XML) should be intuitive and descriptive. There are numerous methods that have been developed for applying a taxonomy as a method of naming. Several have been used over many years and are derived from somewhat dated standards such as the Information Resource Dictionary System (IRDS) and the IBM "of" Language. If these taxonomy practices are well defined, representative of the business enterprise, clear, concise, and intuitive, then they warrant use. However, if they are cryptic and incorporate extensive use of abbreviations and acronyms, alternative taxonomy methods should be researched (see Table 6.1).

Many technology development and engineering practitioners prefer that data and transactions be represented by simple, static structures. This implies that

Chapter 6 Transaction Engineering

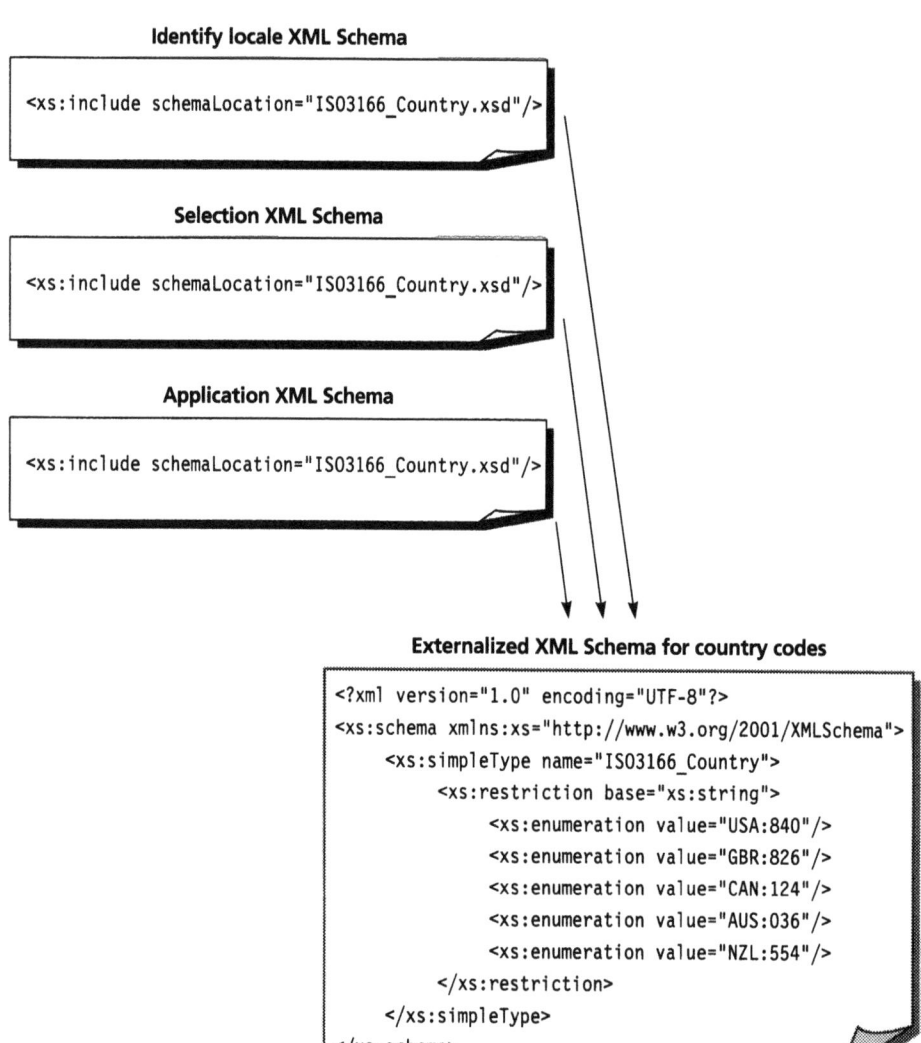

Figure 6.6 External enumeration

every element is uniquely named and identified (e.g., Street_Address_Line_1, Street_Address_Line_2, and Street_Address_Line_3 instead of multiple occurrences of Street_Address_Line). This practice is supported by static database structures and object classes that do not exhibit attribute multiplicity. This practice also supports the simple application of synergistic XML technologies such as XPATH.

Table 6.1 Weak vs. Descriptive Taxonomy

Weak taxonomy	Descriptive taxonomies
<CST_NM_TX>	<CustomerName>
	<Customer_Name>
	<CUSTOMER_NAME>

The problem is that some data concepts (especially those that describe globally diverse data) cannot be readily described by a static structure or transaction. In the interests of data reuse, data sharing, and development efficiencies, it is suggested that abstract container models may be more appropriate solutions for describing data concepts, such as postal address and person name, that are globally and culturally diverse. The challenge with abstract container models is that navigation and processing of the transaction may be somewhat less intuitive and may require additional interrogation of internally defined metadata attributes such as type and order attributes (see Figure 6.7).

When considering globally diverse data and transactions, architects and developers should always consider the potential for change, locale- and culture-specific variations of data, and efficiencies afforded by common and standardized transaction formats. Principles that can help to insure the most effective transaction designs consider the following:

- Transaction purpose and use (both short and long term)
- Complexity of the transaction structure
- The frequency and number of transactions processed at any time
- The potential for ongoing modification and additional data content
- Flexibility (the ability to dynamically expand or contract)
- Extensibility (the ability to add to or extend a transaction)
- Reuse (the ability to reuse or reference standardized transaction definitions)
- Simplicity (intuitive taxonomy)

Beware!

The Web presents a powerful medium for addressing a global marketplace. When supplemented with technologies such as HTML and XML, the ability to capture, exchange, process, and integrate globally diverse data becomes less of a technical

Fixed container model

```
<CustomerName>
    <GivenName>John</GivenName>
    <MiddleName>William</MiddleName>
    <FamilyName>Doe</FamilyName>
</CustomerName>
```

Advantages
- Simple and intuitive

Disadvantages
- Not flexible
- Not easily extended

Abstract container model

```
<CustomerName>
    <Name type="Given" order="1">John</Name>
    <Name type="Middle" order="2">William</Name>
    <Name type="Family" order="3">Doe</Name>
</CustomerName>
```

Advantages
- Dynamically adjusts to additional elements
- Extended without modification
- Includes specific attributes for type and order
- E lements can contain variations of name data

Disadvantages
- Not intuitive
- Not easily navigated
- Additional attribute interrogation logic required

Figure 6.7 Fixed vs. abstract container models

challenge. However, there are numerous nontechnical issues to consider. Although a transaction can be designed and engineered to carry most any data, there may be legal and ethical considerations. Personal privacy is becoming an obvious and visible issue regardless of country, locale, or culture. Capturing and exchanging data that may be identifying, confidential, or sensitive could be regarded as intrusive or unethical, and in some cases may violate specific regulatory acts.

Even when the capture of personal, identifying, or sensitive data is legal and ethical, there may be issues of liability if such information is exposed to unauthorized individuals or organizations. A great strength of XML is the ability to describe the data contained within a transaction. However, XML is also ASCII text. If an XML transaction is captured or interrogated by an unauthorized party, the contained data is not only visible with a text editor, but the location and type of data within the transaction are also readily evident. For these reasons, consideration should be given to secure exchange of personal, confidential, and sensitive data and, where appropriate, encryption should be applied.

Other issues that may arise are generally related to conducting business internationally. The business enterprise should identify legal and regulatory issues regarding liability, warranty, refunds, currency exchange rates, contractual commitments, privacy, nondiscrimination, and copyright, trademark, patent, and intellectual property violations. One example of a potential copyright violation is the application and use of data standards. Several of the most common and recognized data standards are the copyright and intellectual property of standards organizations. The legal use of such standards may require specific licensing and the possibility of a fee for use and acquisition of the data standard.

The advantages of conducting global business using the Web will most often outweigh the disadvantages. However, caution is advised and the enterprise should evaluate all the complexities, challenges, and risks involved.

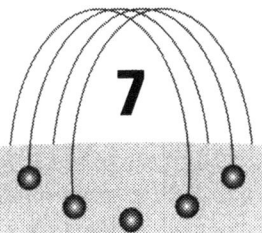

Enterprise Application Integration

Regardless of whether a business is focused on a parochial market or a global market, information is one of the most valuable enterprise assets. Information formalized and structured as granular and specific data is the foundation for tactical day-to-day operations. Alternatively, information that is aggregated, abstracted, grouped, and related supports analytical functions such as decision support and strategic planning. As most technology and business professionals know, the data that describe enterprise information are acquired from many sources, are stored in several databases, and are processed by numerous applications. In many enterprises, customer data are described by several different IDs and characteristics and used by many systems. Each system has its own definition and view of a customer, which introduces redundancy, disparate data definitions, and the inability to directly access, share, or reuse customer data. The problem of enterprise data disparity is not a new one, and is symptomatic of the following:

- Poor application and database design
- Tightly scoped and myopic application development strategies
- Budgeting and planning that is limited to specific system functionality (promoting autonomy)
- Acquisition and implementation of several packaged applications
- Acquisition of other businesses (along with their unique technology environments)
- Exchange of data with several external or collaborative trading partners

Chapter 7 Enterprise Application Integration

The fundamental problems are inability to access system-specific data and highly diverse and varied data structures. In order to identify customer relationships and leverage the information assets of the enterprise, each system needs to read, aggregate, decompose, and parse data from other systems. The most common solution for these challenges is Enterprise Application Integration (EAI). As inferred by this description, the focus is on application processing. However, it is suggested that a more appropriate description would be Enterprise Data Integration or, in the case of globalized Web applications, Global Data Integration. Historically, enterprise data are relegated to vertical systems and applications. Exchange of data between these autonomous systems often results in custom point-to-point interfaces that resemble a spider web (see Figure 7.1). Additionally, even when the information is exchanged

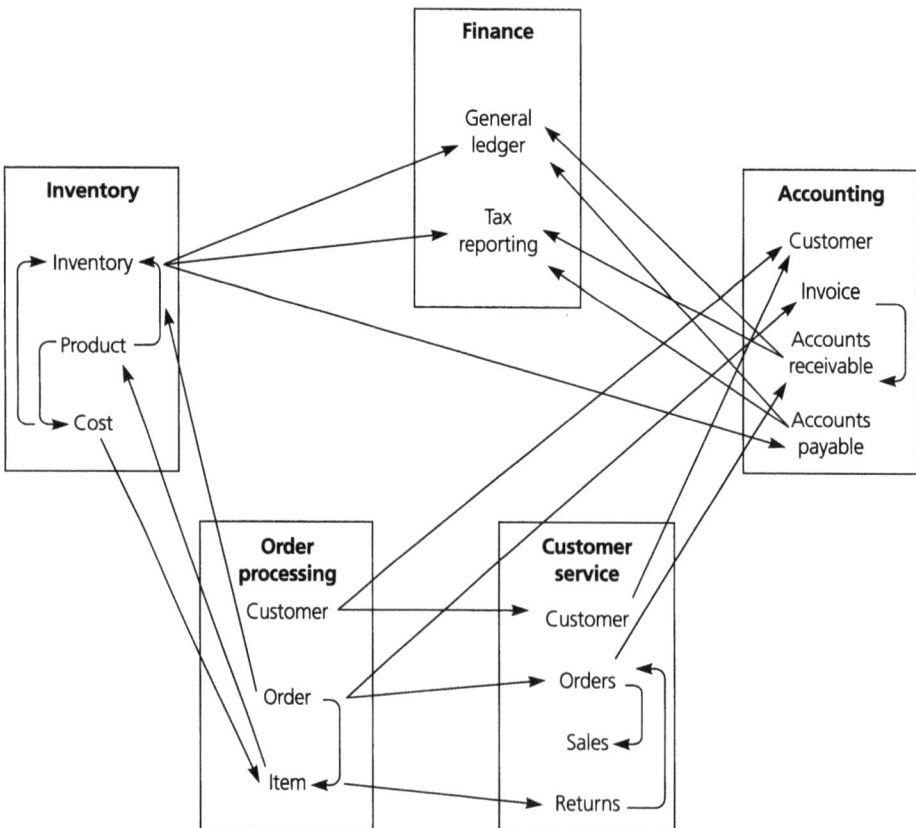

Figure 7.1 Point-to-point interfaces

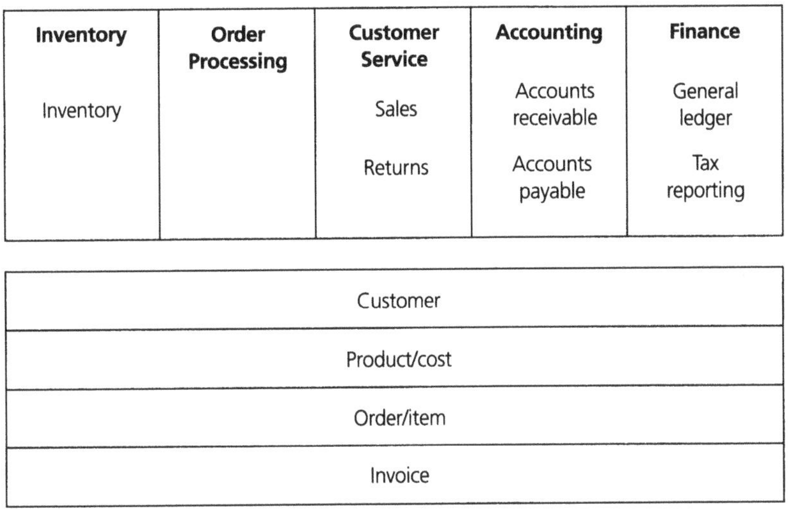

Inventory	Order Processing	Customer Service	Accounting	Finance
Inventory		Sales	Accounts receivable	General ledger
		Returns	Accounts payable	Tax reporting

Customer
Product/cost
Order/item
Invoice

Figure 7.2 Common information concepts

via interface, there is an implied obligation on the part of either the sending or receiving system to resolve structure and format differences.

If the information that is captured and maintained by each of the autonomous systems were described by a common structure, format, and characteristics, applications would have little difficulty sharing and reusing the corresponding data (see Figure 7.2). This approach is often referred to as *horizontal integration*. Common data concepts are defined as crossing all systems and applications, and application-specific functionality is retained by each system. Instead of moving different data representations of data from system to system, the focus is shifted to common data sharing and platform-agnostic access.

Global Data Integration

The topic of global data integration is somewhat self-descriptive. Enterprise data integration is focused on the common storage, access, and processing of data that is diverse in structure, format, and, potentially, definition. However, most traditional enterprise data are defined according to common product, customer, and market characteristics. When integrating globally diverse data, the complexities are compounded. As a simple example, the ability to combine sales data (especially monetary amounts) from various locales becomes a monumental task. Characteristics such as currency type, decimalization, exchange rate, and taxation can no longer be assumed to comply with a single set of financial definitions, structures, and rules.

The solution to global data integration is metadata. *Metadata* is often described as "data about data." This description is somewhat abstract and does not adequately portray the importance and role of metadata. A more comprehensive definition would describe metadata as

- Descriptive taxonomy
- Identifiers
- Structure
- Format
- Allowable values
- Data types and facets

When considering individual data elements or collections of related data elements (e.g., a postal address comprising geographic and address data elements), the infusion of globally diverse data adds additional complexity. The ability to integrate global data with other traditional enterprise data is not always readily evident. The Web or data architect must identify how data from each locale will be stored, managed, and processed. Using the SLKD Auto Rental example, as rental applications are captured from each of the supported locales, it must be determined whether they will be held in a single data store or in separate, locale-specific data stores. In addition, the architect must determine if the application data will be combined and processed with other traditional North American reservations or maintained separately.

It is important to note that no single integration approach applies to every type of business. It is also likely that multiple integration techniques might be necessary for a single business enterprise. Determination of the best approach should consider the following:

- Metadata complexity and diversity of existing enterprise data
- The number of locales expected to be addressed
- The number of different data structures and definitions among enterprise systems
- The capabilities and limitations of the existing business applications
- The capabilities and limitations of the existing technical infrastructure
- The capabilities and limitations of the existing reporting systems (aggregation, separation)
- The cost of development and maintenance
- Regulatory issues (privacy, data retention)

Addressing the listed complexities may result in the need for more than one integration technique. The SLKD enterprise may have determined that existing systems and databases do not currently provide the capability to process global data, and that modifications are cost prohibitive. Similarly, it may be determined that the existing customer database may warrant modification to store and process global data, but that other enterprise systems do not. Another more effective alternative might be to externalize all global data storage but provide application-agnostic interfaces using XML.

After the global data integration approach has been identified, the applicable data concepts and granular data particles will need to be mapped to source and target data stores (i.e., databases). Regardless of whether global data will be stored in combination with traditional data or stored independently, each data concept should include locale characteristics.

A rental application that is accepted by the SLKD Auto Rental Web site will include extensive customer information. By default, each customer will have been aligned with a locale and preferences will have been captured. Locale and preference information is used to drive localized Web site content and to specify characteristic uniqueness. If the global customer data (including locale) were combined with traditional North American customer data, many aggregation processes would be simplified. Similarly, identification of customers by specific locale or locale segment (e.g., currency) would also be possible. Assuming locale data is added to the existing customer database, this approach presents an effective long-term solution by promoting the concept of a single source for customer data. However, design and engineering costs, as well as impact to existing applications can be excessive. Also, additional modifications will be required to convert existing name, address, and telephone data to global data structures.

If the SLKD sample customer data is not combined and stored with traditional North American customer data, aggregation processes will require modification to access, acquire, and process data from two or more sources. This alternative approach assumes that global customer data will be stored in separate data structures (e.g., tables) and aggregated using application logic (see Figure 7.3). This technique avoids (or significantly limits) changes to existing customer databases and requires the development of new global data structures. However, application processing modifications will also be required. Also, the new global database structures will require additional database backup, recovery, maintenance, and disk storage. This second approach may be the most advantageous if the initial scope and project budget are limited.

Regardless of the approach, the complexity of the customer's characteristic data must be resolved, and new interfaces between systems will be required. Some of the ongoing and longer-term costs of either approach may escalate over time, offsetting any potential short-term cost avoidance. At a conceptual level, the majority of global customer data is similar to that of traditional enterprise data (e.g., customer

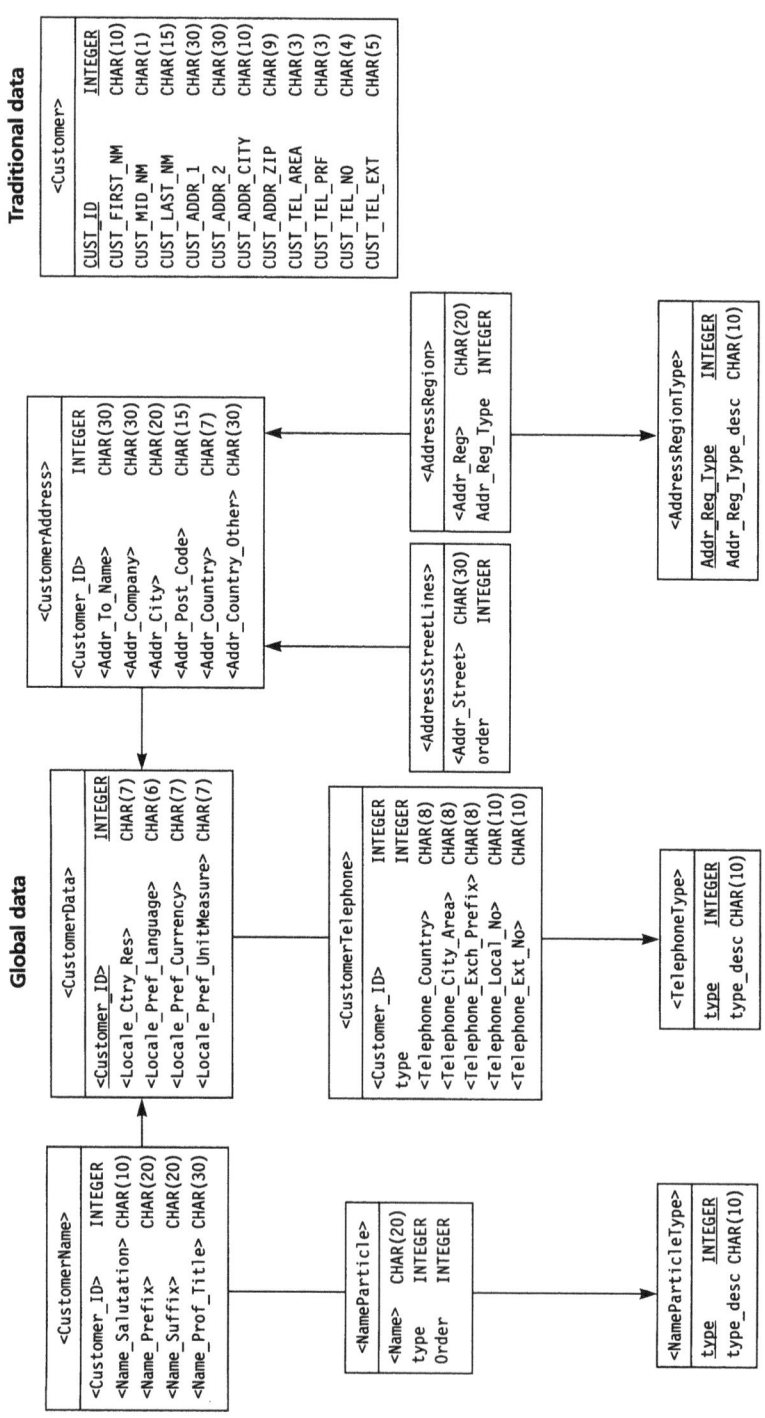

Figure 7.3 Global data vs. traditional enterprise data

Table 7.1 Common types of data disparity

Source	Condition	Target	Description
Element A	=	Element A	Same taxonomy
Element A	=	Element B	Different taxonomy
Element A	< >	Element A	Same taxonomy, context mismatch
Element A	=	Element B + Element C	Decomposition
Element A	=	Element B(1..n)...	Decomposition
Element A + Element B	=	Element C	Aggregation
Element A(1..n)...	=	Element B	Aggregation
Element A + n	=	Element B	Derivation
Element A (substring)	=	Element B	Derivation
Element A(1..n)...	=	Element B(1..n)	Derivation
Element A + Element B	=	Element C + Element D	Derivation
Element A	=	Null	No match
Null	=	Element B	No match

name, address, telephone number). However, at a more granular level, the global data exhibit significant differences.

Using the example of a customer name, cultural diversity may result in names that are comprised of many parts, with the name parts occurring in varying order. The SLKD traditional enterprise definition of a name is limited to first name, middle initial, and last name. Disparity between global and traditional name structures and particles is obvious. Similarly, data disparity at an element level can take on many forms. The most common types of element-level data disparity can be expressed as abstract algorithms (see Table 7.1). Sources of data may be Web sites, internal applications, data exchanges with other businesses, acquired mailing lists or customer data, and so on. Targets can be any number of enterprise systems and supporting data stores.

Resolution for most types of data disparity can be accomplished using a combination of mapping and business logic. Some data disparity can only be resolved by restructuring either the source or target data and performing complex data conversions. In cases of significantly complex data disparity, resolution may not be possible. These cases may require a complete analysis, abstraction, and reengineering effort, or the identification of alternative data sources and targets.

At a summary level, direct matches of both taxonomy and context (e.g., Element A = Element A) do not require resolution, although they may require mapping. Data disparity of mismatched taxonomy (e.g., Element A = Element B) can usually be resolved by mapping elements of the same definition and context. Disparity of elements with matching taxonomy but different definition and context (e.g., Element A < > Element A) are usually not easily resolved. Most examples of mismatched context result from different definitions and metadata characteristics such as data types, lengths, decimalization, or character set. In cases of significant complexity, it may not be possible to resolve this type of disparity.

Decomposition is a common form of data disparity (e.g., Element A = Element B + Element C). In this case, the context of the source must be the same as the context of the target, although in aggregate. Also, the content must be able to be decomposed based upon some identifying characteristic, algorithmic logic, or business rule. Decomposition may also be of the form where the target is a repeating group of like-named elements (e.g., Element A = Element B(1 .. n)). Resolution for this type of disparity is similar but will require additional logic to align with ordinal instances of the target.

Similar to decomposition, aggregation involves multiple instances of data. In one form, multiple source elements of different taxonomy are to be combined in order to match the target (e.g., Element A + Element B = Element C). Logically, this type of disparity is generally simple to resolve by using aggregation algorithms or business rules. Complexity may arise if the aggregation is not intended to result in contextual equality of all source elements to the target element. An alternate form of aggregate data disparity involves multiple instances of source elements that in aggregate will equal a target element (e.g., Element A(1..n) = Element B). In this case, multiple source elements of the same taxonomy are combined to equal the target.

Data disparity that requires derivation introduces the most significant risk and potential for anomalies. The most simple forms of derivative disparity involve logic or business rules that combine the content of a source element with a factor, value, ratio, or similar algorithm to equal a target element (e.g., Element A + n = Element B). Similarly, derivative disparity may involve deriving a segment or part of a source element to equal a target element (e.g., Element A (substring) = Element B). In this case, the result may involve the risk of truncation or the inability to resolve complete equality for integration. Another form of derivative disparity is multiply occurring source elements that target multiple target elements (e.g., Element A(1..n) = Element B(1..n). When the context and ordinal index of the source elements align with the target elements, mapping is generally the resolution. However, when the source elements do not map contextually or by index to target elements, resolution may require application of significantly complex logic and business rules; some cases may not be resolvable. A similar form of disparity involves multiple source elements of different taxonomy to multiple target elements of different taxonomy. Resolution is again most likely complex and, in some cases, resolution may not be possible.

Another somewhat common form of disparity is a direct mismatch—that is, a source element does not have a corresponding target element of taxonomy or context (e.g., Element A = null). This type of disparity is also known as a *gap*. Resolution in many cases is not possible, since the target will not have a matching element. A variation of this type of disparity is when the source does not have an element but the target does. Again, this is a gap and may not be able to be resolved.

Many other types, variations, and combinations of data disparity may be evident. Each presents a challenge for global data integration, and many such cases cannot be resolved. Technologies such as XML can help to simplify some forms of disparity and therefore enable integration. However, XML alone is not the best solution. Successful global data integration requires research, analysis, architectural engineering of new data stores, and significant use of data standards and global classifications in Web applications, as well as with other enterprise applications.

Using the SLKD customer name as an example, there are several types of data disparity (both as data concepts and granular data elements). All data disparity must be resolved before the customer name information can be integrated or processed. The listed forms of disparity must be resolved either at the data storage level, through some form of transformation between systems and data stores, custom application logic, or a combination.

- Different data element names
- Different data structures (variable name and address particles vs. fixed name and address elements)
- Different characteristics (data types, lengths, allowable values)
- Mismatch of elements (missing elements, nonmatching elements)

For the SLKD example, there may be many different solutions for resolving data disparity. One solution would be to modify all existing enterprise systems and databases to use identical data structures. This solution provides a single common globalized database and would be the most desired architectural result. However, the development costs would also most likely be prohibitive. An alternative approach would be to engineer a set of separate, globalized customer data structures that include locale data. Globally diverse structures such as name and address would be managed through relationships between the customer and more granular data particles. This alternative requires additional funding to engineer and maintain the new data structures.

In either case, applications that process customer data would need some modification. If the disparity between the data structures can be resolved by combining transformation rules along with technologies such as XML, modifications and additions could be limited to transforming, reading, and writing XML. Using the example of a customer, name particles would need to be mapped and transformation rules defined. If the receiving or processing application were specific to globalized data, the incoming data from the existing (traditional) enterprise database would be transformed in both taxonomy and structure (see Figure 7.4).

Alternatively, if the receiving or processing application were traditional enterprise processes, the incoming data from the global database would be transformed in taxonomy, structure, and content (see Figure 7.5).

Global data concepts other than customer name also imply the need for recognized data standards. These standards can help to classify and align globally diverse data.

Extensive Use of Standards and Classifications

One of the most common forms of data disparity is when the content of an element is descriptive text. While descriptive text is valuable when viewed by a person, unless some form of rigorous parsing and conversion has been implemented, it is largely unusable for the purposes of comparison, matching, sorting, selection, or application of business logic. Consider the example of a country name. If multiple postal addresses are captured from a globalized Web site and the content of the country element remains a country name, occurrences of an element that contains a descriptive country name for the United States might hold values of the following:

- US
- U.S.
- USA
- U.S.A.
- United States
- United States of America
- Other potential derivations of United States

If this element were part of an address that was processed for the purposes of postal addressing, variations such as those listed might be of minimal significance. However, if the element were assigned as a classification or grouping mechanism for

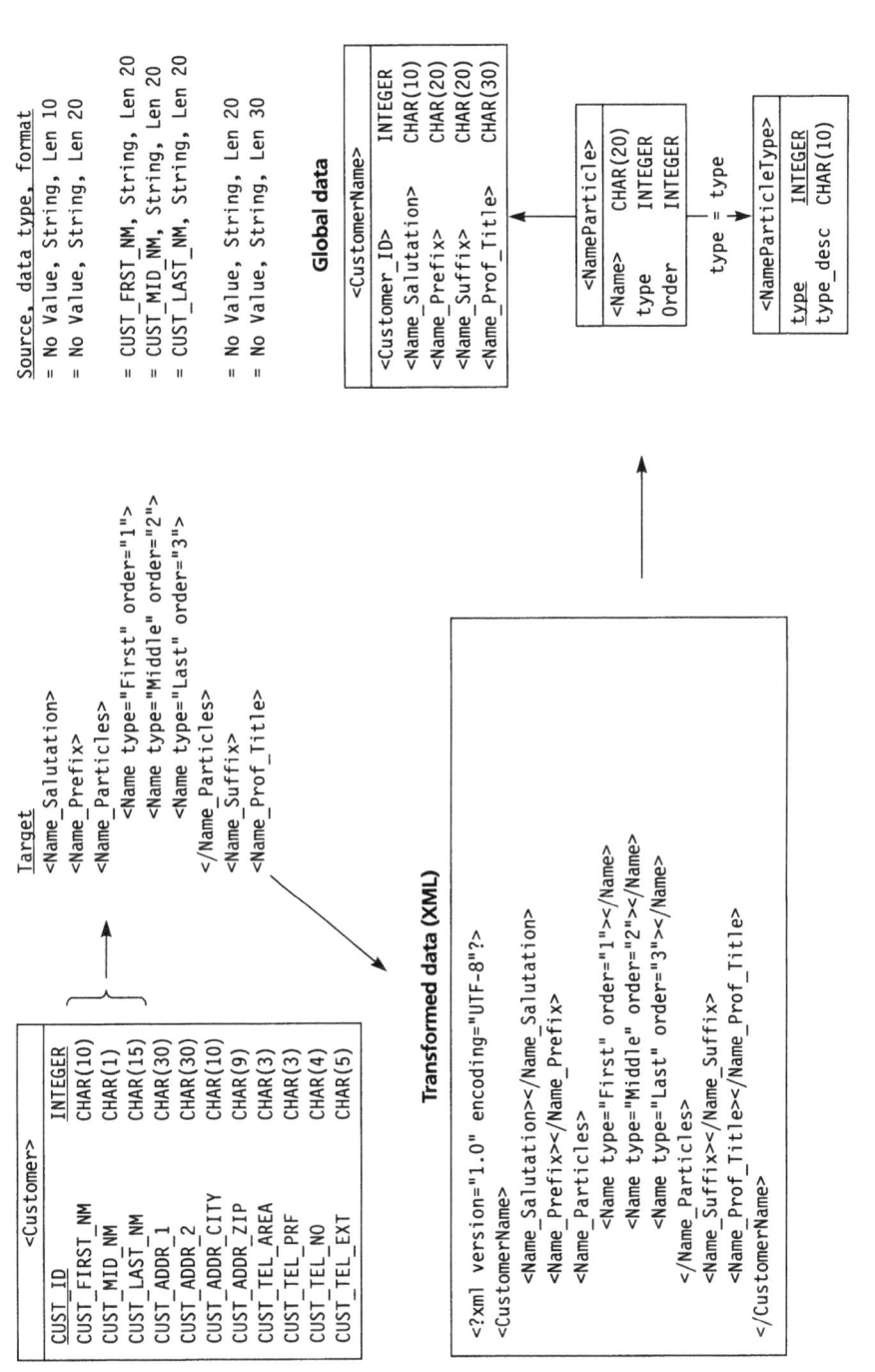

Figure 7.4 Traditional data transformation

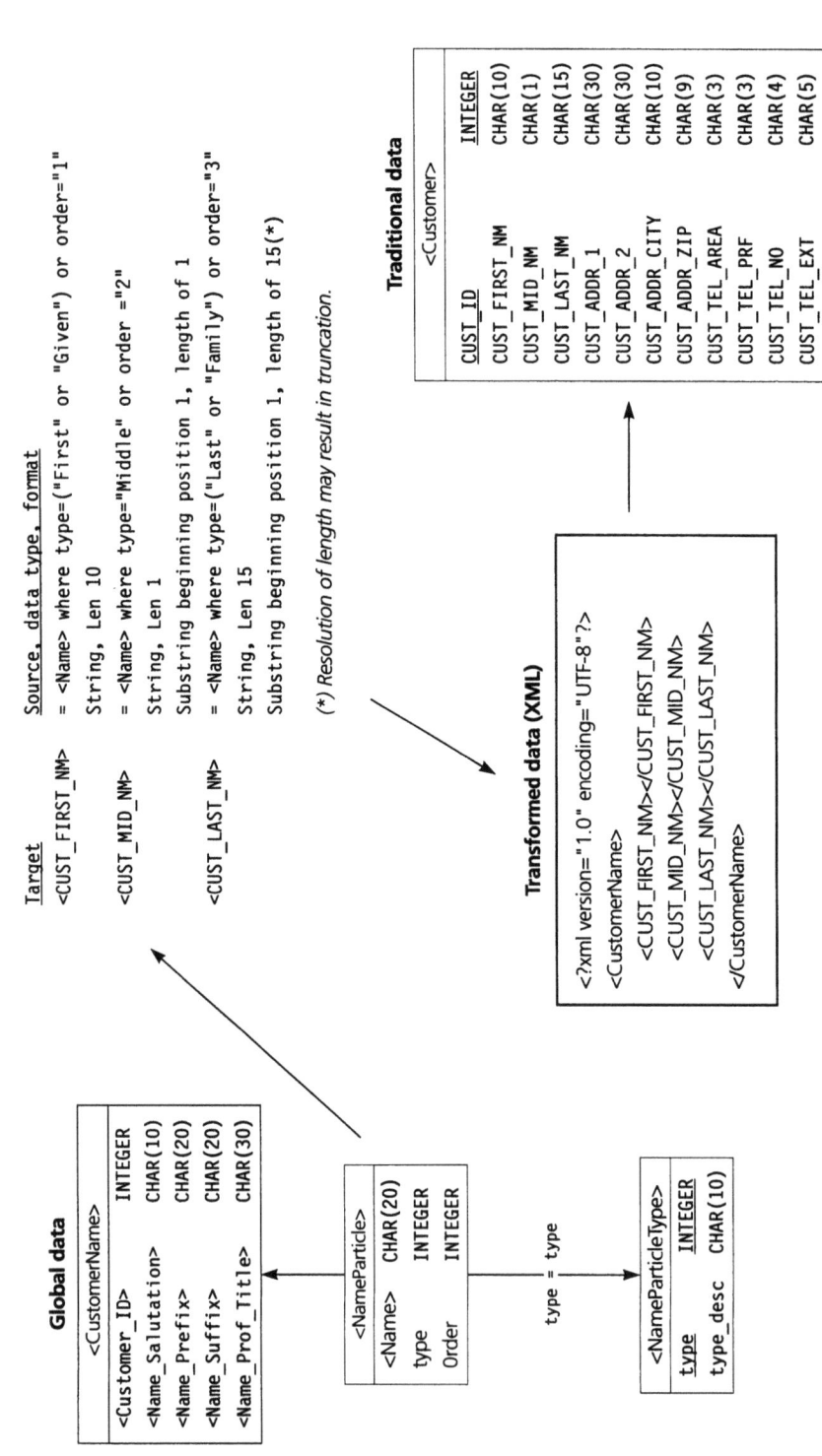

Figure 7.5 Global data transformation

financial reporting, it would be difficult to accurately order and aggregate amounts. Alternatively, if the country element contained standard country code values, classification, matching, ordering, and aggregation would be simplified. The example of country can be extended to global data integration. If address data from multiple locales were collected from a Web site and then inserted into a database, the ability to match and then map country codes would allow the application to identify previous existing address data and potentially avoid duplication. Similarly, when attempting to map and aggregate financial data by region (e.g., country), the ability to correctly match countries is critical.

Beyond the application processes of sorting, matching, and aggregation, reporting for human viewing and consumption requires verbose descriptive text. In this case, it may appear that descriptive country names rather than country codes are warranted. This type of processing can easily be resolved by the use of data standards and reference structures. Global transaction data can be aligned with appropriate data standards and encoding schemes. When application processing requires descriptive text, the reference structure can be used for decoding.

When globalized data are acquired and intended for an internal enterprise target, global data integration becomes a critical consideration. Not only must the common types of data disparity be resolved in order to integrate data, but differences in context, data type, and format also must be addressed. Most data are of three basic types: string, numeric, or date. However, when considering the acquisition of globally diverse data, none of these three basic types will also clearly define the captured data, nor facilitate automated processing.

As described previously, global data such as a person's name or postal address combines multiple elements of primarily string or character data. When considering a single instance of an address, for business processes such as postal addressing, the content of these elements is acceptable. However, when multiple addresses are processed, as in a report or list, sort order and selection become important. In this case, attempting to sort on string data or identify and select a subset of addresses based upon string data is at a minimum difficult and potentially not possible. A more effective solution would be to classify each set of address data by some form of clearly defined code. Similarly, if addresses from many locales are captured from a globalized Web site, integrating that data with like postal addresses in enterprise data stores will require some form of automated matching and selection. Country code is an excellent candidate for this purpose.

When a globalized Web form acquires address data, it is of benefit either to allow the user to select their country, or to convert a key-entered country. The Web user would view and select from a list of possible countries listed by name. Given an example of HTML within the Web page code, the list of countries is directly converted to one or more country code values. The ISO 3166 Country Code standard is often used for this purpose. Rather than having Web users themselves enter a country in the form of "US," "U.S.," "United States," and so on, they would select "United States" from a drop-down list, and the underlying HTML would insert "USA:840" as the value for that form element. When the transaction was received by the Web server and eventually processed through the application server, integration of the address data could be simplified by sorting and selecting addresses based upon country code.

Another valuable application of data standards is the capture of monetary amounts. When a globalized Web site allows an international user to enter monetary amounts in their preferred currency, the content of that HTML form field is just a numeric value. In order to convert to a base currency amount such as the U.S. dollar, the receiving application must be able to identify the currency of the amount as entered. In this case, the ISO 4217 Currency Code standard is an excellent solution. In addition to the monetary amount, the Web user could be prompted to select a currency type from a drop-down list similar to that described for address and country. Although the Web user would view and select a currency code such as "Canadian dollar," the underlying HTML would insert a value of "CAD:124." The receiving application could then use this currency code to identify and apply the necessary exchange rate and conversion logic. If other enterprise processes required descriptive data rather than code values (e.g., reporting, mailing labels, etc.), reference structures would be used to "decode" the code values into their corresponding textual descriptions.

Not all data are identified by or aligned with a coding standard. However, as the global Web application is designed, applicable data standards should have been identified as part of the requirements effort. These standards become an area of alignment between the user interface design and the data and transaction design. The user interface would provide a mechanism for the user to select the necessary data, and the underlying HTML (or other Web technology) would convert those values to standard codes.

The SLKD Web site included a number of data standards that would apply to captured data. Of significant importance are the Web user's locale characteristics and preferences (see Listing 7.1). Each can be described by an applicable data standard. When the Web user's data are captured from the Web application, the locale characteristics and preferences are converted to corresponding standard code values and attached to all subsequent transactions. As the transactions are received by the Web server and processed by the application servers, integration becomes simplified. From the perspective of global data integration, all monetary amounts can be converted from the preferred currency to a base currency such as U.S. dollar, units of measure can be converted, language can be identified (e.g., for later enterprise processing to produce correspondence, quotations, and invoices), and the country can be used to group customers by market, region, and address.

Listing 7.1 Sample locale data with applied standards

```
<?xml version="1.0" encoding="UTF-8"?>
<LocaleTransaction xmlns:xsi="http://www.w3.org/2001/XMLSchema-instance"
xsi:noNamespaceSchemaLocation="LocaleTransaction.xsd">
    <SessionData>
      <HTTP_Header/>
      <TransactionID/>
    </SessionData>
    <LocaleData>
      <Locale_Country_Res>GBR:826</Locale_Country_Res>
      <Locale_Pref_Language>ENG:GB</Locale_Pref_Language>
      <Locale_Pref_Currency>GBP:826</Locale_Pref_Currency>
      <Locale_Pref_UnitMeasure>SI:METRIC</Locale_Pref_UnitMeasure>
    </LocaleData>
</LocaleTransaction>
```

Another consideration for global data integration is the type of information that is captured and how it will be processed or used by the enterprise.

Operational vs. Analytical

The SLKD Auto Rental Web site example is primarily operational—that is, the data and transactions from each user session of the Web site are tactical. They are processed as the basic business operations of the enterprise. Similar to a retail establishment or consumer-oriented business, this type of data is generally the lifeblood of B2C e-commerce.

Alternatively, analytical systems are primarily strategic. They are used for research, analysis, and planning. The most common examples of analytical systems are data warehouse, data mart, and decision support. Data used by these types of systems are generally aggregated, grouped, and sorted. In most cases, transaction data acquired from the operational systems is restructured and copied to alternative platforms. Enterprise personnel can then query the data in numerous ways to view and assess information. Critical planning and strategic decisions are often made from the data reported by these applications.

When the transactional data are moved to analytical systems, they are generally associated with a number of dimensions. In simple terms, a *dimension* is a classification or category for grouping similar data. The underlying data are considered facts. Facts may be associated with or related to many dimensions. This allows for very creative sorting, grouping, and selection. Given a global business scenario, making pricing decisions or planning for new products is not effective when there are a significant number of individual reservations. However, it may be of value to identify groupings of reservation data by locale or locale component. Each locale characteristic and preference becomes an excellent candidate as a dimension.

Analytical processing of global data are also complex. One example is that of monetary amounts in multiple currencies. When operational and transaction data are captured from a globalized Web site, one of the more common types of data is monetary amounts expressed in varying currencies. If the amount is classified by an associated currency, conversion to a base currency is generally possible. However, when performing analysis of aggregate monetary amounts (especially over periods of time such as months, quarters, or years), questions arise as to when a currency amount was converted, the exchange rate used at that time, and the then current value of monetary amounts based upon current exchange rates. While there is no single answer to these questions, they do present a complexity for analytical systems that is influenced by the global nature of the data.

The design and development of a data warehouse or similar analytical architecture requires specific expertise. However, by applying data standards to global transaction data, the data copied to the data warehouse will be of higher quality, and will present opportunities for new dimensions upon which to classify data facts.

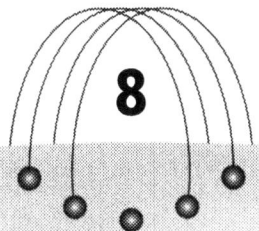

The Complexities of Mobile E-Commerce

The focus of this book has been primarily design and engineering techniques for Web- and Internet-based global e-commerce. The described medium for access of the Web and for transacting global e-commerce is reasonably common and standardized (the personal computer). Currently, consumer Web access is primarily done using a personal computer and a modem. The monitors attached to these personal computers can display significant amounts of data, and navigation within a Web site or between Web sites is done by simply clicking on embedded links or entering a URL in an address bar of a browser. Although connection speeds are dependent upon the local infrastructure (e.g., telephone, cable, DSL, ISDN, etc.) and the service provider, performance is generally reasonable. As you might have come to expect, the described scenario is quite familiar.

However, over the past few years, a new method of Web browsing and conducting e-commerce has come to light: mobile e-commerce. With the evolution of cellular telephones and personal digital assistants, many consumers are beginning to access the Web from wireless devices. Considering the home Web user, wireless networks are also on the rise (e.g., 802.11 wireless networks that are readily available from most computer stores). Within range of a wireless network, the consumer can log onto the Internet from their wireless device and, depending upon the service provider and attachment to the Internet, can achieve speed and throughput that begins to approach broadband.

The ability to transact business on the Web without the restriction of physical attachment presents tremendous opportunity as well as numerous complexities.

Chapter 8 The Complexities of Mobile E-Commerce

When considering a consumer market, the use of wireless devices for the Web provides untold potential and convenience.

The Wireless Globe

The use of cellular telephones and wireless PDAs is increasing. In addition, the supporting technologies and infrastructures continue to improve. Cellular telephone use in Europe and Asia are also on the rise. This increase in usage for consumer-oriented cellular and wireless technology can be attributed to several factors, including the following:

- Decreasing costs for cellular and wireless enabled devices
- Increased availability of cellular and wireless devices
- Improvements in cellular technology capabilities (display, memory, throughput)
- Improvements in network and infrastructure speed
- Increased availability of wireless services (telephone, Web access, Web sites)
- Speed, efficiency, and cost of physical telephone and Internet infrastructures

While not all cellular telephones are Web enabled, the population of cellular telephone subscribers by country is a reasonable indicator of the potential market. Table 8.1 lists the top eight countries based upon the number of cellular subscribers.

Table 8.1 Cellular subscribers

Country	Number of subscribers	Percent of population
United States	100.3 million	36.5%
Japan	66.8 million	52.6%
Germany	48.1 million	58.6%
Italy	42.2 million	73.7%
United Kingdom	40.0 million	67.0%
France	29.1 million	49.4%
South Korea	26.8 million	56.7%
Spain	24.7 million	61.0%

Source: The World Almanac and Book of Facts, "Telecommunications, Worldwide Use of Cellular Phones, 2000," World Almanac Education Group, 2002. Original source of information: International Telecommunications Union.

Table 8.2 Regional wireless subscribers

Region	2000	2001	2002
Latin America	1 million	12 million	38 million
North America	6 million	30 million	72 million
Western Europe	6 million	56 million	151 million
Asia	42 million	113 million	194 million

Regarding the growth of wireless Web technologies, Asia is of particular interest, as there is a high population of both cellular technology and Internet-enabled handhelds (see Table 8.2).[1]

While mobile Web technology presents tremendous opportunities and opens new markets, there are a number of challenges. Many of these challenges are related to the technology, while others are more focused on consumer market acceptance.

Wireless Design Complexities

The design of Web sites that target wireless consumers involves a number of complexities and challenges. Many are specific to the technology. One of the most obvious is commonly referred to as *display real estate*. Most personal computer monitors can present extensive amounts of data on a single screen. When the data exceed the display area of the screen, the user simply scrolls up, down, left, or right. However, many Internet-enabled mobile devices have very limited display areas. Other than high-resolution display phones, many Internet-enabled cellular telephones are limited as to text display lines (generally from 3 to 12 lines of text, at 12 to 20 characters in length). Even with the latest mobile devices that incorporate high-resolution digital displays and graphic-enabled Web browsers, the overall display area is significantly limited. As you might imagine, presenting large amounts of Web page content can be a significant challenge.

Also related to mobile displays are the challenges associated with limited memory and display resolution. Web site content targeted for an international user may contain graphic images. Depending upon the mobile technology, some browsers will

---

[1] "Asia Leads in Wireless Internet Connectivity," *M-Business Magazine*, May 2001, CMP Media, LLC; www.mbizcentral.com.

not render images in the same form as that presented using a personal computer and monitor. However, they may support smaller, one-byte, low-resolution images. Regardless, if the target mobile display device is unknown, eliminating or significantly reducing embedded images may be an effective design approach. Also, most images (even those downloaded and rendered from Web pages to personal computer monitors) are of significant size and may consume a large amount of resources in order to render (e.g., bandwidth for the download and device memory). Again, if the target mobile device is unknown, an effective design approach may be to limit the size and type of image content.

Another design consideration for mobile devices is the display area for text. As described earlier, the processes of internationalization and localization include language translation of Web content. Depending upon the language and dialect, some Web pages may experience increased character counts of 30% or more. When considering mobile devices—in particular, cellular telephones—the display area is already significantly limited. An increase in character usage could thus have a significant impact on the display area. Although a single cellular telephone display may be limited to 3 to 12 lines of text, most mobile browsers provide scrolling and navigation support. However, this introduces another usability challenge.

Web page and Web site navigation using a personal computer, mouse, and browser is as simple as point-and-click. Navigation using a mobile device such as a cellular telephone can be far more limiting. The user may be limited to two or three buttons of the keypad for scrolling. Also, when significant amounts of content are displayed (i.e., text or graphics), the cellular user may be required to perform significant amounts of scrolling. Selective reorganization of global Web content becomes critical.

Another technical complexity that constrains mobile Web application design is device memory. The memory footprint of a typical cellular telephone may be as little as 1kb and a maximum of 512kb. When downloading significant amounts of Web page content, the state of the download must be managed and interaction at the device level must be synchronized with continued content download. When combined with technologies such as the Wireless Access Protocol (WAP), Wireless Markup Language (WML) provides capabilities to address many of the complexities of mobile Web applications.

WML

Wireless Markup Language (WML) is a powerful Web technology that is based upon XML and also resembles HTML. Initially, WML was targeted at mobile telephone technology that exhibited memory, display, and navigation constraints.

Capabilities were added to align with mobile device micro browsers. To facilitate display, navigation, and user interaction, content is organized by decks and cards (see Figure 8.1). Logic and condition-checking capabilities are provided by WMLScript (roughly similar to JavaScript). WMLScript supports variables, functions, and conditional logic.

WML is also compatible with the Wireless Access Protocol (WAP). Requests to download Web pages are specified as conforming Universal Resource Locators (URL). Web pages and content are returned as WML. The mobile or micro browser implemented on the mobile device parses and renders content according to the display characteristics of the device. In addition to the capabilities of the browser, wireless agents and device agents provide navigation capabilities. Web site and Web page navigation and interaction is primarily between decks and cards.

```
<?xml version="1.0"?>
<!DOCTYPEwml PUBLIC "-//WAPFORUM//DTD WML 1.1//EN"
        "http://www.wapforum.org/DTD/wml_1.1.xml">
<wml>
<head>Your Locale</head>
<card id="Card-1" title="Your Locale">
    <do type="prev" label="Back"><prev/></do>
    <p>Country: Canada<br/>
    Language: English<br/>
    Currency: CAN$$<br/>
    U/M: SI-Metric<br/>
    </p>
</card>
</wml>
```

Figure 8.1 Simple WML example (simulated image from dot.WAP v2.0.2 © Inetis D.O.O.*)
* DotWAP is freeware, available from *www.tagtag.com*. Inetis Ltd., info@inetis.com; *http://inetis.com*.

Chapter 8 The Complexities of Mobile E-Commerce

WML has undergone some recent revision and enhancement. WML2 (version 2 of WML) was published in September 2001 on the WAP Web site, *www.wapforum.org*. WML2 includes extensions of Extended HTML (XHTML) that incorporate language and capability features of WML1. It is important to note that, per the WML2 specification, WML2 is targeted to provide backward support for WML1 and is not recommended for content development. Alternatively, XHTML Mobile Profile (XHTMLMP) is recommended for mobile content and the Wireless Access Protocol 2. XHTMLMP extends the XHTML specification to address wireless devices such as mobile phones, PDAs, pagers, and set-top boxes.[2]

The advantages of WML, WML2, and XHTMLMP include synergies with XML, XHTML, and JavaScript that reduce the need for additional technical expertise. As a mobile technology, WML does not relieve the architect of aligning global content with the locale and preferences of the user. Additional challenges are the restructuring of global Web content to conform to the limitations of mobile devices while still providing effective presentation and interaction.

There has been some recent criticism of WAP and WML. The jury is still out regarding the implications of the issues. If these issues are found to be critical to your organization, there are other competing wireless protocols to consider. One of the more popular alternatives is DoCoMo iMode, which originated in Japan. This wireless protocol has a significant following in Japan and Asia and is promoted by NTT (similar to ATT in the United States).

Regardless of the technology chosen, global e-commerce success is dependent upon a number of factors:

- Following a formalized globalization process
- Language-specific user interface and content
- Capability to acquire, capture, present, and process globally diverse data
- Rigorous application of data standards

To gain additional information about global e-commerce, I encourage you to research reference sources on globalization, internationalization, and localization (see Appendixes B and C).

---

2 WAP Forum, XHTML Mobile Profile, October 29, 2001, ©2001 Wireless Application Protocol Forum Ltd.; *www.wapforum.org*.

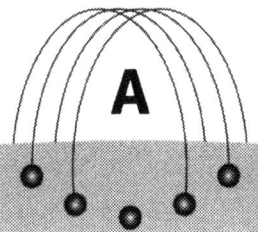

Global Standards References

This section contains sources of reference and originators of various global, international, national, and industry standards and specifications. Web site URLs are not guaranteed but were active when this list was developed. Several standards and specifications are proprietary or copyright property and may require licensing, agreement, and payment of fees. Others may be available as public information.

American Bankers Association (ABA)
www.aba.com
Source of reference, standards, and specifications for bank account routing numbers.

Bureau International des Poids et Mesures (BIPM)
www.bipm.fr
Source of reference, standards, and specifications for international system of units.

Dublin Core Metadata Initiative
http://dublincore.org
Source of reference, standards, and specifications for representing people's names (Dublin Core Metadata).

EAN International
www.ean-int.org

Appendix A

Source of reference, standards, and specifications for
- EAN:UCC
- Global trade item number (EAN:GTIS)

Europa, The European Commission
http://europa.eu.int
Source of reference, standards, and specifications for Euro, single currency for Europe.

European Committee for Banking Standards (ECBS)
www.ecbs.org
Avenue de Tervueren, 12
1040, Brussels
Source of reference, standards, and specifications for
- International bank account number (IBAN)
- International payment instruction (IPI)

Greenwich 2000 (Royal Observatory Greenwich)
http://greenwich2000.com
Source of reference, standards, and specifications for time zones.

International Organization for Standardization (ISO)
www.iso.org
ISO Central Secretariat:
International Organization for Standardization (ISO)
1, rue de Varembé, Case postale 56
CH-1211 Geneva 20, Switzerland
Telephone + 41 22 749 01 11
Telefax + 41 22 733 34 30;
Source of reference and standards for
- ISO 8601 Date and Time
- ISO 5218 Gender Code
- ISO 3166 Country Code
- ISO 4217 Currency Code
- ISO 639 Language Code
- Various other standards

International Telecommunications Union (ITU)
www.itu.int
Place des Nations
1211 Geneva 20
Switzerland
Voice: +41 22 730 5111 (ITU switchboard)

Global Standards References

Fax: +41 22 733 7256
Source of reference, standards, and specifications for
- E.122—Measures to reduce customer difficulties in the international telephone service
- E.123—Notation for national and international telephone numbers, email addresses, and Web addresses
- E.164—The international public telecommunication numbering plan

Legal Information Institute (LII)
www.law.cornell.edu
Source of reference, standards, and specifications for
- Standard time (United States)
- Other legal matters (primarily United States)

Library of Congress
www.loc.gov
Source of reference, standards, and specifications for
- MARC Three-Character Language Codes
- MARC Code List for Geographic Areas

National Institute of Standards and Technology (NIST)
www.nist.gov
Source of reference, standards, and specifications for
- Guide for the use of international system of units
- FIPS 10-4 Countries, Dependencies, Areas of Special Sovereignty, and Their Principal Administrative Divisions
- FIPS 55 Location Codes

NTT DoCoMo
www.nttdocomo.com
Source of reference, standards, and specifications for DoCoMo and iMode.

Open Mobile Alliance (OMA)
(see also WAP Forum)
www.openmobilealliance.org

Uniform Code Council (UCC)
www.uc-council.org
Source of reference, standards, and specifications for the Universal Product Code (UPC).

Appendix A

United Nations—Economic Commission for Europe (UN/ECE)
www.unece.org
Source of reference, standards, and specifications for
- Currency codes
- Country codes
- Codes for units of measure used in international trade

United Nations Statistics Division
http://unstats.un.org
Source of reference, standards, and specifications for
- Composition of macrogeographical (continental) regions and component geographical regions
- Countries or areas, codes, and abbreviations

Universal Postal Union (UPU)
www.upu.int
International Bureau
Weltpoststrasse 4
3000 BERNE 15
SWITZERLAND
Tel.: +41 31 350 31 11
Fax: +41 31 350 31 10
Source of reference, standards, and specifications for
- Addressing formats
- Postal codes

U.S. Census Bureau
www.census.gov
Source of reference, standards, and specifications for
- North American Industry Classification System (NAICS)
- Standard Industry Classifications (SIC)

U.S. International Trade Administration (ITA)
www.ita.doc.gov
Source of reference, standards, and specifications for Safe Harbor (privacy principles).

U.S. Naval Observatory (USNO)
http://tycho.usno.navy.mil
Source of reference, standards, and specifications for time zones.

Global Standards References

WAP Forum (Wireless Access Protocol, Wireless Markup Language)
(see also Open Mobile Alliance)
www.wapforum.org
Source of reference, standards, and specifications for
- Wireless Access Protocol (WAP)
- Wireless Markup Language (WML)
- Other related wireless technologies

World Wide Web Consortium (W3C)
www.w3c.org
Source of reference and specifications for
- XML
- XHTML
- HTML
- Privacy and P3P
- Numerous other Web and related technologies

XML.org (vocabularies)
www.xml.org
Source of reference, standards, and specifications for XML and vocabularies.

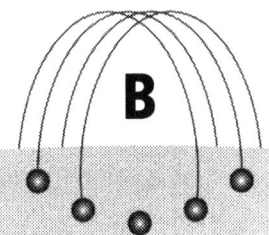

Resources and Recommended Reading

Book of the World Atlas and Factfile
D&K, 1998, ISBN: 0-7894-3623-X

Currency Symbols Range: 20A0–20CF
Unicode Consortium, *www.unicode.org*

DCMI People's Names
Dublin Core Metadata Initiative, Andrew Waugh
February 3, 1998, 1995–2001
http://dublincore.org/documents/1998/02/03/name-representation/

DotWAP
WAP Emulator (currently available as a freeware download from *www.tagtag.com*)
Inetis Ltd.
info@inetis.com, *http://inetis.com*

Essential World Atlas
D&K, 2001, ISBN: 0-7894-7989-3

eXtensible Markup Language (XML) 1.0 (second ed.)
World Wide Web Consortium (W3C)
W3C Recommendation, 6, October 2000
www.w3.org/TR/2000/REC-xml-20001006

Appendix B

Financial Times World Desk Reference
D&K, 2000, ISBN: 0-7894-4894-7

Global Reach, *www.global-reach.biz/globstats/index.php3*

Global Trade Item Number (GTIN)
EAN International, *www.ean-int.org*

Globalization Dimensions
Web Globalization Guide Framework
Relational Logistics Group, James Bean © 1996–2002
www.globalwebarch.com/

Globalization Strategy
Web Globalization Guide Framework
Relational Logistics Group, James Bean © 1996–2002
www.globalwebarch.com/

HTML 4.01 Specification
World Wide Web Consortium (W3C)
W3C Recommendation, 24, December 1999
www.w3.org/TR/1999/REC-html401-19991224

International Bank Account Number (IBAN)
European Committee for Banking Standards (ECBS), *www.ecbs.org/*

International Safe Harbor Privacy Principles
U.S. International Trade Administration (ITA), *www.ita.doc.gov*

International Standard Industry Classification
United Nations, Dept. of Economic and Social Affairs
http://unstats.un.org/unsd/class/family/famlist1.htm

International System of Units
Bureau International des Poids et Mesures (BIPM), *www.bipm.fr*

International Telecommunications Union, *www.itu.int/*

E.122 Measures to reduce customer difficulties in the international telephone service
E.123 Notation for national and international telephone numbers, email addresses, and Web addresses
E.164 The international public telecommunication numbering plan

Resources and Recommended Reading

E.160–E.164 Numbering plan of the international telephone service era, section 3.3 number length

Internet Explorer 6
Used for various reference images
Microsoft © 1995–2000
www.microsoft.com

ISO 639-2, Language Code, RA Registration Authority
International Organization for Standardization (ISO)
http://lcweb.loc.gov/standards/iso639-2/langhome.html

ISO 639-2, Language Code, TC37 Technical Committee
International Organization for Standardization (ISO)
www.iso.ch/iso/en/stdsdevelopment/tc/tclist/
TechnicalCmmitteeDetailPage.TechnicalCommitteeDetail?COMMID=1459

ISO 3166, Country Codes, MA Maintenance Agency
International Organization for Standardization (ISO)
www.din.de/gremien/nas/nabd/iso3166ma/a3ptnorm.html

ISO 3166, Country Codes, TC46 Technical Committee
International Organization for Standardization (ISO)
www.iso.ch/iso/en/stdsdevelopment/tc/tclist/
TechnicalCommitteeDetailPage.TechnicalCommitteeDetail?COMMID=1757

ISO 4217, Currency Codes, TC68 Technical Committee
International Organization for Standardization (ISO)
www.iso.ch/iso/en/stdsdevelopment/tc/tclist/
TechnicalCommitteeDetailPage.TechnicalCommitteeDetail?COMMID=2183

ISO 4217, Currency Codes, UN/ECE United Nations Economic Commission for Europe
International Organization for Standardization (ISO)
www.unece.org/cefact/rec/rec09en.htm

ISO 5218, Representation of Human Sexes, JTC1, SC32 Technical Committee
International Organization for Standardization (ISO)
www.iso.ch/iso/en/stdsdevelopment/tc/tclist/
TechnicalCommitteeDetailPage.TechnicalCommitteeDetail?COMMID=160

ISO 8601, Date and Time, TC154 Technical Committee
International Organization for Standardization (ISO)

Appendix B

*www.iso.ch/iso/en/stdsdevelopment/tc/tclist/
TechnicalCommitteeDetailPage.TechnicalCommitteeDetail?COMMID=3827*

ISO 13616 International Bank Account Number
International Organization for Standardization (ISO)
www.iso.org/

M-Business Magazine, www.mbizcentral.com

Multilingual Computing and Technology Magazine, www.multilingual.com

North American Industry Classification System
United States Office of Management and Budget (OMB)
www.whitehouse.gov/omb/inforeg/statpolicy.html#NAICS

The Platform for Privacy Preferences 1.0 (P3P1.0) Specification
World Wide Web Consortium (W3C)
W3C Recommendation, 16, April 2002
www.w3.org/TR/2002/REC-P3P-20020416/

Pocket World in Figures
The Economist Newspaper Ltd., © 1991, 1992, 1993, 1994, 1995, 1996, 1997
ISBN: 0-471-24838-X

Postal Addressing Systems
Universal Postal Union, *www.upu.int/*

PowerDesigner
Data Modeling Tool
Sybase, *www.sybase.com*

Universal Product Code (UPC)
UCC Uniform Code Council, *www.uc-council.org*

USPS Publications 28, 40, 201, 221
United States Postal Service, *http://usps.com/*

Web Globalization Guide Framework
Global Web Architecture Group, 2002
www.globalwebarch.com

Wireless Business and Technology Magazine, www.WBT2.com

Wireless Markup Language, Version 2
Wireless Application Protocol Forum Ltd., 2001
www.wapforum.org

The World Almanac and Book of Facts
World Almanac Education Group, 2002, ISBN: 0-88687-872-1

World Factbook
U.S. Central Intelligence Agency, *www.cia.gov*

World Trade Organization, *www.wto.org*

XHTML 2.0
World Wide Web Consortium (W3C)
W3C Working Draft, 5, August 2002
www.w3.org/TR/2002/WD-xhtml2–20020805

XHTML Mobile Profile
Wireless Application Protocol Forum Ltd., 2001
www.wapforum.org

XML Globalization and Best Practices
James Bean, Active Education, 2001, ISBN: 1-58264-129-3

XML Schemas
World Wide Web Consortium (W3C)
W3C Recommendation, 2, May 2001
www.w3.org/TR/2001/REC-xmlschema-1-20010502/ (structures)
www.w3.org/TR/2001/REC-xmlschema-2-20010502/ (datatypes)

XML Spy
XML Edit and Development Tool
Altova, Inc., *www.xmlspy.com*

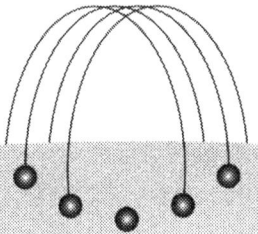

Glossary

abstract container   An abstract container is an XML element that has been generally named or classified, with the intent of having multiple occurrences (e.g., multiple occurrences of <name> rather than <first_name>, <last_name>, etc.).

Business-to-Business (B2B)   Describes a type of Web site that is operated by a business and targets other businesses as the primary customer.

Business-to-Consumer (B2C)   Describes a type of Web site that is operated by a business and targets consumers (individuals, groups).

Component   A decomposed part of a larger concept or object. Using the example of a postal or delivery address, the "city" is a component. Conceptually, the combination of all directly related components will represent the primary object from which they are decomposed.

Consumer-to-business-to-business (C2B2B)   Combination of the business-to-consumer and business-to-business Web sites. The consumer interfaces with a business that in turn interfaces with one or more businesses. The consumer may or may not be aware that businesses other than the primary are involved.

container   In the case of XML, either an element or attribute. An object that contains or holds information (data) or another object.

context   The meaning or definition of an object, information, or item of data.

Customer Relationship Management (CRM)   Combines the business functions of marketing, sales, personalization, customer service, customer retention, and analysis. The abilities to identify, target, attract, service, capture, grow, and retain customers are the basic objectives of customer relationship management.

data concept   A general classification for a type or collection of data in the abstract. Examples of data concepts include "postal address," "person's name," and "telephone number."

211

Glossary

data concept particle A defined set of particles, information fragments, or component parts of a data concept. "Given name" and "family name" are particles of the "person name" data concept.

data disparity Characteristic differences between data concepts or data items. Data disparity is an observable trait between similar but not identical pieces of information. Data disparity must be resolved in order to achieve data integration.

data particle A defined information, particle, fragment, or component part of a data concept. A data particle is at the often considered to be "atomic" (the data particle is at the lowest reasonable level of decomposition).

data standard A representative and accepted definition, set of encodings, form, structure, or allowable values. Data standards are applied to a data concept, data concept particle, or data particle.

e-commerce The electronic transaction of business. Sale and exchanging of goods and services, using the Internet or similar electronic network.

enterprise A business or set of related businesses that operate as a whole. An enterprise includes resources (human and other), processes, information, goals, strategies.

Enterprise Application Integration (EAI) The goal and process for aligning and integrating often disparate processes and information of all enterprise systems.

eXtensible Markup Language (XML) A language derived as a conforming subset of Standard Generalized Markup Language (SGML). XML is often referred to as "a self-describing metadata language." XML is gaining in popularity for use in Web applications and in defining e-commerce transactions. For additional information, see *www.w3c.org*.

global Of or relating to all countries, locations, cultures, and peoples of the world.

Global Customer Relationship Management (G-CRM) Global customer relationship management extends the concept of customer relationship management to incorporate the global and locale characteristics and preferences of a customer.

Globalization (G11N) The concept of globalization extends and complements the activities of internationalization (I18N) and localization (L10N). Globalization not only considers the language and cultural requirements of global e-commerce, but also incorporates rigorous alignment with global data concepts and data standards.

HTML form Hypertext Markup Language form. An extension of HTML that allows for user interaction (data entry, acceptance, limited validation, and submission of data to a Web server or similar application). HTML forms utilize declarative elements (e.g., <INPUT/>, <TEXTAREA/>, and <SELECT/> elements). HTML form elements are also often referred to as HTML form fields.

Glossary

HyperText Markup Language (HTML)   An application of Standard Generalized Markup Language (SGML). Developed to simplify presentation of information over the Web.

integration   A process that results in the derivation, combination, aggregation, or insertion of one or more source information components with a target information component.

international   Of or relating to several nations or countries of the world.

internationalization (I18N)   A process for identification of locales and cultures that will result in the need to uniquely describe or align content. The most obvious internationalization techniques focus on separation of core constructs and content from those that must be localized. The noncore, or locale-specific, constructs are then externalized so that language and culture customization can be implemented while mitigating impact to the primary content or application.

local   Of or relating to a combination of characteristics that describes the geography and preferences of an international user. See also "Locale."

locale   A locale may be defined by a combination of characteristics and describes the geography and preferences of an international user. There is no clearly defined standard for defining a locale. However, most locales can be described as a combination of geography (country, regional area, city, etc.) and preferred language, currency, and unit of measure.

locale characteristic   A combination of characteristics defines a locale. Some of the more common include country, language (and optionally dialect), currency, and unit of measure.

localization (L10N)   The process, tasks, and activities required to develop, present, or express globally diverse content to users of specific locales. Some of the more common characteristics used to identify a locale include geographic location, language, dialect, and currency. The locales defined to each target market must be identified in order to progress an effort from internationalization to a more specific localization process, where tactical language translation will occur.

market   A geographic area, or a collection of peoples or businesses that represents a potential for selling goods and services.

market of opportunity   A market that exhibits characteristics similar to a target market. A market of opportunity may also be referred to as a subtle or hidden market.

metadata   The characteristics, form, allowable values, standards, and rules that describe and define data. Often referred to as "data about data."

Glossary

Personal Digital Assistant (PDA)   A small portable device that provides planning, scheduling, address book, and optional office applications to an individual. Many PDAs also provide wireless communication or connection capabilities.

personalization   An extension of usability that enables Web site customers to feel as if they are interacting directly with representatives of a business, rather than a computer application. Personalization includes usability, presentation characteristics, application of user preferences, forms of navigation, and localization of presentation content.

portal   A type of Web site that provides access and interface to multiple sources of information. The sources of information may be autonomous or tightly integrated.

preferences   A choice or selection made by a person. In the context of globalization, a preference is a selection by an individual from a group of options that represent their locale, a characteristic of their locale, or a similar option.

region/regional   Combinations of nations, cultures, and people. The most common use of the term *region* applies primarily to geography (geographic proximities, borders, closely located nations, or defined market areas). In some cases, a region may be defined as a subset of national borders, countries, or locations.

Relational Database Management System (RDBMS)   A type of database that is founded on matrices, tuples, and relational algebra. The concept of a relational database is most often attributed to the work of E. F. Codd. A relational database not only stores information, but also supports the ability to relate data and view relationships between data.

server   A computer device or application process that provides services to a requestor. Servers may be of various types (e.g., Web, application, data, enterprise).

target market   Market of focus. Also known as the primary or intended market.

usability   Describes the characteristics of an application or user interface as they apply to use by a person (e.g., personalization, intuitiveness, simplicity, ease of use, navigation, interaction).

user interface   Method of interacting with a person that is implemented by one or more technologies. The user interface defines or resides at the presentation layer.

Web page   A defined set of information (also known as content) that is presented to a Web user. A Web page is usually served by a Web server. Web pages may be part of a Web site.

Web server   A type of server. A Web server provides, or serves, Web pages as the resolution of requests that are generally in the form of a Universal Resource Locator (URL).

Web site   A collection of Web pages or similar Web resources. A Web site is generally identified by a Universal Resource Locator (URL).

Glossary

Wireless Markup Language (WML) A language derived from XML that is directed toward wireless devices. For additional information, visit the WAP Forum Web site, *www.wapforum.org*.

XML attribute A type of XML container that is defined to an XML element. An XML attribute may not be defined to exist on its own (without a corresponding XML element). An XML attribute may be defined to contain data. An XML attribute may not be defined to contain other attributes or elements.

XML document A document, file, transaction, or message defined using the syntax of XML.

XML element The most often used type of XML container. An XML element is defined in the form of a tag name stated between a left angle and right angle bracket. An XML container may be defined to contain information (data) or to contain other elements.

XML Schema A type of schema. An XML Schema is the set of metadata (characteristics, format, structure, rules, allowable values) that defines and constrains a referencing XML document. XML Schemas were defined as a "recommendation" of the World Wide Web Consortium (W3C) as of May 2001.

Index

A

ABA (American Bankers Association), 205
abstract containers, 145, 148, 199
acquisition of data. *See* capturing data
actions in B2C technology cycle, 70–73
addresses
    data concept of, 40–44
    data requirements for, 122–124, 133–134
    factors for designing forms, 44
    formatted fields approach, 81–86, 89–90
    formatting, global, 9–10
    free-form entries, 41–42
    locale-specific elements, 81–86
    sample designs for forms, 43
    standards for, 40–44
    transaction engineering of, 170–171
    unformatted fields approach, 79–81
    UPU (Universal Postal Union), 41, 122, 133, 208
    U.S. Postal Service formats, 40–41
    zip codes, 10
aggregation of data
    approaches to, 181
    disparity resolution, 184
American Bankers Association (ABA), 60, 205
American Bankers Association routing numbers, 60
analytic systems, 191–192

ANZSIC (Australian and New Zealand Standard Industry Classification), 59
application function
    common information concepts, 178
    data requirements for, 130–131, 133
    defined, 119
    XML for customer transactions, 159–167
application integration. *See* EAI (Enterprise Application Integration)
architecture, system
    conceptual diagram of, 138
    multiple-language support, approaches to, 76
    reintegration of requirements, 136–137
Australian and New Zealand Standard Industry Classification (ANZSIC), 59
automobile operator licenses. *See* drivers license numbers

B

B2B (business-to-business) model, 2, 199
B2C (business-to-consumer) model
    data concepts. *See* consumer-oriented data concepts
    defined, 199
    described, 1–2
    requirements. *See* business requirements
    technology cycle, 70–74
bandwidth, internationalization of, 22

Index

bank account numbers (routing numbers)
    ABA, 60, 205
    as a business-oriented data concept, 60
    IBAN, 60
    ISO 13616, 213
BBAN (Basic Bank Account Number), 60
BIC (Bank Identifier Code), 60
BIPM (Bureau International des Poids et Mesures), 205
browsers, internationalization of, 22
Bureau International des Poids et Mesures (BIPM), 205
business identifiers, 58–59
business requirements
    combining with market profiles. *See* formalizing the design approach
    cultural. *See* cultural requirements
    data requirements, relation to, 122
    defining for globalization, 94–97
    demographic. *See* demographic business requirements
    functional. *See* functional business requirements
    globalization dimensions, 96, 100–101
    identifying markets. *See* market identification
    market profiles, 99–108
    potential markets. *See* market identification
    SKLD Auto Rental Example, 96–97
business-oriented data concepts
    bank account numbers, 60, 205, 213
    defined, 57–58
    identifiers for businesses, 58–59
    industry codes, 59
business-to-business model. *See* B2B (business-to-business) model
business-to-consumer model. *See* B2C (business-to-consumer) model

C

C2B2B (Consumer-to-Business-to-Business) model, 199
capturing data
    B2C information commonly acquired, 70
    forms for. *See* forms, Web
    purpose of, 66
    requirements for. *See* data requirements
    SLKD Auto Rental example, 79–91
cardinality, 145
cellular telephones
    challenges of Web sites for, 195–196
    display limitations, 195–196
    DoCoMo iMode, 198
    memory limitations, 195–196
    navigation limitations, 196
    number of subscribers by country, 194
    number of subscribers by region, 195
    popularity of, reasons for, 194
    text display problems, 196
    WAP, 197–198
    WML for, 196–198
    WML2, 198
    XHTMLMP, 198
character encodings, 23
character sets
    appropriate selection of, 23–25
    codepages, 24
    defined, 23
    fonts, 23–24
    glyphs, 23
    groupings in, 24
    ISO International, 24
    sorting order of, 21
    Unicode, 25
code sets
    countries, ISO 3166, 48, 129–132, 153–154, 213
    currency, ISO 4217 standard, 50, 126, 154–155, 213
    defined, 31
    examples of, 32
    gender, ISO 5218, 32, 57, 213
    language codes, ISO 639, 32, 154, 213
    SIC, 59
    valid value standards as, 32
codepages, 24
components, 199

Index

confirmation pages
    functional requirement, 119
    place in process, 78–79
    SKLD Auto Rental Example, 87, 91–92
    transactions from, 142, 167–169
consumer-oriented data concepts
    addresses, 40–44
    bank account numbers, 60, 205, 213
    country. *See* countries
    currency. *See* currency
    date. *See* dates
    gender, 56–57
    identifiers for individuals, 39–40
    language. *See* languages, human
    list of, 37
    names of persons. *See* names of individuals
    standards for, 35–37
    telephone numbers. *See* telephone numbers
    units of measure. *See* units of measure
Consumer-to-Business-to-Business (C2B2B) model, 199
containers, 199
context, 199
countries
    data concept of, 47–49
    descriptive text, disparity from, 189
    FIPS, 207
    integration issues, 189–190
    ISO 3166, 48, 129–132, 153–154, 213
    ISO 4217, 213
    telephone data XML Schema, 167
    XML Schema for, 153–154
CRM. *See* G-CRM (global customer relationship management)
cultural profile characteristics, 102, 106–107
cultural requirements
    data requirements from, 126, 128–129
    defined, 102
    functional business requirements, relation to, 112
    language requirements, 128–129
    user interface requirements with, 116

currency
    analytic systems with, 192
    characteristics of, 51
    commas as decimal separators, 50
    consumer-oriented data concept of, 49–52
    data requirements for, 123, 126–127
    decimalization levels, 50
    defined, 49
    design strategies for, 10–11
    exchange rates, 126
    global design for, 7
    integration issues, 190
    ISO 4217 standard, 50, 126, 154–155, 213
    XML Schema for, 154–155
customer data
    addresses. *See* addresses
    capturing, SKLD Auto Rental example, 79–91
    customer application data in transactions, 159–167
    integration of global with legacy, 181
    names. *See* names of individuals
    telephone. *See* telephone numbers
customer relationship management. *See* G-CRM (global customer relationship management)

D

data
    capture of, SKLD Auto Rental example, 79–91
    content, defined, 16–17
    information, compared to, 27–29
    particles, 200
data concept, 199–200
data disparity, 181–186, 200
data integration. *See* integration of data
data requirements
    address formats, 122–124, 133–134
    application function, 130–131, 133
    business requirements, relation to, 122
    cultural requirements with, 126, 128–129
    currency support, 123, 126–127
    dates, 128, 129, 132

Index

data requirements (continued)
- demographic requirements with, 126, 128–129
- drivers license numbers, 134, 135
- economic requirements with, 123, 126–127
- focus of, 119, 121
- formats, importance of, 122
- functional, 129–132
- fundamental purpose of, 110
- geographic requirements, relation to, 122–125
- importance of identifying, 121–122
- language requirements, 128–129
- locale identification, 130
- names of individuals, 126, 128–129
- privacy issues, 136
- product identification, 132
- purpose of, 108, 110
- regulatory dimension, 134–136
- reintegration of requirements, 136–137
- selection, 130
- strategy for globalization, 121
- telephone numbers, 123, 125, 133
- units of measure, 132

data standards, 200. See also standards

dates
- consumer-oriented considerations, 54–56
- data requirements for, 128, 129, 132
- European format, 55
- format standards for, 34
- functional requirements, 112, 116
- global formats for, 7
- ISO 8601, 55, 132, 214
- locales formats, table of, 56
- time zones, 55

decomposition, 184

definition of e-commerce, 1

definition of global, 15–17

delivery addresses. See addresses

demographic business requirements
- data requirements from, 126, 128–129
- defined, 102
- functional business requirements, relation to, 112
- user interface requirements with, 116

demographic profile characteristics, 102, 106–107

derivative disparity, 184–185

descriptive text, disparity from, 186, 189

design approach
- data requirements, 119–136
- functional requirements, 109–119
- key activity identified, 108
- reintegration of requirements, 136–137
- strategy for globalization, 109–111, 121

design mistakes. See mistakes for global Web site designs

dialects, human
- nature of, 19–21
- SKLD Auto Rental example, 77–78

dimensions, data, 192

disparity of data, 181–186, 200

display resolution
- internationalization of, 22
- wireless, 195–198

diversity of global data, 12–13

DoCoMo iMode, 198

dollars, U.S. See currency

down time, 7–8

drivers license numbers, 134, 135

Dublin Core elements, 37, 205

E

EAI (Enterprise Application Integration)
- analytic systems, 191–192
- currency, 192
- customer data, 181
- decomposition, 184
- defined, 180
- derivative disparity, 184–185
- descriptive text, disparity from, 186, 189

Index

dimensions, data, 192
disparity of data, 182–186
existing databases, options for, 181
gaps, 185
global dimensions, 179–180
global v. traditional data diagram, 183
metadata for, 180
operational systems, 191–192
purpose of, 178
transforming global to traditional data, 188
transforming traditional data, 187
types of data disparity, table of, 182
variables to consider in design, 180
EAN International, 205–206
ECBS (European Committee for Banking Standards), 206
e-commerce defined, 1, 200
economic dimension sample table, 105
economic requirements
    currency support, 123, 126–127
    data requirements from, 123, 126–127
    exchange rates, 126
    functional business requirements, relation to, 112, 115
EDI (Electronic Data Interchange), 33
elements, XML, 203
English-speaking audience assumption, 5–6
Enterprise Application Integration. *See* EAI (Enterprise Application Integration)
enterprises
    application integration. *See* EAI (Enterprise Application Integration)
    data, nature of, 177–178
    defined, 200
    standards within, 35–36
enumeration lists for transactions, 169–172
European Committee for Banking Standards (ECBS), 206
events in B2C technology cycle, 70–73
exchange rates, 126
expression standards, 34–35
eXtensible Markup Language. *See* XML (eXtensible Markup Language)

F

fixed container model, 172–174
fonts, 23–24
form elements
    capture for transactions, 159
    changes requirements, 170–171
    XML transactions from, 146–148
formalizing the design approach
    data requirements, 119–136
    functional requirements, 109–119
    key activity identified, 108
    reintegration of requirements, 136–137
    strategy for globalization, 109–111, 121
format standards, 33–34
forms, Web
    addresses, design factors, 43–44
    change requirements for, 170–171
    currency, 51
    elements of. *See* form elements
    formatted fields approach, 81–86, 89–90
    free-form entries, 41–42
    HTML forms, defined, 200–201
    language, 53
    local preference selection, 49, 63
    problems with, 29
    telephone numbers, 47
    transactions, capturing, 159
    units of measure, 54
    XML from. *See* XML transactions
functional business requirements
    application, 119
    confirmation, 119
    cultural requirements, relation to, 112
    data requirements from, 129–132
    date formats, 112, 116
    demographic requirements, relation to, 112
    economic requirements, relation to, 112, 115

Index

functional business requirements (continued)
  fundamental purpose of, 110
  geographic requirements, relation to, 111–114
  identification of locale, 119
  market profiles, 106, 108
  names of individuals, 112, 115, 116
  navigation, 115
  purpose of, 106, 108
  regulations, 119–120
  reintegration of, 110–111, 136–137
  selection, 119
  sizing Web pages, 110
  strategy, place in, 111
  targets of, 110
  technological availability planning, 110
  units of measure, 106, 115, 116
  user interaction considerations, 115
  user interfaces, table by country, 117–118

G

G11N. *See* globalization
gaps, 185
G-CRM (global customer relationship management)
  CRM defined, 199
  customer application data for, 159
  data needed for, 29
  defined, 200
  establishing relationships, 68
  interested party state, 68–69
  locale, importance of, 67–68
  objectives of, 66
  personalization, 68
  potential customer state, 68–69
  states of relationships, 67
  typical relationships, 68–70
  visitor state, 68–69
  Web user state, 68–69
gender
  consumer-oriented considerations, 56–57
  ISO 5218, 32, 57, 213

geographic requirements
  data requirements, relation to, 122–125
  dimension sample table, 103–104
  functional business requirements, relation to, 111–114
geography, global presentation issues, 7–9
global customer relationship management. *See* G-CRM (global customer relationship management)
global data requirements. *See* data requirements
global, defined, 15–17, 200
global marketplace, defined, 15–16
global nature of the Web, 2–4
global standards, 35–36
Global Trade Item Number, 206
globalization
  defined, 16–17, 200
  dimensions of, 96, 100–101
  process of. *See* process of globalization of Web sites
glyphs, defined, 23
graphics, expression standards, 34–35
Greenwich 2000 (Royal Observatory Greenwich), 206
GTIN (Global Trade Item Number), 132

H

hiring localization staff, 25–26
horizontal integration, 179
HTML (Hypertext Markup Language)
  data capture for transactions, 159, 170–171
  defined, 200
  forms. *See* forms, Web
  XML, transforming form elements to, 145–146

I

I18N, 201
IBAN (International Bank Account Number), 60
icons, expression standards, 34–35

Index

identification of locale as a functional requirement, 119
identification of markets. *See* market identification
identification standards, 31
identifiers for individuals, 39–40
industrial standards, 35–36
industry codes, 59
information defined, 27–29
integration of data
    analytic systems, 191–192
    common information concepts, 178
    country data, 189–190
    currency, 190, 192
    customer data, 181
    decomposition, 184
    defined, 201
    derivative disparity, 184–185
    descriptive text, disparity from, 186, 189
    dimensions, data, 192
    disparity of data, 182–185
    EAI as solution for, 178
    existing databases, options for, 181
    fragmentation, reasons for, 177–178
    gaps, 185
    global dimensions, 179–180
    global v. traditional data diagram, 183
    horizontal integration, 179
    locale characteristics, 190–191
    metadata for, 180
    mismatched elements, 185
    operational systems, 191–192
    point-to-point interfaces, 178
    sort order for multiple instances, 189
    transforming global to traditional data, 188
    transforming traditional data, 187
    variables to consider in design, 180
intellectual property concerns, 175
interested party state
    defined, 68–69
    example of, 78

international, as a modifier, 15, 18, 201
International System of Units of measure, 54
International Telecommunications Union (ITU), 44–47
internationalization
    concepts included in, 21–22
    defined, 201
ISIC (International Standard Industry Classification), 59
ISO 639, language, 32, 154, 213
ISO 3166, country, 48, 129–132, 153–154, 213
ISO 4217, currency, 50, 126, 154–155, 213
ISO 5218, gender, 32, 57, 213
ISO 8601, dates, 55, 132, 214
ISO 13616, bank account numbers, 213
ISO (International Organization for Standardization), 206
ITA (U.S. International Trade Administration), 208
ITU notation for telephone numbers, 44–47, 206–207

L

L10N. *See* localization
languages, human
    codes for, ISO, 20–21
    dialects, 19–21, 77–78
    ISO 639, 52, 154, 213
    multiple, supporting, 7, 76
    nature of, 19–21
    XML Schema using ISO 639, 154
legacy system globalization problems, 180–181
Legal Information Institute (LII), 207
legal issues. *See* regulations
Library of Congress, 207
LII (Legal Information Institute), 207
local, defined, 201
local markets, 18–19
locale characteristic, 201
locale identification
    data requirements for, 130
    functional requirements of, 119

Index

locale identification (continued)
  SKLD Auto Rental Example, 75–77
  techniques for, 61–63
locales
  affinity drivers from, 62–63
  characteristics of, 62
  data integration issues, 190–191
  defined, 21, 61–62, 201
  G-CRM, importance for, 67–68
  identification as a functional requirement. See locale identification
  opportunities, identifying, 62
  preferences, selecting, 62–64
  SLKD Auto Rental example, 63–64
  transaction example, 150–155
  of users, identifying, 29
localization
  defined, 19, 201
  language skills necessary, 25
  locale identification process, 21
  validation of expertise in, 25–26

M

market identification
  commercial publications recommended, 100
  country, defining by, 98
  invalidation, 101
  issues in, 94–96
  markets of opportunity, 98
  overview, 97–99
  profiles, developing, 99–101
  reference Web sites, 99–100
  regulatory requirements, 106
  SKLD Auto Rental example, 98–99
  validating markets, 98, 101–108
market profiles
  combining with business requirements. See formalizing the design approach
  cultural characteristics, 102, 106–107
  demographic characteristics, 102, 106–107
  developing, 99–101
  economic dimension sample table, 105
  functional dimension, example table, 108
  geographic dimension sample table, 103–104
  regulatory dimension, example table, 108
markets
  defined, 201
  identifying. See market identification
  of opportunity, 98, 201
  profiles. See market profiles
  target, 202
  validation of, 101–108
measurements. See units of measure
metadata
  defined, 27, 180, 201
  as solution to global data integration, 180
  usability resulting from, 30
metric system, 54
mistakes for global Web site designs
  address formatting, 9–10
  currency, 7, 10–11
  date formats, 7
  English-speaking audience assumption, 5–6
  geography, ignoring, 7–9
  multiple-language support assumption, 7
  North American market assumption, 5
  regulations, lack of awareness of, 11
  telephone number formats, 7
  time zones, ignoring, 7–9
  transaction data, neglecting importance of, 9–10
mobile e-commerce
  cellular telephones, popularity of, 194–195
  challenges of wireless Web sites, 195–196
  display limitations, 195–196
  DoCoMo iMode, 198
  importance of, 193
  memory limitations, 195–196
  navigation limitations, 196
  OMA, 207

text display problems, 196
WAP, 197–198
wireless technologies, 193
WML for, 196–198
WML2, 198
XHTMLMP, 198
money. *See* currency
multiple-language support
architectural approaches, common, 76
assumption, 7
general language problems. *See* languages, human
welcome pages, 76

N

NAICS (North American Industry Classification System), 59
names of businesses, 58–59
names of individuals
capture alternatives, 38–39
capturing, SKLD example, 88
data requirements from, 126, 128–129
disparity of data, 185–186
Dublin Core elements, 37, 205
factors in selecting techniques, 39
formatting issues, 10–11
functional requirements, 112, 115, 116
standards for, 37–39
transaction engineering, 170
XML representation of, 145
NANP (North American Numbering Plan), 44
National Institute of Standards and Technology (NIST), 207
national standards, 35–36
nations. *See* countries
navigation
functional requirements for, 115
internationalization of, 22
wireless devices, 196
NIST (National Institute of Standards and Technology), 207
North American market design assumption, 5

O

OMA (Open Mobile Alliance), 207
operational data systems, 191–192
order data capture, 79–91

P

page size. *See* sizing Web pages
Pareto's Law, 16
particles, data, 200
PDAs (Personal Digital Assistants). *See* mobile e-commerce
personalization, 68, 202
point-to-point interfaces for data, 178
portals defined, 202
postal addresses. *See* addresses
postal codes, 10
potential customer state
defined, 68–69
example, 78
potential markets. *See* market identification
preferences defined, 202
presentation
characteristics of, 65–66
defined, 16–17
path of globalization, 27–29
privacy issues
data requirements, 136
ITA, 208
transaction engineering, 175
process of globalization of Web sites
activities in, 93–94
business requirements, defining, 94–97
formalization of. *See* formalizing the design approach
market identification, 97–108
overview, 93–94
product identification
data requirements for, 132
GTIN (Global Trade Item Number), 132
transaction design for, 140
UPCs for, 132, 207

Index

product selection
    SKLD Auto Rental example, 77–78
    transactions for, 155–159

R

RDBMS (relational database management systems), 202
real estate, visual. *See* sizing Web pages
regional, defined, 17–18, 202
regulations
    data requirements for, 134–136
    functional requirements and, 119–120
    lack of awareness of, 11
    market identification, expertise requirements, 106
    SKLD Auto Rental Example, 97
reintegration of requirements, 136–137
relational database management systems (RDBMS), 202
relationships, customer
    establishment of, 68
    interested party state, 68–69, 78
    personalization, 68, 202
    potential customer state, 69–70, 78
    states of, 67
    typical global B2C, 68–70
    visitor state, 68–69, 77
    Web user state, 68–69
requirements
    business. *See* business requirements
    cultural. *See* cultural requirements
    data. *See* data requirements
    demographic. *See* demographic business requirements
    economic. *See* economic requirements
    functional. *See* functional business requirements
    geographic. *See* geographic requirements
residence addresses. *See* addresses
results, in B2C technology cycle, 70–73

S

sales data integration, 179–180
schemas, XML, 144, 148–150. *See also* XML Schema
security for transactions, 175
selection
    data requirements for, 130
    functional requirement of, 119
    transactions for, 155–159
servers, defined, 202
SI (International System of Units), 53–54
SIC (Standard Industry Classification), 59
sizing Web pages
    display resolution, 22
    functional business requirements, 110
    wireless devices, 195
SLKD Auto Rental example
    address collection, 79–86, 89–90
    business requirements for, 96–97
    confirmation pages, 78–79, 87, 91–92
    customer identification information, 88–91
    data capture, 79–91
    locale identification, 75–77
    locale preferences, 63–64
    localization of content, 77
    market identification, 98–99
    market validation, 102–108
    names of customers, capturing, 88
    overview, 74–75
    preferences, expressing, 129
    product selection phase, 77–78
    profile characteristics, 100–101
    telephone numbers, capturing, 88–89
sorting order of character sets, 21
standards
    addresses, 40–44, 122, 133
    allowable values in XML Schema, 169–170
    code sets. *See* code sets
    country codes, 48, 129–132, 153–154, 213
    currency, 50, 126, 154–155, 213

Index

dates, 55, 132, 214
enterprise, 35–36
expressions. *See* expression standards
formats. *See* format standards
gender, 32, 57, 213
global, 35–36
identification, 31
industrial, 35–36, 59
language codes, 32, 154, 213
market profiles for identifying, 99
national, 35–36
references for, 205–209
structures. *See* structure standards
telephone numbers, 44–47
types of, 30–31
valid values. *See* valid value identification standards
vocabulary. *See* vocabulary standards
XML Schemas using, 148
strategy for globalization, 95, 109–111, 121
structure standards, 32–33
symbols, internationalization of, 22

T

target markets, defined, 202
taxonomy
  transforming, 187–188
  weak, 171–173
technological availability planning, 110
technology cycle, B2C, 70–74
telephone numbers
  capturing, SKLD Auto Rental Example, 88–89
  country XML Schema, 167
  data requirements for, 123, 125, 133
  global design for, 7
  international access codes, 45
  ITU notation, 44–47, 206–207
  maximum length of, 46–47
  NANP (North American Numbering Plan), 44
  sample form designs, 47

separators, 46
standards for, 44–47
time
  global presentation issues, 7–9
  Greenwich 2000, 206
  locales formats, table of, 56
  stamps of, 8–9
  U.S. Naval Observatory, 208
  zones, 55
traditional enterprise data, integrating, 180–184
transaction design
  application functionality, including in, 140–142
  capturing content, locale with, 66
  complexity of global data, 139
  confirmations, 142
  goals of, 139
  locale identification, 139–140
  overview, 137–139
  principles for, 173
  product selection data, 140
  sample fields, 140–142
  set of transactions types, need to minimize, 139
  techniques for, 139
transaction engineering
  abstract containers, 145, 148, 173–174
  addresses, 170–171
  application transaction example, 160–162
  avoiding pitfalls, 171–174
  change, inevitableness of, 169–171
  confirmation pages, 167–169
  constraints, applying, 144
  countries, using ISO 3166, 153–154
  currency, using ISO 4217, 154–155
  customer application data, 159–167
  data type support, 150, 155–156
  definitions of structures, 144–145
  design principles, 173
  enumeration lists, 169–170, 171–172

Index

transaction engineering (continued)
- externalizing type data standards, 171–172
- fixed container model, 172–174
- intellectual property concerns, 175
- introduction, 143–144
- languages, using ISO 639, 154
- locale transaction example, 150–155
- names of individuals, 170
- non-technological issues, 175
- parameters requiring evaluation, 148
- parsers, XML, 144
- privacy, 175
- rules, applying, 144
- schemas, XML, 144
- security issues, 175
- selection transactions, 155–159
- session data schema, 152–153
- static structures for, 172–174
- taxonomy, weak, 171–173
- telephone country data schema, 167
- units of measure, 155
- variable transaction structure, 147
- Web technologies available, 143
- XML, reasons for using, 144
- XML Schema in. See XML Schema

transactions
- basic premise of, 144
- importance of, neglecting, 9–10
- non-technological issues, 175
- time stamps for, 8–9

transforming traditional data, 187–188
transforms, XSLT. See XSLT (XML Stylesheet Transform)

U

UCC (Uniform Code Council), 207
UN/ECE (United Nations—Economic Commission for Europe), 208
Unicode, 25
Uniform Code Council (UCC), 207
United Nations, 208

units of measure
- BIPM, 205
- business requirements for, 106
- data requirements, 132
- English units, 53–54
- functional requirements, 115, 116
- International System, 54
- standards for, 52–54
- XML Schema using, 155

Universal Postal Union (UPU), 41, 122, 133, 208
UPC (Universal Product Code), 132, 207
UPU (Universal Postal Union), 41, 122, 133, 208
U.S. Census Bureau, 208
U.S. Naval Observatory (USNO), 208
U.S. Postal Service address formats, 40–41
usability, 202
user interfaces
- cultural dimension, 116
- defined, 202
- demographic dimension, 116
- economic dimension, 115
- forms for. See forms, Web
- functional dimension, 117–118
- geographic dimension, 113–114
- regulatory dimension, 119–120
- reintegration of requirements, 136–137

V

valid value identification standards, 32
validating markets, 101–108
vehicle data, XML Schema for, 159
visitor state
- defined, 68–69
- example of, 77

vocabulary standards, 33

W

W3C (World Wide Web Consortium), 209
WAP (Wireless Access Protocol), 197–198, 209, 215

Web forms. *See* forms, Web
Web pages, defined, 202
Web servers, defined, 202
Web site, defined, 202
Web user state, 68–69
welcome pages, SKLD Auto Rental example, 75–76
wireless e-commerce
    cellular telephones, popularity of, 194–195
    challenges of Web sites for, 195–196
    display limitations, 195–196
    DoCoMo iMode, 198
    importance of, 193–194
    memory limitations, 195–196
    navigation limitations, 196
    text display problems, 196
    WAP, 197–198
    WML for, 196–198, 203
    WML2, 198
    XHTMLMP, 198
WML (Wireless Markup Language), 196–198, 203
WML2, 198
World Wide Web Consortium (W3C), 209
World Wide Web, global nature of, 2–4

X

XHTMLMP (XHTML Mobile Profile), 198
XML attributes, 203
XML documents, 203
XML elements, 203
XML (eXtensible Markup Language)
    abstract containers, 145, 148, 199
    advantages for transactions, 143–144
    application transaction example, 160–162
    attributes, 203
    confirmation pages, 167–169
    containers, 199
    customer application data, 159–167
    definitions of structures, 144–145
    documents, 203
    elements, 203
    HTML forms, transforming from, 145–146
    locale transaction examples, 150–155
    names of individuals, representation of, 145
    parsers, 144
    schemas, 144, 148–149
    selection transactions, 155–159
    transformations, 145–146
    vocabulary standard, as a, 33
    WML subset, 196–198
    XML.org, 209
    XSLT transformations. *See* XSLT (XML Stylesheet Transform)
XML Schema
    advantages of, 148, 149
    allowable values example, 150
    allowable values specification, 169–170
    application transaction example, 162–167
    confirmation pages, 167–169
    countries, using ISO 3166, 153–154
    currency, using ISO 4217, 154–155
    customer application data, 159–167
    data type support, 150–151, 155–156
    defined, 203
    enumeration lists, 169–170
    externalizing type data standards, 171–172
    languages, using ISO 639, 154
    locale transaction examples, 150–155
    reuse of elements, 148, 153
    selection transactions, 155–159
    session data example, 152–153
    telephone country data, 167
    units of measure, 155
    vehicle data, 159
    W3C, 215
XML transactions
    abstract containers, 145, 148, 173–174
    addresses, 170–171
    application transaction example, 160–162
    architectural diagram with, 138
    change, inevitableness of, 169–171
    confirmation pages, 167–169

Index

constraints, applying, 144
countries, using ISO 3166, 153–154
currency, using ISO 4217, 154–155
customer application data, 159–167
data type support, 150, 155–156
definitions of structures, 144–145
enumeration lists, 169–172
externalizing type data standards, 171–172
fixed container model, 172–174
introduction, 143–144
languages, using ISO 639, 154
locale transaction example, 150–155
names of individuals, 170
parameters requiring evaluation, 148
parsers, XML, 144
rules, applying, 144

schemas. *See* XML Schema
selection transactions, 155–159
session data schema, 152–153
static structures for, 172–174
taxonomy, weak, 171–173
telephone country data schema, 167
units of measure, 155
variable transaction structure, 147
Web technologies available, 143
XML, reasons for using, 144
XML Schema. *See* XML Schema
XPATH, 173
XSLT (XML Stylesheet Transform), 145

Z

zip codes, 10

www.ingramcontent.com/pod-product-compliance
Ingram Content Group UK Ltd.
Pitfield, Milton Keynes, MK11 3LW, UK
UKHW050412240426
12048UKWH00020B/1468